PROBLEM-BASED LEARNING FOR TEACHERS, GRADES 6–12

DANIEL L. KAIN

Northern Arizona University

Boston   New York   San Francisco
Mexico City   Montreal   Toronto   London   Madrid   Munich   Paris
Hong Kong   Singapore   Tokyo   Cape Town   Sydney

Series Editor: *Traci Mueller*
Editorial Assistant: *Krista E. Price*
Marketing Manager: *Elizabeth Fogarty*
Editorial-Production Service: *Omegatype Typography, Inc.*
Manufacturing Buyer: *Andrew Turso*
Composition and Prepress Buyer: *Linda Cox*
Cover Administrator: *Kristina Mose-Libon*
Electronic Composition: *Omegatype Typography, Inc.*

For related titles and support materials, visit our online catalog at www.ablongman.com.

Between the time Website information is gathered and then published, some sites may have closed. Also, the transcription of URLs can result in unintended typographical errors. The publisher would appreciate notification where these occur so that they may be corrected in subsequent editions.

Library of Congress Cataloging-in-Publication Data

Kain, Daniel L.
    Problem-based learning for teachers, grades 6–12 / Daniel L. Kain.
        p.   cm.
    Includes bibliographical references and index.
    ISBN 0-205-33920-4 (alk. paper)
    1. Problem-based learning.   2. Problem-solving—Study and teaching (Secondary)   I. Title.

LB1027.42 .K345 2003
373.139—dc21

                                                                                2002074767

Printed in the United States of America

10 9 8 7 6 5 4 3 2 1   07 06 05 04 03 02

CONTENTS

PART II   PROBLEMS FROM TEACHERS' WORK   28

CHAPTER THREE

What Should We Do about Andy?   28

A child study team cannot come to agreement about what is best for a middle-school student's IEP.

CHAPTER FOUR

Whose Discipline Problem Is This?   46

A principal at a combined middle school and high school demands that teachers adopt a single policy/procedure for classroom management.

CHAPTER FIVE

Change This Grade!   65

A high-school athlete is denied the opportunity to participate in basketball due to his failing English grade; a teacher committee must rule on his grade appeal.

CHAPTER SIX

An Afrocentric Curriculum?   84

An ad hoc parent committee demands that the high school curriculum be altered to serve the neglected African-American students in the school.

CHAPTER SEVEN

To Team or Not to Team?   101

Consultants must help a school staff decide on whether to implement the recommendations from a national commission to have team teaching in their school.

CHAPTER EIGHT

Math Makes Tracks   120

A middle school committee must respond to charges that the elimination of honors math sections is merely an example of political correctness interfering with best practice.

CHAPTER NINE

Raise Those Scores!   142

A superintendent calls for schools to institute a "test-prep" program in order to enhance the schools' performance on the state standardized test.

CHAPTER TWELVE

Reflecting on the Place of Problem-Based Learning   202

This chapter guides your reflection on PBL and your experience as a learner in this particular model.

CHAPTER THIRTEEN

Using PBL in Your Classroom   215

This final chapter takes you through the process of developing a PBL unit for use in your classroom.

PREFACE

This text may be unique among the texts you encounter in your professional education. For one thing, it's doubtful that you'll make your way through this text in the order it has been set out. It's more likely that your instructor will guide you to read part of a chapter, work with it, return to finish the chapter, and then maybe skip three chapters for your next work. That's the sort of flexibility I hope instructors will exercise and students will tolerate. But even more unusual, this is a textbook that, with a few exceptions, *doesn't have the answers in it.* I don't mean answers to practice problems, such as you find in the back of a math text. I mean **answers.** The whole purpose of this text is to provide you with a framework to learn how to raise questions about issues that are important to your work as a teacher, and then to help you learn how to go about finding those answers. If the book is successful, it will lead you to finding answers, but more importantly, to a disposition to continue learning throughout your professional life.

And one more thing. This book may lead you into some uncomfortable new territory, especially if you fit well with the way schools currently operate. It is my hope that your experience as a learner through the problems in this text will help you to see another way of organizing learning for the students with whom you work. Just as I am confident that good teachers can be trusted to seek answers, I am confident that your students, with a bit of guidance, can be trusted to seek answers. It strikes me that the essence of true learning is not only memorizing facts—which happens to us all as we use them—but learning how to raise questions and seek good answers.

HOW TO USE THIS TEXT

Several features of this text demand a bit of explanation. You will find the book divided into three parts. Part I provides introductory information about problem-based learning (PBL). The first chapter explains what is generally meant by PBL, with an eye to the recent history of the model. Chapter 2 provides coaching for you on how to get the most out of your PBL experience.

Part II of the text holds the core of what this book is about. In this section, you will encounter a series of problems that are similar to what you might face as a classroom teacher. For instance, Chapter 9, "Raise Those Scores," leads you to investigate what might happen when a school district decides to devote all its energy to improving standardized test scores, regardless of the consequences to programs, personnel, or learning. You will be asked to assume the perspective of a relatively new teacher in one of two high schools in the district, the older and lower performing school. After examining what the superintendent is calling for in the system, you will address the school board as part of a team to endorse, modify, or oppose the superintendent's test-prep plan.

Each chapter follows a similar pattern. A brief introduction sets the context for the general issue represented in the case. Although the particulars of each problem are built around unique situations, the issues at stake span across most schools. Following the introduction, each chapter lays out the particulars of the problem (for example, details about policy or the community) and the basic parameters of the solution you will be asked to come up with. These parameters will be somewhat loose, because—*and here's an asset of PBL*—you may define the problem in a manner significantly different from some of your colleagues. Where one group sees a problem with ineffective school leadership, another sees a problem with curricular organization or assessment.

A series of problem documents comes next in each chapter. These documents are modeled after the sorts of documents teachers encounter in their work. Some of the documents will look familiar to you, as in the case of a newspaper editorial that slams the work of educators. Other documents may seem strange, almost in need of translation. You will find, for example, a psychoeducational assessment of a student in the problem documents for Chapter 3. You may find that this assessment becomes clear after a couple of readings; you may find you need to seek some help from others to understand it. In either case, you will profit from wrestling with this sort of document in a safe learning environment rather than seeing such an assessment for the first time when you are contributing to a decision that will have a significant impact on a young person's future.

My intent for you is to stop reading the chapter after you have examined the problem documents. Work through the problem, propose a solution, discuss the experience with your peers, and then return to finish the chapter. Each chapter includes guides to reflection on some of the issues that may have been raised in your solving of the problems. I know that no group will raise all the questions I have included in reflection, and I know that nearly every group will raise questions I had not anticipated. The main focus of a problem may be determining whether to overturn a teacher's grade (Chapter 5), but multiple intelligences in the curriculum emerges as a key issue for one group while another group becomes fascinated with school district policies. Such is the nature of PBL. Indeed, if you were to come back to any given chapter after more experience as a teacher, you would see new issues emerge.

Each chapter concludes with a set of discussion questions and an annotated list of further readings. Clearly, no such list can be exhaustive. As I've worked with these problems and my students, they always find even better readings than the ones I've collected for them. You will, too, if you look. But I've given you a starting point.

As I indicated earlier, your instructor will guide you to the problems she or he finds most productive for your learning experience. The problems in Part II are not placed in a sequence that needs to be respected. If you do Chapter 7 before Chapter 6, that's fine. In fact, this text works best when it is seen as part of a whole program of teacher education (pre-service or graduate) rather than the textbook for a single course. Some problems focus on student characteristics and needs, which suggests one course, while others focus on policy, school structures, or curriculum. Thus, using the text throughout a program reinforces the method of learning (PBL) while allowing you to explore many potential difficulties you may face in your career.

Part III concludes the book with two chapters. Although each problem chapter asks you to reflect on issues in the problem, the first chapter in Part III asks you to reflect more specifically on how you learn in this model and what you have learned about yourself. The final chapter guides you through the process of creating your own PBL unit. Some people think it is necessary to go through this process before participating in PBL activities, and they recommended that I put this chapter up front. Working with many students from middle school to graduate school, I have found that my students have the greatest success when I immerse them in several problems before I ask them to try to create problems of their own. For that reason, I have left the chapter at the end of the book. However, I encourage you to glance at this chapter whenever you feel it would be of most help. The chapter reveals how I create problems as a means to encourage you to create problems of your own. Ultimately, I am hoping that your experience with PBL will lead you to create such learning experiences for your students.

PREVIEW

You were thrilled to find out you had received a position teaching at a desirable local high school. This was your dream job—a good school, a great community, and a better-than-average teaching load for a newcomer in this established school. In fact, you were so pleased with the job that you spent a tremendous amount of your time over the summer preparing to be the best possible teacher. You organized all your units for the year, complete with several excellent projects, outside learning opportunities, numerous cooperative learning opportunities, and a thorough assessment plan.

On the first day of school, you decided to begin with a careful explanation of what your class was all about and the vision you had for the year. It went very well the first and second periods, but then came third period. You had barely begun the class when a counselor interrupted you and called you to the door. Standing in the hallway, she introduced you to a new student. You invited the student to take a seat, but the counselor held you back in the hall for a moment longer. She explained that the student had a condition called "Asperger's syndrome." She added that the student appeared to do fairly well in highly structured independent work, but fell apart in group situations.

What should you do? What does it mean to have a student in class with Asperger's syndrome? What is that? And what about all the plans you had made for an exciting classroom? Would those plans stand? Who might you turn to for help? What do other teachers do in such situations? What resources are there for you? Ultimately, how will you adapt your plans, your activities, your vision of the classroom to this new reality? *Or should you?*

In determining how you would adapt to this situation, you are at the beginning of a problem-based learning experience. You are also at the edges of what it means to be a teacher—where you continually confront new situations with less information than you would like, situations that demand that you consider possibilities, inquire about facts, and come to decisions about what is the best solution. Welcome.

ACKNOWLEDGMENTS

I wish to thank a number of people for their assistance with this project. Dr. Mary McLellan, Dr. Felicia McGinty, Dr. Minnie Andrews, and Russell Randall all reviewed problems or portions of problems included here. Dr. Pat Hays and Dr. Peggy Raines experimented with problems to assist in their refinement. Also, I appreciate the comments of the reviewers: Mavis Brown, University of Richmond; Fred Groves, University of Louisiana at Monroe; Robert Gryder, Arizona State University; Charles Pryor, University of Louisiana at Monroe; and Tracy Smith, Appalachian State University. Traci Mueller provided helpful editorial assistance. And above all, I wish to thank Kerry Olson Kain for her assistance throughout.

CHAPTER ONE

WHY PROBLEM-BASED LEARNING FOR FUTURE TEACHERS?

Teachers work. Teachers work hard to accomplish the complex goals they have for their students. Teachers work with a variety of pressures on them from all directions, and if anyone were to enter the profession with a naive notion that teachers' work is simply standing in front of a class and explaining ideas, the system would shock them sorely.

Of course, teachers do stand in front of the class to explain important ideas, and good teachers use a host of other teaching models and techniques to help their students succeed. The process of becoming an effective teacher involves a negotiation among all the responsibilities that await you when you face those first days in an empty classroom, contemplating the waves of young people passing through your door period after period. *Do I really have to make bulletin boards? How do I use this curriculum guide to make any meaningful learning go on? Where do I get the materials I need? What do you mean, I have to go to a department meeting? How can I handle all this grading of papers? How do I make a grade anyway? You mean some of these students don't even speak English? They can't read? Lunch duty—you're kidding!* It's overwhelming at times. And that's before you consider the committee work for arranging a school-wide motivation system and another committee to decide about adopting a textbook and another to examine a suggested change in the daily schedule and another to. . . . You get the idea.

Teachers' work goes well beyond making a lesson plan—though it always also involves making lesson plans that effectively help your students develop greater skills and understandings. This book is designed to help you at two levels on your journey to becoming the best teacher you can be. First, the book will guide you *as a learner* in a powerful means of acquiring knowledge while enhancing critical thinking and problem-solving skills: problem-based learning. Your experience as a learner will help you to empathize with your own students and provide you with insight about how to use the teaching/learning technique effectively. Second, the book will focus your attention on some of the complex issues that constitute teachers' work. You will have an opportunity to address some of the problems that may await you in your job—but in the relative safety of a community of learners.

1

WHAT IS PBL?

Problem-based learning is not new. In a sense, informal education has always incorporated the essential elements of PBL: A person encounters a puzzling situation, formulates some understanding of what *might* need fixing, gathers information, and tries out a solution. I imagine early farmers did this when they noticed the eastern portion of a crop flourishing while the section west of the stream was struggling. *What could be wrong? Is it the soil? the water? the sunlight? the seed? What are other farmers doing? What if I plant this section later in the season?* At a more formal level, PBL has roots in the "project method" of William Kilpatrick (1918). Kilpatrick argued that students don't so much need to be provided with answers as with experiences in learning to pose the questions and to work out solutions. He gave a wonderful illustration in response to his critics. Someone correctly observed that Kilpatrick's method would have children rediscover what we already know well—for example, how to grow corn. He responded that if it is corn we want, then the criticism is fine. But if it is children we want to grow, not corn, then we need to let them discover how to solve the corn-growing problem themselves.

There are important differences between "project-based learning" (Wolk, 1994) and problem-based learning, which we will address later. However, it is worth knowing that the PBL approach to educating children has a tradition in American education. Moreover, this tradition has focused on the importance of connecting students' interests with the real-world problems they encounter. John Dewey (1938/1963), a progressive educator, advocated that we organize learning around experiences, though he clarified that not all experiences are equal. He helped us understand that an experience is "educative" if it helps young people grow in positive ways. The task of the educator is to match the needs and capacities of the learner with the subject matter in meaningful experiences. The subject areas of the curriculum, he argued, should connect to "ordinary life-experience," and PBL does just that.

In a problem-based learning experience, students encounter carefully selected, but ill-structured, problems *before* they experience any instruction in the particular focus area (Bridges & Hallinger, 1992). The problem becomes the vehicle for learning. Motivation to learn is generally high because of the shift in focus: Instead of doing school work for the sake of school, the children attack real problems and the learning is embedded in solving those problems. Linda Torp and Sara Sage (1998) record examples of high school students solving problems related to waste from the school cafeteria, flooding associated with retention ponds, wolf reintroduction, and more. Taking on issues relevant to the local situation, students learn investigation skills (Internet, interviewing, reading), communication skills, perseverance, content-related concepts, and so on. In a summer program for middle school and high school students at Northern Arizona University, for example, students investigate the problem of getting 5 million visitors through the Grand Canyon National Park on a restricted and crowded system of roads. The students propose solutions to the Canyon's traffic problems, taking into consideration the social, historical, and environmental issues.

A basic version of PBL, which will be elaborated later, is as follows. Students encounter a problem situation. They inquire into the problem situation using a sim-

FIGURE 1.1   Basic Structure of Inquiry

What do we know?

↓

What do we need to know?

↓

How can we find it out?

Source: Based on Stepien & Gallagher, 1993.

ple three-part structure (Figure 1.1). They ask, what do we know, what do we need to know, and how will we find out (Stepien & Gallagher, 1993). As they cycle through this inquiry process, teachers coach the students on how to ask questions and where to seek information. Ultimately, the students present a solution to the problem in an "authentic" context—if not the real thing, then a close approximation.

Project-Based Learning versus Problem-Based Learning

How does PBL differ from project-based learning? It is a matter of focus. The project-based learning experience focuses on an outcome, which, though it will vary from student to student, has essentially the same characteristics. Having students create a videotaped news program about immigration in the 19th century would be an example of a project. Each group of students would select different events to highlight, use varying costumes and settings, and inject their own humor (or lack of humor) to present their information. But the basic projects would be similar, and the learning process from the start would focus on the product (project). In contrast, problem-based learning focuses on the process of inquiry. Instead of starting with instructions for creating a news program, a PBL experience might cast students in a role where they must inquire into a sudden change in immigration patterns. Students would investigate this puzzling situation, and perhaps some would decide to represent their discoveries in a documentary format. Some students would focus on political changes in America, while others might highlight social and economic changes in Europe. Some might decide that the problem is not really a question of immigration, but a pattern of natural disasters, and that what has been labeled as the problem is merely a symptom of the real problem. Their solution would, perhaps, completely neglect immigration laws, while some other group might focus exclusively on such laws. In short, while both project-based learning and problem-based learning provide engaging opportunities for students to learn, the focus on what one learns in each is different.

Case Study versus Problem-Based Learning

Problem-based learning has similarities, also, to the case study method. Indeed, the teacher education program developed at the University of Colorado, Boulder, in the mid-1980s was built around a position midway between the elaborate case studies from the Harvard Business School and the brief medical problem cases from McMaster University (Kraft & Haas, 1989). Case studies have been popular in many professional education programs, including teacher education. Numerous collections of cases appear each year.

In fact, many people view PBL as a version of the case study method. Let me offer a distinction. For the most part, case studies are presented as narratives, sometimes as brief as a paragraph, sometimes as long as a book chapter. Traditionally, students read and reflect on a case study, often writing responses, before engaging in a discussion with tutors and peers. The case study authors frequently include discussion questions to focus the learner's attention, but the centerpiece of learning is the discussion itself. In contrast, the PBL approach as presented here provides the learners with a series of artifacts that are not collapsed into a narrative summary. Learners must examine the documents, determine the nature of the problem, and propose an actual solution. Following this, a discussion similar to the case study discussion ensues.

Brief History of PBL in Professional Education

Some people might contend that learning to be a teacher (or a better teacher) is too important to trust PBL. For such critics, the popularity of PBL in other professional education programs may be worth consideration. In the late 1960s, medical educators at McMaster University and Case Western Reserve began using PBL to educate future physicians (Barrows, 1996). The technique has been applied to the education of architects, social workers, managers, economists, lawyers (Boud & Feletti, 1991), and educational administrators (Bridges & Hallinger, 1992; Bridges & Hallinger, 1995) among others. Those charged with educating professionals have found PBL to be effective in allowing learners to assume the role of problem-solvers in areas relevant to their studies.

How successful has this approach been? More data comes in all the time, but it seems that we do know a few things. Bridges (1991) reports that his students—school administrators—had superior attitudes and application of knowledge through PBL. Problem-based learning improves the diagnostic skills of medical students (Schmidt et al., 1995) and increases students' ability to retain and apply knowledge (Albanese & Mitchell, 1993; Norman & Schmidt, 1992). A longitudinal study of students in the professions of business, marketing, and nursing at Alverno College indicated that PBL enhanced the problem-solving skills graduates brought to their professions (O'Brien, Matlock, Loacker & Wutzdorff, 1991). Woods (1996), who helped establish the PBL approach for a school of chemical engineering, maintains that PBL is superior to conventional instruction in every respect. Barrows (1996) suggests that PBL may avert some of the destructive tendencies of other forms of instruction, because conventional instruction inhibits or destroys clinical reasoning abilities in students. Hmelo's (1998) longitudinal comparison of PBL and non-PBL students in medical schools found evidence that PBL students used scientific concepts and effective reasoning better than non-PBL students. She concluded that the PBL curriculum moved students "along the path to novice physician" more rapidly than the non-PBL curriculum (p. 202).

The Use of PBL in Today's Schools

In recent years, problem-based learning has been promoted by a number of scholars and practitioners for use in the public schools (Arends, 1997; Delisle, 1997; Fogarty, 1997; Glasgow, 1997; Jones, Rasmussen & Moffitt, 1997; Krynock & Robb, 1999; Savoie & Hughes, 1994; Stepien & Gallagher, 1993; Stepien, Senn & Stepien, 2000; Torp & Sage, 1998; Wiggins & McTighe, 1998). The Illinois Math and Science Academy incorporates the technique. There is a Center for Problem-Based Learning, with a website that features samples of the approach and a discussion of issues related to PBL (www.imsa.edu/center/cpbl/cpbl.html). Indeed, many schools are incorporating the practice (see Glasgow, 1997, for an example).

The research into the effects of PBL on learning in the public schools is still emerging. However, initial results are encouraging. In his action research study of PBL in a biochemistry course, Richard Dods (1997) found that students acquired content knowledge at about an equal rate through PBL and traditional lectures, though they retained more of the information in the PBL approach. Also, the depth of understanding was greater in the PBL condition. This finding is similar to Gallagher and Stepien's (1996) analysis, showing that students in the PBL model did as well on multiple-choice tests as students in the traditional model, with better depth of understanding.

Increasingly, educators are realizing the benefits of PBL as a means to help students become thinkers, rather than passive recipients of information. Martin Haberman (1991) saw this sign posted over a high school's main entrance: "We dispense knowledge. Bring your own container." Such a statement stands in stark contrast to what a PBL school would use for a motto. Students acquire information, yes, but in a context where they are seeing the application of that knowledge, and its relevance to their own lives.

In addition, students can become better at problem-solving in general (Gallagher, Rosenthal & Stepien, 1992). Certainly the nature of life in an information age justifies an emphasis on creating flexible thinkers who know how to solve problems. The process of solving problems encourages a number of important dispositions in students:

- They become *collaborative learners,* capable of working together to solve problems.
- They learn *critical thinking skills,* such as problem identification.
- They *apply knowledge* and connect to prior learning.
- They realize the *relevance* of their learning experiences.
- They learn to *assume responsibility* for their own learning.
- Over time, they become more *self-directed learners.*

The idea of students becoming self-directed learners is particularly appealing. For too many students, the move through school is a bland repetition of mind-numbing sameness, with little to engage their curiosity. Seymour B. Sarason (1998) offers an inspiring goal when he describes what he would like schools to provide children: *"I*

*would want all children to have at least the same level and quality of curiosity and motiva-
tion to learn and explore that they had when they began schooling"* (p. 69, original emphasis). Given that PBL has a record of success in sparking such curiosity and
motivation, it is well worth considering as another tool to engage students.

PBL AND LEARNING TO TEACH

People preparing to become secondary teachers and practicing secondary teachers
often express the desire to focus exclusively on the subject matter they will be
teaching. *Give me more math. I need to read more British novels. Let me explore the inva-
sion of the Armada in greater depth.* While it is true that expertise in your subject area
will serve you well, that's not the whole story. The love of subject matter expressed
by college majors is not generally shared by public school students. It is crucial,
then, that future instructors have a variety of tools to use in order to make their
teaching more effective.

By experiencing PBL firsthand, you will be better prepared to become an
instructional leader in your school. Working through the problems in this book will
assist you in learning the features of a good problem. For example, you will see
how different kinds of documents and artifacts can help make learning more relevant to the lives of students. You will witness from the inside the sorts of group
considerations you will want to bear in mind as you coach (Stepien & Gallagher,
1993) your own students through the learning process. At one level, then, your
experience in this process becomes a model for how you might help your own students. But there is more. . . .

PBL and Becoming a Professional

The problems you will address as you experience PBL through this book are not
what most people think of as teaching issues. Yet they are the essence of becoming
a professional. Beyond the teaching of English and math and science and the rest,
teachers face a host of issues that come under the umbrella of *occupational realities*
of teaching (Pellegrin, 1976). All the business surrounding the job of teaching—the
business of dealing with other adults and setting policies and making decisions—
forms a crucial part of your future occupational world.

Richard Arends (1997) writes about the "two big jobs" of teaching. These are
the interactive aspects and the leadership aspects of teaching. Interactive aspects
include what most people think of as teaching: explaining ideas, guiding students in
practice, showing films, and so on. The leadership aspects include planning the
lessons, managing the classroom, and assessing student progress. But there's
another part to this job, and it's deserving of the label the "third big job of teaching."
This third job involves the broader working world of being a professional educator.

In general, teachers-in-training focus almost exclusively on the instructional
components of the teacher's work world—the interactive and leadership aspects.
However, the "third big job" deserves attention. Consider an analogy. To prepare

for a long backpacking trip, hikers train their muscles through simulations of the kind of walking they will be doing. They prepare their shoulders to be able to endure the pressure of the packs. But they also carefully plan their routes and the materials they will lug with them. Even though they will be walking, mainly, they need to be prepared for the other aspects of the experience. So, too, though teachers mainly teach, there are other aspects of the job that require careful attention in the preparation stage and systematic reflection on the job. The problems you will address in this book are designed to help prepare you to deal with the complexities of teachers' work. That said, you should know that most problems you face in your career will bear similarities to what you face in this safe practice arena. You will want to hone the skills of collaboration, inquiry, and problem-solving so that you can be a fully-rounded, effective member of the faculty of your school.

Even more important, the problems you will consider here help to move you to the position of being an architect and builder of a positive school environment. Not only will you consider issues surrounding the occupation of teaching—from the viewpoint of an active participant in conversations to make the place better—but you will also begin to develop that habit of inquiry that promises to keep the profession stimulating to you. Sarason (1998) recounts a story about trying (vainly) to beat a dead horse into action, and then he writes, "Schools are to their inhabitants uninteresting, unstimulating, impersonal places where respect for individuality is rarely found—or even possible. Contexts for productive learning do not exist for teachers. *When those contexts do not exist for teachers, teachers cannot create and sustain those contexts for students*" (p.13, original emphasis). Perhaps a focus on teachers as learners can help to make the context of schools more stimulating for all.

An Alternative View of Coming to Know

In their essay on cognitive apprenticeships, Collins, Brown, and Newman (1989) focus on learning to read, write, and do mathematics. However, many of the principles they describe present a useful way of thinking about developing as a professional educator. Collins, Brown, and Newman criticize traditional education for its narrow focus on conceptual and factual knowledge, with little attention given to how experts actually *use* knowledge. By failing to place knowledge in the context of its uses, educators doom the learners to acquiring inert facts. In contrast, a traditional apprenticeship, they argue, provides an excellent context for learning; there the learner could observe a master, be coached as he or she practices, then have the master's presence fade into the background until it was needed in another new or troubling situation.

Most of the learning that goes on in schools is not the same as a traditional apprenticeship, especially when that knowledge is not external and observable. Still, this apprenticeship model is an effective way to learn to think like experts, to solve the problems that experts solve. In preparing to become a teacher or to enhance your teaching, there are many facts and concepts you will need to master. However, learning to think like a teacher is more in line with a cognitive apprenticeship than memorizing information from a textbook. Much of the cognitive apprenticeship is carried out in the student teaching or intern relationship, especially if the mentor teacher deliberately talks through her or his thinking about actions. But more can be done for this cognitive apprenticeship even before student teaching—or after the first few years of teaching. The use of a problem-based learning approach to professional education and graduate education allows teachers to build together a "culture of expert practice" where learners articulate the elements of problem solving. Problem-based learning also helps establish "situated learning," which is a learning environment where "students carry out tasks and solve problems in an environment that reflects the multiple uses to which their knowledge will be put in the future" (Collins et al., 1989, p. 487). Interactions with your instructor allow you to see how an expert goes about solving problems. Thus, the chief elements of coming to know through a cognitive apprenticeship are in place through problem-based learning.

A WORD ON MAGIC PILLS

This text offers an immersion into a form of learning that has proven to be engaging and effective for many learners. Any given individual may find it personally challenging or frustrating. In fact, *most* learners will find it to be frustrating at first. As you will see in the next chapter, some learners have had to adjust to PBL much the same as people grieve the passing of loved ones: the loss of a comfortable means of learning is hard to handle.

This is, however, especially important for future teachers to think about. Many of your learners will feel uncomfortable with one or another of the techniques you use. It never hurts to have a bit of empathy. More important, however, is the realization that this approach to learning is not offered to you as *the* solution to all teaching situations. It is not. There are places where a lecture is exactly the right approach or where self-paced learning centers will be far more effective for the purposes you have in mind. As educators, you must consider where your purposes and techniques match.

Indeed, PBL has its set of critics. Fenwick and Parsons (1997), for example, criticize PBL because it makes all of professional practice seem to be a matter of problem-solving. They worry that PBL creates an elite class of professionals, governed by rationality to the exclusion of other ways of knowing. Such criticism (and there are flaws in their critique, I think) reminds us that teaching is a complex act that requires openness to many means of accomplishing our goals. While PBL is not presented as a magic pill, neither is it a placebo or a poison. It is an important resource that responsible educators do well to experience.

THE PLAN FOR THIS TEXT

In the next chapter you will find a discussion of how you can best prepare for problem-based learning. One of the themes of that chapter, and this book as a whole, is that you can make much of your own education to the extent that you take responsibility to learn. You will need to be willing to pursue ideas and ask questions.

Part II of the text consists of a series of problem situations for you to experience. In each case, you will find a basic introduction to the broader issues, a few details to contextualize the situation, a series of "problem documents," a reflection section, and some suggested further readings.

Part III of the text provides you with an opportunity to reflect on your experience (both what you've learned and how you learn) and to examine how you might create PBL experiences for your own students.

DISCUSSION QUESTIONS

Throughout this text you will find discussion questions to assist you in processing the information. Such questions are best used for discussion. That is, you ought to talk with your colleagues about these ideas so that you can experience the kind of growth in understanding that Britton (1993) and others attribute to the exchanging of ideas. In the context of discussion, you are able to articulate, adapt, and advance your ideas.

1. Given the application of PBL to education in other professions, what does this mean for teachers? Is it appropriate to use the same training techniques as future physicians, nurses, architects, and so on? What shift in focus is required of future teachers when teacher preparation moves from teaching techniques and content to issues related to professionalism? And what does this form of education offer for the continuing education of teachers?

2. Based on your emerging understanding of problem-based learning, how is PBL different from the traditional use of problems in education? Consider the problems at the end of the chapter in a math text, for example.

3. Advocates of PBL recognize that its use always involves a trade-off. Problem-based learning allows students to go into much greater depth when examining an issue, but the time required means that there is less "coverage." What do you see as the advantages and disadvantages of this trade-off for your own education or development as a teacher?

4. This chapter has hinted at a variety of non-instructional tasks teachers must face. At this point, what kinds of tasks do you think would fit in this category? Based on conversations with practicing teachers and other educators, what do you see as the surprising elements of being a teacher? If you've been teaching for some time, what are some of the non-instructional tasks that took you by surprise?

FURTHER READING

Delisle, R. (1997). *How to use problem-based learning in the classroom*. Alexandria, VA: ASCD.
    Delisle's book has a clear description of what PBL is, with a good rationale for using this approach. Such a rationale is helpful if parents or administrators have difficulty accepting

a teaching/learning technique that is not familiar to them. Delisle also includes several sample problems at the secondary level, including a chemistry problem for grades 11 and 12, a biology problem for the ninth grade, and a seventh-grade mathematics problem.

Glasgow, N. A. (1997). *New curriculum for new times: A guide to student-centered, problem-based learning.* Thousand Oaks, CA: Corwin.

This book is a little less careful about some of the definitions of different models of teaching, but it does provide an excellent narrative account of one high school's use of the PBL technique. Glasgow's school is a member of the Coalition of Essential Schools, so the book provides a fine portrait of a "school-within-a-school." His Center for Technology, Environment, and Communication (C-TEC) becomes a model for how secondary teachers can break the mold of how schools have always been.

Stepien, W. J., Senn, P. R., & Stepien, W. C. (2000). *The Internet and problem-based learning: Developing solutions through the web.* Tucson, AZ: Zephyr.

This book makes a thoughtful link between PBL and using the Internet in the classroom. The authors provide a variety of units, including some from history, English, science, and consumer sciences, with reproducible classroom handouts. The intersection of Internet skills and PBL is a useful model. To some extent, using prepackaged units cancels out some of the greatest benefits of PBL (the local relevance issue), but experiencing these units will certainly assist in creating similar experiences for your students.

Torp, L., & Sage, S. (1998). *Problems as possibilities: Problem-based learning for K–12 education.* Alexandria, VA: ASCD.

Their book is an excellent, concise guide to how to do PBL in the classroom. Torp and Sage include numerous examples from the schools they have investigated, and they provide a set of templates that will assist you in developing units. The book is a fine resource for your work in moving students to become inquirers.

WEB SITES

Center for Problem-Based Learning
www.imsa.edu/center/cpbl/cpbl.html
Features samples and relevant discussion.

Let's Get Real, Academic Competition
www.lgreal.org/index2.html
This site organizes a competition among K–12 students, giving them the opportunity to work on real problems posed by actual companies. The web site allows you to see some of the problems and solutions proposed.

Samford University School of Education, Problem-Based Learning
www.samford.edu/schools/education/pbl/pbl_index.html
Samford uses PBL prominently in its programs, and this web site provides background and samples of the procedure.

REFERENCES

Albanese, M. A., & Mitchell, S. (1993). Problem-based learning: A review of literature on its outcomes and implementation issues. *Academic Medicine, 68*(1), 52–81.

Arends, R. I. (1997). *Classroom instruction and management.* New York: McGraw-Hill.

Barrows, H. S. (1996). Problem-based learning in medicine and beyond: A brief overview. In L. Wilkerson & W. H. Gijselaers (Eds.), *Bringing problem-based learning to higher education:*

Theory and practice (New directions for teaching and learning No. 68) (pp. 3–12). San Francisco: Jossey-Bass.

Boud, D., & Feletti, G. (Eds.). (1991). *The challenge of problem based learning.* New York: St. Martin's Press.

Bridges, E. (1991). *Problem-based learning in medical and managerial education.* Paper presented at the Cognition and School Conference of the National Center for Educational Leadership and the Ontario Institute for Studies in Education, September 26–27, Nashville, TN.

Bridges, E. M., & Hallinger, P. (1992). *Problem based learning for administrators.* Eugene, OR: ERIC Clearinghouse on Educational Management.

Bridges, E. M., & Hallinger, P. (1995). *Implementing problem based learning in leadership development.* Eugene, OR: ERIC Clearinghouse on Educational Management.

Britton, J. (1993). *Language and learning: The importance of speech in children's development* (2nd ed.). Portsmouth, NH: Boynton/Cook.

Collins, A., Brown, J. S., & Newman, S. E. (1989). Cognitive apprenticeship: Teaching the crafts of reading, writing, and mathematics. In L. B. Resnick (Ed.), *Knowing, learning, and instruction: Essays in honor of Robert Glaser* (pp. 453–494). Hillsdale, NJ: Lawrence Erlbaum Associates.

Delisle, R. (1997). *How to use problem-based learning in the classroom.* Alexandria, VA: Association for Supervision and Curriculum Development.

Dewey, J. (1938/1963). *Experience and education.* (first published, 1938 ed.). New York: Collier Books.

. Dods, R. F. (1997). An action research study of the effectiveness of problem-based learning in promoting the acquisition and retention of knowledge. *Journal for the Education of the Gifted, 20*(4), 423–437.

Fenwick, T. J., & Parsons, J. (1997). *A critical investigation of the problems with problem-based learning* (Report ED 409 272). Antigonish, Nova Scotia: St. Francis Xavier University.

Fogarty, R. (1997). *Problem-based learning and other curriculum models for the multiple intelligences classroom.* Arlington Heights, IL: IRI Skylight Training and Publishing.

Gallagher, S., Rosenthal, H., & Stepien, W. (1992). The effects of problem-based learning on problem-solving. *Gifted Child Quarterly, 36*(4), 195–200.

• Gallagher, S. A., & Stepien, W. J. (1996). Content acquisition in problem-based learning: Depth versus breadth in American studies. *Journal for the Education of the Gifted, 19,* 257–275.

Glasgow, N. A. (1997). *New curriculum for new times: A guide to student-centered, problem-based learning.* Thousand Oaks, CA: Corwin.

Haberman, M. (1991). The pedagogy of poverty vs. good teaching. *Phi Delta Kappan, 73*(4), 290–294.

Hmelo, C. E. (1998). Problem-based learning: Effects on the early acquisition of cognitive skill in medicine. *The Journal of the Learning Sciences, 7*(2), 173–208.

Jones, B. F., Rasmussen, C. M., & Moffitt, M. C. (1997). *Real-life problem solving: A collaborative approach to interdisciplinary learning.* Washington, DC: American Psychological Association.

Kilpatrick, W. H. (1918). The project method. *Teachers College Record, 19*(4), 319–335.

Kraft, R. J., & Haas, J. D. (1989). PROBE: Problem-based teacher education at the University of Colorado, Boulder. In J. L. DeVitis & P. A. Sola (Eds.), *Building bridges for educational reform: New approaches to teacher education* (pp. 161–178). Ames, IA: Iowa State University.

Krynock, K., & Robb, L. (1999). Problem solved: How to coach cognition. *Educational Leadership, 57*(3), 29–32.

Norman, G. R., & Schmidt, H. G. (1992). The psychological basis of problem-based learning: A review of the evidence. *Academic Medicine, 67*(9), 557–565.

O'Brien, K., Matlock, M. G., Loacker, G., & Wutzdorff, A. (1991). Learning from the assessment of problem solving. In D. Boud & G. Feletti (Eds.), *The challenge of problem based learning* (pp. 274–284). New York: St. Martin's.

Pellegrin, R. J. (1976). Schools as work settings. In R. Dubin (Ed.), *Handbook of work, organization, and society* (pp. 343–374). Chicago: Rand McNally.

Sarason, S. B. (1998). *Political leadership and educational failure.* San Francisco: Jossey-Bass.

Savoie, J. M., & Hughes, A. S. (1994). Problem-based learning as classroom solution. *Educational Leadership, 52*(3), 54–57.

Schmidt, H., Machiels-Bongaerts, M., Hermans, H., ten Cate, O., Venekamp, R., & Boshuizen, H. (1995). *The development of diagnostic competence: A comparison between a problem-based, an integrated, and a conventional medical curriculum.* Paper presented at the Annual meeting of the American Educational Research Association, April 18–22, San Francisco, CA. (ERIC Document Reproduction Service No. 385190).

Stepien, W., & Gallagher, S. (1993). Problem-based learning: As authentic as it gets. *Educational Leadership, 50*(7), 25–28.

Stepien, W. J., Senn, P. R., & Stepien, W. C. (2000). *The Internet and problem-based learning: Developing solutions through the web.* Tucson, AZ: Zephyr.

Torp, L., & Sage, S. (1998). *Problems as possibilities: Problem-based learning for K–12 education.* Alexandria, VA: Association for Supervision and Curriculum Development.

Wiggins, G., & McTighe, J. (1998). *Understanding by design.* Alexandria, VA: Association for Supervision and Curriculum Development.

Wolk, S. (1994). Project-based learning: Pursuits with a purpose. *Educational Leadership, 52*(3), 42–45.

Woods, D. R. (1996). Problem-based learning for large classes in chemical engineering. In L. Wilkerson & W. H. Gijselaers (Eds.), *Bringing problem-based learning to higher education: Theory and practice (New directions for teaching and learning No. 68)* (pp. 91–99). San Francisco: Jossey-Bass.

CHAPTER TWO

GETTING READY FOR THE PROBLEM-BASED LEARNING EXPERIENCE

One of the mistakes we often make as teachers is to jump into learning experiences without adequate preparation for the vehicle of learning. Think about what probably seems a simple matter to you: driving a car with a manual transmission. You skim along the roads, talking with your passengers, adjusting the radio, deciding about which turns to take, slowing, shifting, speeding, deciding, talking, and so on. The actions associated with shifting gears are essentially invisible. But recall how complex the act of shifting gears seemed when you first learned it. For most people, just getting the sequence of steps and the delicate balance of foot work under control takes full concentration. Never mind all that other stuff that goes on while we drive. In the same way, learners just beginning a new means of acquiring understanding need to focus on the learning process before they can set out to use is as it is meant to be used. This chapter will help prepare you to learn in a new way.

LEARNING IN NEW WAYS

Think for a moment about the students you are currently teaching or hope to be teaching in the near future. Suppose you find yourself in a situation where the students have been socialized through years of practice to view "real" school as a pattern where students listen and work quietly, passively, while the teacher does all the explaining. Anything outside of that pattern feels awkward and wrong to them. You decide the best way to help them understand an important concept in your subject area is to involve them in peer teaching through a jigsaw activity (Aronson, Blaney, Sikes, & Snapp, 1978), in which students become experts on portions of the target concepts. Your main target for teaching is to move them to a deeper conceptual understanding of an important concept, but you know that you can do that and more through this cooperative approach. However, before your students can succeed in understanding the concept, they have to understand and work through the format of learning. It's likely that the first few times you use the new approach, your students will be a little confused and frustrated. You will be acutely aware that if you had used the traditional explanation method, the students would probably have caught on more quickly. Still, in the long run, you believe that their understanding will be deeper and more long-lasting if you use a jigsaw. (And if you don't know what a jigsaw is, it's well worth investigating.) In addition, you'll be able to use this teaching technique for a variety of concepts once the students have mastered the basic approach.

What's happening in this example is something like what Michael Fullan (1991) calls an "implementation dip" (p. 91). Whenever a school or system or teacher makes a change, things get worse before they get better. The teaching/learning technique is awkward for all parties. The immediate impulse is to abandon the new way of learning and return to the old ways, just as a tennis player wants to return to bad habits that worked rather than persevere through the difficulties of learning to serve correctly—even if that tennis player spent a lot of money to master a new serve.

In fact, students themselves will sometimes pressure teachers to return to ineffective, but familiar, means of teaching if the newer models don't feel right (Haberman, 1991). A group of teachers and researchers looking into the experience of eighth-graders in PBL found that the shift to new forms of learning disrupted community expectations and created student anxieties (Sage, Krynock, & Robb, 2000), almost as though the teachers were changing the rules of the (school) game after the students had already figured it out. As Sage, Krynock, and Robb put it, "Students struggled with the work inherent in their new role as active learners. They were, by the eighth grade, well versed in the expectations of what they considered school to be: the teacher lectures or gives us information, we write it down and then give it back on a test" (p. 170).

Learning Styles Misapplied

There is also a myth or misconception that deserves some thoughtful attention. In an effort to be sensitive to learners, we may do them a disservice. There has been much discussion about learning styles or preferences (Woolfolk, 1998) or multiple intelligences (Gardner, 1995; Gibson & Govendo, 1999), concepts that can help us reach more learners and generate more variety in teaching. Too often, however, this discussion becomes a means of placing limits on our students rather than a means of pushing them to greater accomplishments. Young people who come to see themselves as "visual learners," for example, may develop the habit of dismissing other kinds of learning as not suited for them. David Strahan (1997) quotes one sixth-grade student who identifies her "main intelligences," but who goes on to write, "I am shy so I *can't* and hate to work in groups" (p. 80, emphasis added). It's unfortunate that someone that young has already decided she can't learn in certain ways. Joyce and Weil (1996) describe research that shows how students not only demonstrated different learning styles, but also managed to direct their teachers toward those styles. Students who are comfortable with group learning situations thrive in group learning. However, as Joyce and Weil point out, it is the young people who are uncomfortable in group settings who most need to learn to succeed there. "Hence, the challenge is not to select the most comfortable models but to enable the students to develop the skills to relate to a wider variety of models, many of which appear, at least superficially, to be mismatched with their learning styles" (1996, p. 389).

Joyce and Weil (1996) acknowledge the stress of new ways of learning for *both* the students and the teachers. After providing an array of models for teachers to use, the authors report some discouraging research to indicate that relatively few teachers (5 to 10 percent) will even try a new teaching strategy unless they are provided with a support system, such as coaching partners. "Even then," they write, "during the first half dozen trials, most teachers found the use of the new teaching strategies, whatever they were, to be extremely uncomfortable" (p. 338).

So there is a two-headed threat facing you as you prepare for becoming a teacher or as you focus on improving your teaching. First, you must consider what will push you to incorporate a variety of teaching strategies, *even when these strategies make you and your students uncomfortable.* Second, you face the prospect of being a learner in some discomfort, which, though it promises greater growth, is not exactly enticing.

Grieving or Learning?

To get less abstract and more personal, let's consider what the learning you are about to embark on will be like. People attracted to the teaching profession are generally those who found school to be a comfortable place, a place where they could succeed. In general, the traditional approaches to teaching and learning suit future teachers, because that's what they have used for success. Problem-based learning, however, pushes learners to make some fairly substantial changes—and change induces anxiety.

Donald R. Woods has been a leader in the expansion of PBL for professional education. He guided the development of a PBL program for chemical engineering at McMaster University, where the medical school also uses PBL. In one of his books, Woods (1994) describes the changes his students (at the university level) experience as they begin work in PBL. He compares the impact of the changes to the typical grieving cycle a person goes through when he or she suffers a significant loss. *Grieving?* Shifting to PBL prompts the same emotions as losing a loved one? That's the comparison. Of course, the degree of emotional response is obviously different, but the nature is similar.

Woods (1994) explains that the grieving cycle moves a person through eight stages. Your performance as a student, which has probably become a predictable element of your life, encounters a change in instructional processes, and the grieving cycle begins. As Woods summarizes them, these eight stages are as follows: 1) shock, 2) denial, 3) strong negative emotion, 4) resistance and withdrawal, 5) surrender and acceptance, 6) struggle to affirm the new reality, 7) sense of direction and desire to make it work, 8) integration of the new approach. In recognizing that such a response to change is normal, you may be better equipped to deal with your feelings as you encounter PBL experiences. At the very least, this understanding is crucial for you to have so that you can resist the temptation to dismiss PBL or give up trying before you've had the opportunity to work through several attempts.

WORKING WITH YOUR COLLEAGUES—NOW AND LATER

The McMaster model of PBL, like most versions, involves solving problems in a group (Barrows, 1996). There is an important reason for this in medical education: often the solution to a given problem requires the integration of various professionals' expertise. Likewise, in education, the natural context in which many of the problems of our work are addressed is in a group of colleagues. Committees make decisions about curricular issues; faculties join to decide on school policy; departments or teams collaborate to work through such issues as incorporating standards, re-evaluating resources and practices, or creating motivational plans. While little in teacher preparation addresses the collaborative elements of the profession, much of the work you do as a teacher requires good group skills. Indeed, there are increasing calls for teachers at the secondary level to learn to work together (Carnegie Council on Adolescent Development, 1989; National Association of Secondary School Principals, 1996) in the substance of their teaching.

Researchers have found that some of the best schools are characterized by a work environment that encourages teachers to work together (Little, 1982; Rosenholtz, 1989). Ironically, the teaching profession in general is characterized by a sense of loneliness and isolation (Hargreaves, 1993; Little, 1990; Lortie, 1975; Roberts, 1992), and this isolation gets in the way of teachers' professional growth (Ashton & Webb, 1986; Maeroff, 1993). The image of the teacher privately working away in an egg-crate classroom may be accurate, but it is not hopeful for the profession. As a teacher, your capacity to work with your colleagues will do much to determine both your success and the success of your school.

Fine, you say. *In my work as a teacher, I'll be willing to work with my colleagues. But now I'm working as a student, and these are my grades, and I prefer to do it myself.*

The problem with that line of thought is fairly obvious. If you practice teaching as an isolated activity, you'll learn it as an isolated activity. If you develop a habit of working through the issues of schooling alone, you'll become good at working alone. Despite the relative safety of a teacher-preparation program or a graduate course, you will have failed to learn and practice the skills of working together, skills that employers report to be most seriously lacking in new hires.

Working together goes pretty smoothly when you select people like you to work with. However, there are two major problems with doing that. First, the potential for generating the multiple perspectives that lead to excellent solutions is severely limited by creating groups only of similar people. In fact, William Dyer (1995), a group researcher, argues that groups of friends worry too much about maintaining their friendships and lack the diversity that leads to innovative, creative ideas. A second problem with only working with the people you select is that this is simply not the way of the working world—whether in education or elsewhere. You will find, if you have anything like a typical career, that you will have to work with obnoxious people and lazy people and annoying people—in addition to creative, exciting, committed people. In short, your work world requires you to be flexible, cooperative, and somewhat thick-skinned.

Another consideration is how much you will learn through the PBL experience. Researchers of PBL learning situations have found that when groups function effectively, attendance at group sessions goes up and achievement in terms of learning course outcomes increases (Van Berkel & Schmidt, 2000). For the sake of your own learning, it is worth your time to invest some energy in helping your PBL groups to function effectively.

Role-Playing Group Functions and Activities

One way to head off some of the potential difficulties of working with a group of colleagues is to play out some of the potential conflicts *before* they arise. As part of your preparation for learning in a group for PBL experiences, join with colleagues to work through some of the following typical group snags. The best way to do this is for different groups to take on one of the situations described here, and then to perform for the rest of the larger group. Follow each role-play with a discussion about what challenge each group faced, how the group handled its particular challenge, and what might be some alternate strategies.

A note about doing role-plays: It's fine to talk through the situation briefly, but it's far more effective to move quickly into a dramatic mode, where you construct the situation together. Work through the "scene" several times, but feel free to innovate as you recreate your situation in front of your colleagues.

Situation One.   Construct a group meeting/discussion where one of the group members continually pulls the rest of the group off task. Your group is a committee of teachers that has been asked to come up with a solution to the complaints coming from nearby businesses about students' behavior during the lunch hour. Your role-play should provide a brief demonstration of the challenging member's behavior and then focus on a productive means of dealing with this person.

Situation Two.   Create a group meeting/discussion where one member is domineering, pushing his or her ideas all the time. Assume your group is a mixture of teachers and parents who are trying to decide on a plan to institute more work experiences for the young adults in this high school. Conduct the meeting long enough to demonstrate the problem, but focus your attention on the solution to this domineering member your group thinks would be most effective.

Situation Three.   Construct a group meeting/discussion in which one member is apparently uninterested and a nonparticipant. This member does not do anything to disrupt the meeting, but simply does not contribute. Assume the group is a committee of teachers that has been appointed to recommend a solution to the controversy about using computers at your school: some teachers want a second fully-funded computer lab, while other teachers would prefer to distribute the computers to the departments to use as they see fit. Remember, use the situation to focus on showing the problem of the nonparticipant and how your group could effectively draw this person into the group's task.

Situation Four.   Design a role-play in which two members of your group are obviously at odds. There may be some conflict between them over the ideas the group is dealing with, but it is apparent that there is also much personal animosity between the two members. Assume your group is made up of teachers who have volunteered to help a high school principal decide on a new mission statement and motto for the school. Act out enough of the meeting to establish the conflict, but focus your efforts on how the group can address this problem of conflicting members.

For each of the role-play situations, be sure to discuss ways of handling similar problems. An important point for you to consider here is that the experience of anticipating common group difficulties may help you address similar difficulties later in your own group work. Beyond that, bringing potential problems out into the open may assist all participants in recognizing their own limitations or negative tendencies when they are involved in group work.

Group Structure

As you have probably already discovered in working with groups, effective cooperative learning requires that group members have an interdependency, but also an individual accountability. In your group work in PBL, you will discover that there are a number of predictable duties. To keep group members accountable, it is important that the group keep some sort of records—perhaps a log of decisions made and a list of things to do. Someone must keep such a record. It is also important that your group interact with your instructor. Someone must conduct such liaison. It is important that your group have a clear sense of direction. Someone must perform such leadership. The actual roles that group members take can change from problem to problem or even within a problem, but confusion about who is doing what will damage the effectiveness of your group's work. At a minimum, your groups should address these roles:

Leader.   This person is primarily responsible for keeping the group focused on the task at hand. Interestingly, teachers resist taking on leadership roles because of their sense of equality among colleagues (Kain, 1997). However, there is no claim of superiority by virtue of being the leader. The importance of keeping the group focused is simply too great to ignore this job.

Recorder.   You don't want to lose track of the decisions made or duties assigned. It's amazing how different each member's recollection of a group meeting can be, so to avoid this, have someone who will take minutes.

Liaison.   The leader can do this, but it is probably more effective for you to share duties. When you need to contact the instructor or another group, a liaison will be prepared to focus on that task.

Inquirer.   Peter Senge (1990) writes about the important roles of inquiry and advocacy. To get sound decisions, he argues, it is crucial that we consider options seriously. Ideally, every member of your group will be willing to question ideas instead of merely conceding. However, if you charge a group member with trying to see the other side, you will be more likely to have broad perspectives. This is not to be confused with the PBL inquiry process that every group member will conduct. The inquirer's role is simply to bring up counter positions as the group moves toward a solution.

HOW TO ATTACK A PROBLEM—A PBL PROCESS

Having examined the emotional reactions PBL might engender and the challenges of working in groups, it is now time to consider how best to attack a problem in PBL. This section will provide some guidance about what you should do as a learner in the PBL context. One note of caution: Often the pace of being a university student causes learners to want to hurry through tasks. Learners develop a checklist mentality, where their sense of accomplishment is tied to completing projects. *I finished that reading; I've written that paper; I've prepared for yet another mid-term exam. Now I get ice cream!* This checklist mentality is likely to cause you to rush to solutions prematurely in PBL. Your pace should be slow enough to allow you to experience the full range of issues and understandings embedded in each problem.

The major steps of solving the problems, which often must be repeated, are these: define the problem, seek information, generate options, select a solution, formulate and present the solution according to the parameters of the problem, debrief your experience.

Defining the Problem

Woods (1994) writes that "unsuccessful problem solvers tend to spend most of their time *doing* something whereas successful problem solvers spend most of their time deciding *what* to do" (pp. 3–6, original emphasis). That "deciding what" begins with deciding what the *real* problem is in a PBL experience. Good problem solvers tend to spend a good deal of time in what some have called "problem finding" (Bridges & Hallinger, 1995; Gallagher, Rosenthal, & Stepien, 1992) or problem identification (Adams, 1979). Rather than assuming that the most obvious issue is the real problem, good problem solvers dig into the problem details for a while, messing around with the facts and descriptions before they decide what the real problem is.

This messing about with the facts is especially important when we think about the way most problems come to us. Most problems come to us filtered through someone's perspective, and often that someone has embedded his or her view of what the solution should be into the problem description. Remember the last time you were told, "You know what *your* problem is? You . . . " In general, such statements assume a lot about "your problem." The principle of being cautious about defining a problem is illustrated well in a monologue from Robert Pirsig's (1974) novel, *Zen and the Art of Motorcycle Maintenance:*

> In Part One of formal scientific method, which is the statement of the problem, the main skill is in stating absolutely no more than you are positive you know. It is much better to enter a statement "Solve Problem: Why doesn't cycle work?" which sounds dumb but is correct, than it is to enter a statement "Solve Problem: What is wrong with the electrical system?" when you don't absolutely *know* the trouble is *in* the electrical system. What you should state is "Solve Problem: What is wrong with cycle?" and *then* state as the first entry of Part Two: "Hypothesis Number One: The trouble is in the electrical system." You think of as many hypotheses as you can, then you design experiments to test them to see which are true and which are false. (p. 101)

Another excellent example, not from the literary world, comes to us from James Adams's (1979) book, *Conceptual Blockbusting.* Adams recounts how people spent a good deal of time and money trying to devise machinery that could pick tomatoes without damaging the skins. These people were solving a problem of the *picking technology,* when in fact the problem was broader than that. The real solution came when the problem was defined as the issue of *damaged fruit*—and the solution was in genetically creating tomatoes with tougher skins!

Once your group feels confident it has explored a number of possible problems, you should state what you think is the problem fairly concisely—a sentence or two. However, as you gather more information, you may need to revisit your problem statement and revise it to match your emerging understanding. As Larry Cuban has written, "There is, after all, no worse lie than a problem poorly stated" (1989, p. 801).

To practice identifying "real" problems, look at the following samples (Figures 2.1 and 2.2). These are two practice scenarios that were used with eighth-grade students to develop the capacity to form problem statements. Notice that in the first sample, students had a multiple-choice practice, while in the second sample, the problem statement is left open-ended.

Seeking Information

In the brief introduction to PBL in the last chapter, I presented a three-part structure for seeking information. Learners gather to generate answers to these three questions: What do we know? What do we need to know? and How will we find out?

Answers to the first question come from the problem documents or artifacts and the general knowledge of the participants. Each member of the group should carefully read the problem documents to determine what facts are present. Be care-

FIGURE 2.1   Scenario for Forming Problem Statements, Sample 1

The principal of a middle school expresses her frustration with the way the students in her school crowd each other, shove in the hallways, and make each other late for class. It seems as though the halls have actually become hazardous, and some of the teachers are worried that there will be a major disaster soon. The principal considers this situation to be out of hand, and she's not going to put up with it any more.

The *real* problem is
A. Children in this school are rude and do not know how to behave. They probably should have classes in proper public behavior.
B. The school is overcrowded. The school district needs to build another middle school to eliminate the problem.
C. The locker arrangement is poorly designed. The principal should remove the lockers and replace them with smaller ones.
D. The passing schedule puts all the students in the hall at the same time. A new schedule should be implemented that has kids going to their lockers at different times.

FIGURE 2.2   Scenario for Forming Problem Statements, Sample 2

The PE teachers at the middle school have approached the principal with a proposal. They say that their students continually fail to "dress out" for PE. Students refuse to put on the required outfit. Students make up excuses, such as not feeling well or that they forgot their outfits or that their mom was washing it. The teachers have proposed that students who do not have the gym uniform one time be given an hour of after-school detention and that students who do not have the uniform two times receive an F in the course. The teachers think this is the only way to get students to take this requirement seriously.

The *real* problem is

ful, however, not to mix up facts and conclusions drawn from those facts. For example, problem documents might make it clear that a student has a difficult time with English. That fact is not the same thing as saying the student is an English as a Second Language (ESL) student (one *possible* explanation for the difficulties with English) or the student has a processing problem (another possible explanation) or the student's home life is a disaster (a stretch). We must also be careful about the sort of general knowledge we list as what we already know. For example, if we say that language use is an important factor in learning, we're on safe ground (though it is always helpful to back up such statements with research). On the other hand, if we say that nonnative speakers don't do as well as native speakers of English, we're probably turning what appears to be common sense into a fact when it is not.

Based on our initial hunches and questions from a careful reading of the problem documents, the next question is, "What do we need to know?" For most PBL experiences, you will find there is some information included in the problem documents that has no real bearing on the actual problem. That's the nature of real problems—the problem solver must learn to sift through material to find out what is important and what is not. But you can be certain that each problem will have gaps in the information provided, and you will need to seek answers to questions. For example, if the problem has something to do with a teaching technique, does that teaching technique have a record of effectiveness? We need to know. If the problem addresses a new school schedule, has that schedule been implemented elsewhere? What happened where it was tried? We need to know. The group generates a list of such questions.

Armed with questions, the group then decides how to find out the answers. This probably involves two kinds of decisions. First, where are the answers available? Some questions would be appropriate to address to practicing teachers or other school personnel. Some questions might require venturing into the library or conducting an Internet search. Second, who will seek the answers? There is little point in every member of the group duplicating the efforts of every other member. It makes much more sense to consider how to divide the labor. As the group fleshes out the plan for how it will find information, make and record assignments for each group member.

At your group's next meeting, you will essentially be able to revisit the three-part structure. *What do we know?* has changed by virtue of the research conducted. Group members share what they have discovered and the list of what we know expands. At the same time, the list of things we need to know has changed. New information generates new questions. *How will we find this out?* The cycle continues.

Generating Options and Selecting a Solution

Your group has done some fact finding in a messy description, defined a problem, and conducted inquiry/research into the problem. It is now time to generate some solutions. Notice the plural there. Too many people and groups are satisfied to latch onto the first solution that comes to mind. Recall what I said about a "checklist mentality." A solution presents itself, and it is just easier to go for it. This way of thinking is not likely to lead you to the best solutions.

To avoid early closure, discipline your groups by requiring that you consider at least three possible solutions to any one problem. That way you will have some perspective, and though you may end up selecting the first solution that came to mind, at least you will do so because it is a *better* solution, not the only possible solution.

Once you have decided on the solution to a problem, you will probably need to conduct more research. Perhaps you'll only need to briefly revisit some of the resources you've already examined; perhaps new gaps will be apparent. Now you will have a refined focus for your research as you build support for your case.

Presenting the Solution

In the real-world context of problem solving, the next step would be to implement your solution. For example, if you had decided that the solution to an overcrowded lunch room was to build a new cafeteria, you would start the construction. In the context of PBL, such implementation is not possible. Instead, most problems will require you to make some sort of presentation of your solution (which is often true in real-world problem solving as well). You might be asked to address a school board or a parent committee, for example. In this context, as in the real world, you will want to present yourself as an informed professional. If you were to address the school board in your school district, you wouldn't come to the meeting in casual attire, speaking off the cuff, and presenting unfounded opinions. You would argue your case with supporting facts and in a manner that demonstrated your careful professionalism. In the same way, your PBL presentations of solutions should demonstrate preparation and professionalism.

Pay careful attention to the parameters of the solution presentations and the context described in each problem. If, for example, a presentation can be fifteen minutes long, don't make yours thirty. While instructors are sometimes generous with time limits, it's a rare school board that will let a speaker go on beyond the established time. As a group, rehearse your presentation. Listen to each other carefully for the effects of the presentation, as well as for the supporting evidence. It is crucial that teachers learn to make defensible decisions that are open to public scrutiny.

Debriefing the Experience

Again, in the real world of problem solving, the final step would be to evaluate your solution and its effect on the problem. In PBL, your evaluation takes on a different form. You will undergo a debriefing of each problem in two stages.

First, after each PBL presentation, you should meet with your group to discuss your performance. What went well? What needs improvement? Ask yourselves, *If we were in the actual context, such as a school board meeting, how would people have viewed our work?* Your group should discuss its performance, and it should also share in examining any feedback your instructor or colleagues may provide.

Second, you should join with all the groups that have addressed this problem for a debriefing of the issues represented by the PBL experience. This does not mean you will hear from someone what the "correct" solution is for the problem. Each problem has been selected so that there are multiple solutions, each with advantages and disadvantages. Instead, the debriefing should allow you to discuss the relative merits and potential disadvantages of differing solutions. In addition, your debriefing should be a time to raise points on which you still have questions. As a teacher examining professional issues, do you see questions generated by the experience that need further clarification from your colleagues or instructor? You must take the initiative to raise such questions for discussion.

Figure 2.3 lists some generic debriefing questions for you to consider. Not all of these questions will be appropriate for all of your PBL experiences. However, the basic pattern is sound, and the practice of reflecting on your experience is one that will help to sharpen your problem-solving skills and to make connections among the parts of your learning experience. Your instructor may ask you to respond to these prompts in writing, or your instructor may use the prompts as a discussion guide.

Following each problem, you will find a section in the text that leads you to reflect on some of the issues embedded in the problem. It is important that you use

---

FIGURE 2.3   Debriefing the PBL Experience

Directions: Use these questions as a guide to assist you in reflecting on your experience. Questions can be used for personal reflection or for group debriefing of the problems.

1. What worked well in the problem-solving process? (e.g., "We changed our definition of the problem, which led to new solution ideas.") _____

    _____

2. What key issues were raised by this problem? _____

    _____

3. What did you learn about these issues? _____

    _____

4. What questions remain after working through one solution? _____

    _____

5. In terms of working with peers, what did you learn through addressing this problem? _____

    _____

6. As a teacher, what is one thing you can apply to your professional work from this problem? _____

    _____

these readings as a means to debrief the problem *after* you have worked through a solution. If you read the reflections while you are working out your solutions, it is likely you will be led in directions that do not match your own inquiry. This will take discipline, but the reflections will be much more valuable to you after having struggled with the problems themselves.

A Note on Learning Objectives

As educators, we tend to think in terms of objectives for each learning experience. That's a good practice, but it has limitations when students are operating in ill-defined problem-solving situations. Still, keep this issue before you as you work through the problems in your program. The objective for your work is not that you solve these particular problems, but that you learn through your experience of solving these problems. Ideally, you will learn much about problem solving and working with colleagues and the substantive issues of the problems, and even the use of PBL for your classroom. The key issue, however, is learning.

DISCUSSION QUESTIONS

1. Problem-based learning can induce stress in learners, particularly those who have been successful in learning through traditional means. Are there any potential benefits to stress in a learning situation? What are some means of coping with stress that you have found to be effective? How can you use other people to assist you in dealing with stress?

2. Most manifestations of PBL involve learning in groups, yet many people complain that their group learning experiences have not been positive. What are some of the features of the best groups you've been a part of? What specific behaviors have made group membership a means for your own growth?

3. This chapter proposed several roles as a means of sharing responsibility for group performance and as a means of remaining accountable to one another. If you were helping your students lay the groundwork for successful group work, what roles would you have them take on? How can the idea of performing a specific task in the group limit a person's effectiveness? What does a group member do to make sure the role is productive for him or her?

4. Problem-based learning is obviously a version of problem solving. What are your personal strengths and weaknesses in problem solving? What approach do you find most effective? Is problem solving essentially the same whether in groups or on your own? Indeed, is problem-solving something one can teach?

5. Problem-based learning is above all a means of organizing the learning experiences for particular learners. How can you effectively keep the focus on learning? What role does the instructor assume in the context of a focus on learning? What means can a learner use to connect the disparate pieces of understanding acquired through an open-ended format, such as PBL?

FURTHER READING

Gallagher, S. R. (1997). Problem-based learning: Where did it come from, what does it do, and where is it going? *Journal for the Education of the Gifted, 20*(4), 332–362.
> A brief article that provides some of the basics about PBL from the perspective of teachers in the schools. Gallagher includes information about the history of PBL, some guides for teachers to become tutors, and some information about research on PBL.

Levin, B. B. (Ed.). (2001). *Energizing teacher education and professional development with problem-based learning.* Alexandria, VA: Association for Supervision and Curriculum Development.
> A short edited volume that provides a number of useful perspectives for teachers. The book includes a brief description of PBL, samples of how teachers use the technique, and a helpful chapter of questions and answers.

Woods, D. R. (1994). *Problem-based learning: How to gain the most from PBL.* Waterdown, ON: Author.
> The unique element of this book is that it is directed to the student in a PBL situation. Most other texts take the instructor's perspective. By focusing on what the student experiences and ways to succeed as a PBL learner, Woods provides a terrific resource for enhancing the benefits you might receive through PBL. In particular, Woods includes a great many diagrams and checklists that promise to guide reflection on the process you will be going through.

WEB SITE

Problem-Based Learning Initiative
> http://pbli.org/core.htm
> This site is available to support teachers at any level ("kindergarten through infinity") in work with problem-based learning.

REFERENCES

Adams, J. L. (1979). *Conceptual blockbusting: A guide to better ideas* (2nd ed.). New York: W. W. Norton & Company.

Aronson, E., Blaney, S. C., Sikes, J., & Snapp, M. (1978). *The jigsaw classroom.* Beverly Hills, CA: Sage.

Ashton, P. T., & Webb, R. B. (1986). *Making a difference: Teachers' sense of efficacy and student achievement.* New York: Longman.

Barrows, H. S. (1996). Problem-based learning in medicine and beyond: A brief overview. In L. Wilkerson & W. H. Gijselaers (Eds.), *Bringing problem-based learning to higher education: Theory and practice* (Vol. 68, pp. 3–12). San Francisco: Jossey-Bass.

Bridges, E. M., & Hallinger, P. (1995). *Implementing problem based learning in leadership development.* Eugene, OR: ERIC Clearinghouse on Educational Management.

Carnegie Council on Adolescent Development. (1989). *Turning points: Preparing American youth for the 21st century.* New York: Carnegie Corporation.

Cuban, L. (1989). The "at-risk" label and the problem of urban school reform. *Phi Delta Kappan, 70*(10), 780–784, 799–801.

Dyer, W. G. (1995). *Team building: Current issues and new alternatives* (3rd ed.). Reading, MA: Addison-Wesley.

Fullan, M. G. (1991). *The new meaning of educational change* (2nd ed.). New York: Teachers College Press.

Gallagher, S., Rosenthal, H., & Stepien, W. (1992). The effects of problem-based learning on problem-solving. *Gifted Child Quarterly, 36*(4), 195–200.

Gallagher, S. A. (1997). Problem-based learning: Where did it come from, what does it do, and where is it going? *Journal for the Education of the Gifted, 20*(4), 332–362.

Gardner, H. (1995). Reflections on multiple intelligences: Myths and messages. *Phi Delta Kappan, 77*(3), 200–209.

Gibson, B. P., & Govendo, B. L. (1999). Encouraging constructive behavior in middle school classrooms: A multiple-intelligences approach. *Intervention in School & Clinic, 35*(1), 16–22.

Haberman, M. (1991). The pedagogy of poverty vs. good teaching. *Phi Delta Kappan, 73*(4), 290–294.

Hargreaves, A. (1993). Individualism and individuality: Reinterpreting the teacher culture. *International Journal of Educational Research, 19*(3), 227–246.

Joyce, B., & Weil, M. (1996). *Models of teaching* (5th ed.). Boston: Allyn & Bacon.

Kain, D. L. (1997). Misplaced camels, crowded captains, and achieving greatness: Leadership on middle school teams. In T. S. Dickinson & T. O. Erb (Eds.), *We gain more than we give: Teaming in the middle school* (pp. 403–424). Columbus, OH: National Middle School Association.

Levin, B. B. (Ed.). (2001). *Energizing teacher education and professional development with problem-based learning.* Alexandria, VA: Association for Supervision and Curriculum Development.

Little, J. W. (1982). Norms of collegiality and experimentation: Workplace conditions of school success. *American Educational Research Journal, 19*(3), 325–340.

Little, J. W. (1990). The persistence of privacy: Autonomy and initiative in teachers' professional relations. *Teachers College Record, 91*(4), 509–536.

Lortie, D. C. (1975). *Schoolteacher: A sociological study.* Chicago: University of Chicago.

Maeroff, G. I. (1993). *Team building for school change: Equipping teachers for new roles.* New York: Teachers College Press.

National Association of Secondary School Principals. (1996). *Breaking ranks: Changing an American institution: A report of the National Association of Secondary School Principals in partnership with the Carnegie Foundation for the Advancement of Teaching on the high school of the 21st century.* Reston, VA: NASSP.

Pirsig, R. M. (1974). *Zen and the art of motorcycle maintenance.* New York: Bantam.

Roberts, H. (1992). The importance of networking in the restructuring process. *NASSP Bulletin, 76*(541), 25–29.

Rosenholtz, S. J. (1989). *Teachers' workplace: The social organization of schools.* White Plains, NY: Longman.

Sage, S. M., Krynock, K. L., & Robb, L. (2000). Is there anything but a problem? A case study of problem-based learning as middle school curriculum integration. *Research in Middle Level Education Annual, 23,* 149–179.

Senge, P. M. (1990). *The fifth discipline: The art and practice of the learning organization.* New York: Doubleday.

Strahan, D., Bowles, N., Richardson, V., & Hanawald, S. (1997). Research on teaming: Insights from selected studies. In T. S. Dickinson & T. O. Erb (Eds.), *We gain more than we give: Teaming in middle schools* (pp. 359–384). Columbus, OH: National Middle School Association.

Van Berkel, H. J. M., & Schmidt, H. G. (2000). Motivation to commit oneself as a determinant of achievement in problem-based learning. *Higher Education, 40,* 231–242.

Woods, D. R. (1994). *Problem-based learning: How to gain the most from PBL.* Waterdown, ON: Author.

Woolfolk, A. E. (1998). *Educational psychology* (7th ed.). Boston: Allyn & Bacon.

■ ■ ■ ■ ■ ■

CHAPTER THREE

WHAT SHOULD WE DO ABOUT ANDY?

INTRODUCTION AND PROBLEM BACKGROUND

Beginning teachers are often surprised to find out just how much the schools expect of them in relation to special education issues. Just when you feel you've mastered enough of your content material to teach your course effectively, you realize that you will also be expected to adapt that material to a host of different levels. If that weren't enough in itself, you will also be expected to meet with other teachers, counselors, administrators, psychologists, and parents to determine what the best possible placement and program might be for a particular child.

These placement meetings are generally called student study teams (child study teams is another term). Sometimes such meetings are polite discussions about how to support a particular student. But other times, such meetings are characterized by high levels of disagreement and emotion. In some cases, the various participants disagree intensely about the causes and cures for a young person's behavior or performance. The psychologist may offer an explanation that supports a parent's view of his or her child, while the teachers may maintain that this view tries to justify immature or malicious misbehavior. Or the parents may find themselves opposing all the school personnel. What happens then?

This problem-based learning experience asks you to examine just such a situation. While it would be convenient if there were a straightforward, single solution to every student's multiple needs, the real world offers no such simplicity. And while the players in the decision-making process struggle to make their cases, it is the young adult whose future is at stake. What should we do about Andy?

PROBLEM CONTEXT SOLUTION PARAMETERS

Context

King Middle School* in Paris, Arizona, is a relatively new school serving 261 students in grades six, seven, and eight. Up until two years ago, special education stu-

*For all problem documents included in this book, the people, places, and institutions are fictional. Any resemblance to people, living or dead, is purely coincidental.

dents received services in separate classrooms, isolated from other students. With the hiring of a new superintendent, all schools in the district have implemented "integration" of special needs students into the regular classroom. Initially, the professional staff strongly supported this move; after one semester, this support dissipated.

Andy P. is an eighth-grade student who has spent most of his school time in special education classes. He has a well-documented learning disability (reading comprehension and written expression), but he has most often been addressed as a behavior problem. Early in the first semester, his student study team met to review his individualized education plan (IEP), and the meeting broke up after the participants could not come to any agreements. Andy's mother refused to sign off on a new plan because she felt Andy should be treated like a regular education student; the teacher representative disagreed strongly with her. In an effort to resolve this constructively, the principal suggested an independent team review Andy's situation. For now, Andy has simply stayed in a regular class assignment with no special support.

Problem

Your group is a committee of educators working at King Middle School. You have been asked to assist in this contentious student study team. Disagreements about what is best for Andy P. have arisen among his classroom teachers, the school counseling staff, the administration, and his custodial parent. These disagreements are evident in the statements produced by each (included in the problem documents). In addition, your committee has access to the latest pyschoeducational evaluation conducted on Andy, as it is represented in his previous IEP.

Solution Parameters

You will need to make a brief presentation to the original student study team, consisting of one of Andy's teachers, a counselor, his mother, and an administrative representative. What recommendations do you make for addressing Andy's school situation? How can you persuade the student study team that your ideas are best for a child like Andy? Consider the legal and ethical obligations in this situation. The maximum time for your committee to speak is 15 minutes; up to 10 minutes discussion time will follow.

You will also need to provide the principal with a written committee report that summarizes your recommendations and the reasons for these recommendations. Be sure that you support your recommendations carefully, drawing on what is known about LD students, school delivery systems, teaching techniques, and so on.

········**WORK THE PROBLEM** ⟶

PROBLEM DOCUMENTS

The following documents are provided for your examination in formulating a decision about Andy's situation (but remember, you will need to go beyond these particular documents to solve the problem):

3.1 Andy's latest Individualized Education Plan (IEP), which includes information from the psychoeducational assessment completed by the school psychologist

3.2 A statement from Andy's mother about his placement

3.3 A statement from one of Andy's teachers in response to the initial student study team

3.4 A statement from Andy's school counselor

3.5 A statement from the assistant principal in charge of discipline

3.6 The progress reports filed by Andy's math and social studies teachers for consideration by the initial student study team

3.7 Andy's grade transcript from sixth and seventh grades

3.8 King Middle School daily schedule

PROBLEM DOCUMENT 3.1   *Andy's Latest IEP*

Paris School District, Special Education Programs
INDIVIDUAL EDUCATION PLAN

IEP DATES: Beginning ___8/25/03___   Valid to ___8/24/04___

IEP status: _____ Initial   __X__ Review   _____ Change of placement

Exit date: _____

Personal Information

Student name: _Andy P._   Student #: _511–100–511098_   DOB: _4/12/91_

Grade: __7__   School: _King Middle School_

Parent (X) or Guardian ( ) _____ _Amaldea B._ _____

Home phone: _____   Work phone: _____

Vision screening date: ___5/17/01___   P _X_ F __

Hearing screening date: ___9/22/00___   P _X_ F __

Psychological evaluation date: ___9/15/02___   Diagnostic category: _SLD_

Special Education Services

Special Education Teacher assigned: _____

Related Services

Type	Eval date	Initiate date	Duration	Frequency	Specialist
Speech					
Counseling					
OT					
PT			*None*		
VI					
HI					
OI					
Other					

TIME IN SPECIAL ED: _____ 0% _____   Time In Regular Ed: _____ 100% _____

CLASS SCHEDULE:

	S	R			S	R
Social Studies		X	Science			X
Math 8		X	Reading			X
English/Language Arts		X	Electronic music			X
P. E./Health		X				

Indicate areas in which student will participate with students who have no disabilities:

____ Recess   ____ Athletics   ____ Clubs   ____ Recreational Activities

_X_ Lunch   _X_ Assemblies   ____ Employment   _X_ Passing Periods

____ Other _____

Evaluation/Review of progress

Previous Year IEP Goals and Objectives: _____ 7 _____ *Written* and _____ 3 _____ *Met*

STATEMENT OF CURRENT LEVEL OF PERFORMANCE:

Strengths: _Andy displays average intellectual ability. Test results indicate adequate perceptual organization, visual-motor integration, and processing speed._

Needs: _Andy exhibits weaknesses in verbal and reading comprehension and in written skills. He displays poor visual-sequential memory skills which may impact his reading and spelling skills. Andy's behavior is often marked by inattention and distractibility and some excessive motor movements. He has difficulty initiating seat work, comprehending instructions, and staying on task._

Additional parental comments: _____

Assessment Data (Standard Scores)

WRAT	Woodcock-Johnson		K-TEA	Other Testing:
Date: _____	Date: _9/15/02_		Date: _____	
___ Reading	_92_ Letter/ Word ID	___ Broad Math	___ Read. Decod	_____
___ Math		_70_ Dictation	___ Read Comp.	_____
___ Spelling	_78_ Passage Comp	_75_ Writing samples	___ Total Read	_____
	___ Broad Reading	___ Broad Written Lang.	___ Calculation	_____
	_90_ Calculation		___ Applied Prob	_____
	_88_ Applied Problem		___ Total Math	_____
			___ Spelling	_____

Interpretation of assessment results: _Letter/word ID, applied problems, and calculation are within the average range. Passage comprehension, writing samples, and dictation represent discrepancies between ability and achievement._

Goals

Short-Term Objectives	Begin/ Master	Methods of Evaluating	Instructional Methods, Materials, Adaptations
1) Andy will obtain a daily assignment sheet for parents to check with 100% compliance.	9/25/03 12/5/03	Parent report; secretary report	Assignment sheet
2) Andy will complete all assignments with 70% accuracy.	9/25/03 12/5/03	Percent determined from log of sheets.	Longer time permitted for Andy to complete assignments and tests.
3) Andy will turn in all assignments, even if only attempted, with 85% turned in.	9/25/03 12/5/03	Percent determined.	Assignments can be completed in resource room if necessary.

Are Limited English Proficient (LEP) services needed? __X__ yes ____ no

Language of Instruction: _____

Indicate LEP modifications incorporated in student's program:

____ Use of home language   ____ Hands on activities   ____ Interactive teaching

____ Multicultural activities   ____ Simplified language   ____ Cooperative activities

____ Individualized instruction   ____ Use of visuals, graphics,   ____ Guarded (controlled)
                                              audiovisuals   vocabulary
____ Other:

The above modifications will be implemented in the following settings:

____ Special Education   ____ Regular Education   ____ Other:

Least Restrictive Environment Plan

The I.E.P. Review Committee recommends:
New Placement: Category _____   IEP from _____ to _____
Student continues as _____SLD_____   IEP from _9/25/03_ to _9/24/04_
Student exits from the _____ program. Date: _____
Change of placement from _____ to _____.
(Reevaluation and/or justification documentation required.)

Are related services needed to benefit this student's educational program? ___ Yes _X_ No

Continuum of Alternative Placements

Site

_X_ Regular school within district

___ Regular school outside district

___ Special school outside the district

___ Home-bound

___ Residential treatment center

___ Hospital

___ Other: _____

Instructional Setting

___ Regular education with supplementary aides and/or consultation

___ Regular education with itinerant support

_X_ Regular education with resource support

___ Special education integrated with regular classroom

___ Special education, self-contained classroom

___ Special education, individual

___ Other: _____

Explain why the site and instructional setting indicated above is **appropriate** and **least restrict**ive: _Andy's ability levels warrant his inclusion in the regular classroom. Andy can profit from learning to comply with basic academic and behavioral standards in the context of peer interaction._

If less restrictive options were determined to be inappropriate, explain why: _Andy's self-esteem could be injured if he were placed outside the regular classroom._

Describe any potential negative effects of this placement on the student: _Andy may have difficulty keeping up with normal classroom demands and customary classroom behavioral expectations._

SITE AND SETTING DETERMINATION

1. The site selected is the school the student would attend if he/she did not have a disability. _X_ Yes ___ No

2. The site selected is as close as possible to the student's home. _X_ Yes ___ No

3. The instructional setting selected is based on the student's IEP. _X_ Yes ___ No

4. To the maximum extent appropriate and feasible, the student will be educated among nondisabled students. _X_ Yes ___ No

Explain any "no" responses:

_____

_____

Test exemption: ___ Yes _X_ No   Tests: _____

Behavior plan needed: ___ Yes _X_ No

Extended school year needed: ___ Yes _X_ No

Parents' rights explained: _____ (Parent's initials)

(Signature page filed with district office)

PROBLEM DOCUMENT 3.2   *Statement from Guardian (Andy's mother)*

Andy has never done very well in his classes because the teachers don't seem to understand him. He was pretty good as a student when he was younger. Maybe teachers were more patient. He didn't spend half his time in the office for trouble-making. He's basically a good kid, but he needs lots of attention. And that obviously isn't his fault. If his father had been any kind of father he would have helped the kid, even after the divorce. But it seems like now even visiting his dad makes Andy crazy. You should see the pictures he draws after that. And he's always talking about guns and stuff. In class, Andy just doesn't get interested if the teachers don't notice him and give him some time. I don't expect college work or anything like that. We all know Andy is no genius and he will have to learn some kind of trade. He just needs to know enough to get some kind of job, and he's never gonna learn that if he keeps getting kicked out. But you can't put him in with the special ed classes. What's a kid gonna learn there? He's not a little kid anymore and we need to get him ready for a real world where there aren't special ed classes.

PROBLEM DOCUMENT 3.3   *Statement from Ms. R (Andy's teacher)*

Andy is a difficult case. He's been identified as a special needs student, and I understand he's received services in the past. It's really hard to say what his needs are in that sense, because he is so needy in so many other ways. I understand he's from a broken home, and it's probably not his fault. That's not the issue anyway; we all just want whatever is best for Andy. His placement in my class is probably a mistake, because Andy is so unmotivated that he's getting nothing out of the time he spends in class. I hear from other teachers that they have the same problem with him. If the goal has been to give Andy some lessons on social adaptability, it's been a terrific failure. The one area he cannot handle is social. He speaks out of turn; he interrupts his classmates; he says "off the wall" things all the time. In fact, I've sent him to the time-out room five times just for inappropriate language. What I have not seen from this kid is any efforts whatsoever. I suspect he needs the full-time surveillance of a paid aide, but he hasn't got that in my class. I have 27 normal kids in that class who all need my help; I also have three other special education kids who don't have Andy's potential, but who don't disrupt class continually. At least they try when I give them work; Andy finds any excuse to get all eyes on him. I've simply exhausted all possibilities for Andy and I don't see why the class as a whole should pay for the ignorance of some short-sighted law! He will not make it in class.

PROBLEM DOCUMENT 3.4   *Statement from Mr. C (Andy's counselor)*

Andy is exactly the sort of kid who can make inclusion work. If there was a case for 94-142 to prove, Andy is it. I'm sure that patient, caring professionals could find a way to bring out this kid's abilities. He's not dumb. I think his I.Q. score was around 90, and that's probably higher than some of our teachers! He just has what Dr. T, the visiting school psychologist, calls a disability in written expression and reading. So why can't teachers allow him to talk, maybe find some alternative assignments? Isn't that flexible professional behavior? In all my dealings with this kid, I find him to be courteous, reasonable, intelligent. It would be a mistake to place him in a special ed classroom when he can make it elsewhere.

PROBLEM DOCUMENT 3.5   *Statement from Ms. H (assistant principal in charge of discipline)*

Andy P. has managed to offend just about every teacher in this school, except for a couple that he seems to run to when he's about to get hammered. And too often they cover for him. What I guess bothers me most about this kid is that he has been covered for throughout his life. His mother likes to blame all his problems on Dad; the counselors are quick to blame his teachers; the teachers won't face it either. Who is there to blame Andy? The kid has had enough chances, now it's time to live out some choices. I think Andy will never make it in a regular classroom because he sees it as an audience for him. I would like to be able to support my teachers, who complain about a lot of frustrations with this kid. And I think that we'll have too many other kids suffering from Andy's obnoxious behavior. Andy ought to go into a holding pattern: another year and a half in special education classrooms, and Andy could move on to some vo-tech training, where he belongs. I guess that's the ideal world. The real world is there are laws that maybe don't know what's best for kids. And there are parents, who are the bottom-line clients in a school. Unless we can work out something else, I've got to go with Mom's decision here.

PROBLEM DOCUMENT 3.6

Progress Reports Completed by Mr. Rios and Ms. Ostrum

Student Study Team: Progress Report

Teacher: Mr. Rios   Student: Andy P.

Date: 9/19/03   Subject: Math

Please address the indicated concerns to the best of your ability. Attach extra sheets or documentation as necessary.

The things I see as this student's greatest strengths:

Andy is able to complete straightforward assignments involving basic calculation skills. Working with numerical symbols seems easier than dealing with word problems. Andy can be a lively, fun student. He seems bright, but he's not working up to his ability.

The things I see as this student's greatest weaknesses:

Andy seems confused when working on word problems. He appears unable to understand the material and thus can't work toward any solutions. He then gives up quickly and begins to talk to nearby classmates. He can be very distracting to others, as well as easily distracted himself. He turns in assignments that are done in class, but rarely completes homework. Tests reflect his difficulty with word problems and an apparent lack of studying.

Current grade: C

Attendance: Generally good.

Other concerns:

I wonder if Andy's English proficiency is impacting his performance.

Student Study Team: Progress Report

Teacher: _Ms. Ostrum_   Student: _Andy P._

Date: _9/19/03_   Subject: _Social Studies_

Please address the indicated concerns to the best of your ability. Attach extra sheets or documentation as necessary.

The things I see as this student's greatest strengths:

Andy has a good sense of humor and can be very enjoyable in one-on-one conversation. He seems most interested in special activities like creating topical maps or other hands-on projects.

The things I see as this student's greatest weaknesses

Andy doesn't seems to put much effort into any assignments involving reading or writing. Much of his work is either incomplete or not turned in. On written tasks, he fails to develop or organize ideas and lacks mechanical skills. It seems that he never reads the textbook. Andy rarely enters into classroom discussions. He does tend to get into noisy conversations with friends and can seem restless and distracted.

Current grade: _F_

Attendance: _poor_

Other concerns:

I honestly doubt that Andy has the capabilities or motivation to pass this class.

Grade 6

Course	Grades				Course	Grades			
English/Language Arts	D	D	F	D	Math	C	D	F	D
PE/Health	C	C	D+	C	Science	D	D	F	D-
Geography	F	D-	F	F	Vocational Elective Experiences	B	C	D	B

Grade 7

Course	Grades				Course	Grades			
Reading	D	F	F	F	Math	C-	D	D	D
PE/Health	B	D+	C	C	Science	D	F	F	D-
Social studies	F	D-	F	D-	Art	B	C	-	-
English	D	F	F	F	Computers	-	-	D	D

Period	Times	Period	Times
1	7:40–8:24	5	11:49–12:33
2	8:28–9:12	6	12:37–1:21
3	9:16–10:00	7	1:25–2:09
4	10:04–10:49		
Lunch	10:49–11:19		
Advisory*	11:19–11:45		

Note: 6th-grade double periods (English/Language Arts) may use the passing time for breaks if the teachers elect to do so.

*Advisory period may be used as study hall at the teacher's discretion. Teachers are discouraged from using the advisory period for resource room support.

····PROPOSE A SOLUTION ⟶

SOLUTION SUMMARY

Before proceeding to the reflection section of this chapter, write a brief summary of your team's solution here:

Our team defined the "real" problem here as _____

_____

_____

_____

_____

_____

_____

_____

The key features of our solution were _____

_____

_____

_____

_____

_____

_____

_____

My personal view of the problem and solution is _____

_____

_____

_____

_____

_____

_____

_____

TIME FOR REFLECTION

As you considered Andy's case, you probably found a variety of issues you needed to think about and discuss. This reflection section is designed to add to your deliberation by focusing on the nature of inclusion, the complicated role of teachers, and the importance of learning about the network of colleagues available to assist you in your work.

The Nature of Inclusion

An unhappy reality in too many schools is the half-hearted compliance with inclusion laws. Teachers, generally under-prepared for the demands of inclusive teaching, are told this is something else they must do. So new students are assigned to their classes, without help for the teachers or the students. And as Rogan and his colleagues put it, "Inclusion without support is abandonment" (Rogan, LaJeuness, McCann, McFarland, & Miller, 1995, p. 35).

One of the tasks all teachers face, in the midst of the complex and demanding world of teaching, is acquiring a student's perspective on the issue of inclusion. Inclusion isn't a matter of doing yet another chore demanded by the bureaucracy or an interruption to the smooth flow of neatly planned lessons. This is a question of a student's learning. And more, it's a question of this student's continuing development of successful approaches to learning, successful attitudes about school, and a sense of efficacy about his or her own abilities. From the perspective of the included young person, it's not a matter of inconvenience, but of opportunities. For many secondary students, it's also a matter of years of feeling bad about themselves as students.

There is some evidence that providing students who have learning disabilities with support in the form of learning strategies can help them catch up with their peers, but far too often the included students find themselves simply dumped into lower track classes with no support at all (Rogan et al., 1995). Yet there are many options available for schools to create more inclusion-friendly environments (Fisher, Sax, & Pumpian, 1999; Sage, 1997).

The starting point is coming to the understanding of inclusion as helping these young people, as opposed to merely inconveniencing their teachers. Then the task becomes, in part, gaining a balanced perspective—what Virginia Roach (in Fisher, Sax, & Pumpian, 1999) calls the three legs of the achievement stool: curriculum, instruction, and placement. Fortunately, it turns out that much of what we do to help special needs learners is helpful to all students. For example, using groups for learning, using hands-on activities, and providing organizational supports are all solid recommendations for teaching most learners. Becoming a good inclusion teacher builds on becoming a good teacher (Capper, Frattura, & Keyes, 2000; Tomlinson, 1999).

You don't need to know all about inclusion and inclusive teaching techniques to start teaching, *as long as you are willing to be a learner throughout your career.* Tomlinson (1999) suggests a gradual approach, where each year you expand your capacity to differentiate curriculum in order to address the many needs of all your students. If you are growing year by year, you will find yourself increasingly able to help all learners succeed.

Teachers or Counselors?

As you worked through the details of Andy's case, considering the stresses placed on him from home and school, it may have occurred to you that this situation calls on the teacher to be a lot more than a teacher. To what extent, you fairly ask, is a teacher also a counselor or surrogate parent?

While the tradition of a caring parental figure has a long history in elementary schools, the idea that "caring" is important has recently found acceptance in secondary schools. The National Middle School Association, for example, has argued that each child should come into contact daily with an adult who knows and cares for him or her (1995). Nel Noddings (1995a; 1995b) makes the case that schools are obligated to make themes of care a part of every day. Deborah Meier (1996) sees the kindergarten model as an ideal for all levels of schooling to aim at. In short, there are increasing calls for teachers to be more than technicians of instruction, but also to be role models and confidantes.

There are, of course, limits. You should become familiar with the counseling resources at your school and the legal issues surrounding teacher-student interactions. You are not expected to be a trained counselor, and you should be certain to refer students to the appropriate resources as you see the need. For example, your response as an educator to the possibility that Andy's time with his father is unproductive is completely different from your response to evidence that Andy may be experiencing abuse. The first situation calls on you to be empathetic and supportive; the second calls on you to report through official channels.

Consider how you can be an empathetic, caring person who connects to students. Your success in teaching most students will be enhanced when they sense that you do care for them.

The Network of Colleagues

One of the potential frustrations in this problem is the need to deal with so many people: a parent, an administrator, regular teachers, special educators, a psychologist, and a student. However, by seeing these forces as frustrating, we may be losing sight of one of the most important aspects of helping special needs students—the network of professionals that can assist teachers.

As you begin to uncover the complexities of working with included students, you should also be uncovering all those resources that are there to help. You may find that there is a classroom aide, and with clear expectations for how you will work together (Giangreco, 1997), this aide can become a powerful ally. You may encounter a speech therapist, a physical therapist, an occupational therapist, a counselor, a psychologist, and more. What is essential is that you enlarge your view of the resources that you can draw on—without passing off the student to other "experts" to handle. Early in your teaching assignment, it's a good idea to find out just what resources—human and material—are available for you. For the most part, don't view your place in this as an independent contractor. Instead, learn to see yourself as a part of a team that is sincerely concerned about the student's welfare. Success is much more likely in the context of a supportive instruction team (Bauer & Shea, 1999). You may be surprised how much you can improve life for your students by making a quick visit to a special education teacher and asking what is working for various students. A simple adjustment, such as giving a student copies of your notes, can make dramatic improvements. The specialists in your school will not only have generic suggestions like providing notes, but they may also know particular techniques that work for the particular students you have in class.

This awareness of the "team" you have to work with should expand your thinking to reflect on the whole school context. Whenever you enter a school, you gradually become aware that there is a culture to this school. That culture is made up of the beliefs and practices and traditions and hero stories of the school. Some cultures are positive; some are negative. You can often see the difference by comparative trips to the teachers' lounges. However, it is important for you to realize that the cultures will have an effect on your efforts and your ability to work with the support team for inclusion of special needs students. Anne Wheelock (1998) writes, "The rhetoric of *all students achieving* is little more than empty promise without a school culture, including the norms, values, routines, and beliefs about learning that define school practices, that nurtures that vision" (p. 27). If the prevailing attitude in the school is that special education students are included because they have to be and teachers just endure it, the culture will work against real successes. Given this, consider how you might contribute to creating a school culture that honors positive, motivating relationships between adults and the children. For example, in discovering that longer class periods provide better opportunities to address the needs of included students (Bauer & Shea, 1999), you may help your school come to the realization that lengthened periods might benefit all students.

DISCUSSION QUESTIONS

1. The perspectives of Andy's mother and the teachers were clearly at odds in this situation. How does a teacher balance the focused concern of a parent with the accumulated wisdom of other teachers? When is it reasonable for a teacher to oppose what a parent thinks is best? And how do you weigh varying perspectives of parents, particularly in a case where the child's time is split between parents who do not live together?

2. A student's behavior and a student's disability may have the same effect in a classroom, but these issues are quite different when thinking about what serves that particular student. How can you keep the behavior and disability separate, and still create the classroom atmosphere you wish to promote?

3. In the teams that address needs of students, teachers are in an interesting position. They generally know the students better than anyone else, but they may be in a position of lower status than their colleagues. How can a teacher establish and maintain credibility and a spirit of cooperation with the specialists in the school?

4. Just how much should a teacher be expected to adjust his or her lessons or teaching style to meet the needs of individual students?

5. Considering the PBL process, what did you notice about your own frustrations with this particular approach to learning?

FURTHER READING

Giangreco, M. F. (Ed.). (1997). *Quick-guides to inclusion: Ideas for educating students with disabilities.* Baltimore: Paul H. Brookes.
  This book is a collection of ideas to help teachers succeed with inclusion students. Written as a series of "quick," reproducible recommendations, the book is user-friendly. You can easily find sections that will assist your work. The five major categories the guide addresses are these: including students with disabilities in the classroom, building partnerships with parents, creating partnerships with paraprofessionals, getting the most out of support services, and creating positive behavioral support. The book has many practical, promising suggestions.

Jarrett, D. (1999). *The inclusive classroom: Mathematics and science instruction for students with learning disabilities: It's just good teaching.* Eugene, OR: Northwest Regional Educational Laboratory.
  This brief publication focuses on math and science, but it provides a number of practical ideas for how to make a classroom friendly to students with learning disabilities. For example, Jarrett points out the importance of cooperative learning and peer tutoring for students with learning disabilities. She also explains how to use inquiry-based science instruction with these students and how to enhance the students' problem-solving abilities in mathematics. Jarrett gives a number of general strategies for making textbooks more accessible to students who have trouble with the written word. The subtitle of this monograph, *It's Just Good Teaching*, is an important reminder that much of what we do for students identified as having special needs is simply effective instruction that all students could benefit from.

Sage, D. D. (Ed.). (1997). *Inclusion in secondary schools: Bold initiatives challenging change.* Port Chester, NY: National Professional Resources.
  This compilation presents the way a number of secondary schools address issues of inclusion. Throughout the text there are examples of innovative approaches to organizing education, such as exhibitions for assessment, schools-within-schools, teacher teaming, and so on. Of particular interest is the chapter on Grand Avenue Middle School, in Milwaukee, Wisconsin. This account of one middle school's work with inclusion provides a number of features worth thinking about. The school has been creative in deploying staff and organizing students into a "family" structure, where students and staff work in smaller groups. The curriculum offered builds on the ideas of multiple intelligences and integrated studies, making it a more natural process to create appropriate IEPs for included children. The account includes sample assessment approaches, schedules, and stories about inclusion.
  For a similar account, with a focus solely on high schools, see *Inclusive High Schools* (Fisher et al., 1999). This book profiles three schools, with an analysis of what the schools are doing well to restructure into schools that have system-wide support for diverse students.

Tomlinson, C. A. (1999). *The differentiated classroom: Responding to the needs of all learners.* Alexandria, VA: Association for Supervision and Curriculum Development.
  In her short book, Tomlinson builds a compelling case for teachers to create learning environments and experiences that help students grow and succeed. Her book has numerous examples of teachers adapting the curriculum (differentiating) to students of varying abil-

ity levels. The examples run the full range of public schools. In addition, she provides a list of many specific ways to adapt the learning environment and experiences for students. Lest the reader be overwhelmed by the demands of such a list, Tomlinson provides practical suggestions for how to ease into differentiation and continue to grow as a learner. This is a book well worth reading for inspiration and guidance on the issue of adapting the curriculum.

WEB SITES

Disability Rights Education and Defense Fund, Inc.
www.dredf.org/index.html
This site focuses on issues of the law as it pertains to questions of disabilities. The site includes a summary of IDEA changes for 1997 and 1999: www.dredf.org/idea10.html

IDEA Practices
www.ideapractices.org
This site includes an index of resources and practical ideas for addressing inclusion of special needs students.

Internet Resources on Disabilities
http://busboy.sped.ukans.edu/disabilities
This web site is from the University of Kansas.

REFERENCES

Bauer, A. M., & Shea, T. M. (1999). *Inclusion 101: How to teach all learners.* Baltimore: Paul H. Brookes.

Capper, C. A., Frattura, E., & Keyes, M. W. (2000). *Meeting the needs of students of ALL abilities: How leaders go beyond inclusion.* Thousand Oaks, CA: Corwin.

Fisher, D., Sax, C., & Pumpian, I. (1999). *Inclusive high schools: Learning from contemporary classrooms.* Baltimore: Paul H. Brookes.

Giangreco, M. F. (Ed.). (1997). *Quick-guides to inclusion: Ideas for educating students with disabilities.* Baltimore: Paul H. Brookes.

Jarrett, D. (1999). *The inclusive classroom: Mathematics and science instruction for students with learning disabilities: It's just good teaching.* Eugene, OR: Northwest Regional Educational Laboratory.

Meier, D. (1996). Supposing that. . . . *Phi Delta Kappan, 78*(4), 271–276.

National Middle School Association. (1995). *This we believe: Developmentally responsive middle level schools.* Columbus, OH: Author.

Noddings, N. (1995a). A morally defensible mission for schools in the 21st century. *Phi Delta Kappan, 76*(5), 365–368.

Noddings, N. (1995b). Teaching themes of care. *Phi Delta Kappan, 76*(9), 675–679.

Rogan, J., LaJeuness, C., McCann, P., McFarland, G., & Miller, C. (1995). Facilitating inclusion: The role of learning strategies to support secondary students with special needs. *Preventing School Failure, 39*(3), 35–39.

Sage, D. D. (Ed.). (1997). *Inclusion in secondary schools: Bold initiatives challenging change.* Port Chester, NY: National Professional Resources.

Tomlinson, C. A. (1999). *The differentiated classroom: Responding to the needs of all learners.* Alexandria, VA: Association for Supervision and Curriculum Development.

Wheelock, A. (1998). *Safe to be smart: Building a culture for standards-based reform in the middle grades.* Columbus, OH: National Middle School Association.

■ ■ ■ ■ ■

CHAPTER FOUR

WHOSE DISCIPLINE PROBLEM IS THIS?

INTRODUCTION AND PROBLEM BACKGROUND

"Don't smile until Christmas." How many beginning teachers have received this bit of advice in starting off their school years? How many students may have suffered under artificial hostility as a result? The serious business of maintaining a safe, orderly environment in schools spawns an industry of systems and packages that promises help for the dedicated teacher. But the array of options can be paralyzing—and too often the advocates of any one approach to discipline come across as hawkers for the one true answer to a multifaceted challenge.

It's hard to overplay the importance of the discipline/management issue, either from the perspective of teachers facing unruly students or from the perspective of a concerned public. Surveys regularly discover that the biggest concern of the general public about education is discipline and safety in the schools (Rose & Gallup, 1999). At the same time, researchers document the importance of a well-managed classroom in promoting student learning (Wang, Haertel, & Walberg, 1993). In short, we often hear it said of a teacher that she or he "has a discipline problem," and this is a strong indictment of a teacher's abilities. An alternative reality may be that *schooling* has a discipline problem.

Perhaps it's worth looking at some of the extreme examples. A few teachers seem to manage classes effortlessly. They may not be able to articulate any "system" that they use, claiming instead that it's just a matter of relating well to the children. Some teachers will say they have no discipline problems, as though this were simply an innate quality. More often, teachers make deliberate and sustained efforts to run their classes well, and sometimes with quite mixed results. Consider the teacher who wants to create the supportive, nonconfrontational classroom. Students learn quite early that anything goes. The teacher may plead with students, play on their sense of guilt, and occasionally express profound disappointment. But the environment created here is not terribly supportive, maybe not even safe. Boundaries for behavior are fuzzy, and the guiding principle for the teacher's actions—a feel-good ethic—does not match the crowded and contrived gathering that constitutes a classroom. At the other extreme, a teacher may replace feel-good passivity with domineering aggression. Such teachers will brook no contradiction, no challenges to their authority. The primary weapon of such teachers becomes the harsh tone of voice, fueled by an array of put-downs ever at the ready. Students know they will incur the wrath of their teacher in any moves away from quiet compliance. Yet there is some mysterious attraction to sending that teacher over the edge of control. Whole schools can become sites of conflict and coercion. Here's the way one teacher–student interaction in the hallway of such a school was recorded:

> "You! Yes you! Come here!"
> "Yeah?"
> "Let me see your pass."
> "Pass?"
> "Come on, come on. Your pass."
> "Here."
> "This thing isn't any good!"
> "Huh?"
> "It isn't signed."
> "No?"
> "Let me see your program card."
> "I'm in Mister Brown's class."
> "I don't remember seeing you around. You better come with me."
> "But why?"
> "Because! Because you don't have a pass. YOU DON'T HAVE A PASS!"
> (Rothstein, 1987, p. 59)

There are intermediate positions as well. Some teachers work for democratic environments with clear expectations. Some create well-oiled classroom machines. In the 1984 movie *Teachers,* one educator, known to his students and peers as "Ditto," had created such a routinized classroom that it ran well for several periods even after he had died in the back of the room!

The nature of public schooling guarantees that classroom management and discipline will always be an issue. Public schools draw together people who would not normally associate. Schools crowd these forced companions into small spaces and give them tasks to do which too often seem unpleasant to students (Jackson, 1968/1990). These crowded companions—the students—then find they need somehow to assert themselves and establish some sort of status in the group. It is, of course, a formula for challenges. So whether we talk about an invitational school (Purkey & Novak, 1984), a quality school (Glasser, 1990, 1993), a community of learners (Kohn, 1996), a positive school (Jones, 1987), or any other sort of school, discipline issues will be awaiting us.

This chapter invites you to think about the issue of discipline at a level that may not have occurred to you yet. Of course each teacher needs to form policies and practices and routines for the classroom he or she inhabits. However, discipline may be an issue that spills out the individual classroom door and into the school more generally. In fact, there are schools where every teacher must use the same discipline approach, just as there are schools where every classroom is distinct from its neighboring room in this regard. One text on classroom management (Froyen & Iverson, 1999), for example, argues that the real starting place for good discipline is at the schoolwide level: "Professional educators need to think about management at a systems level (e.g., ecological systems theory). This means fitting classroom management plans into the schoolwide discipline policy, the culture of the school, and the culture of the community" (p. 31).

The problem you will investigate invites you to think about the bigger picture of discipline. When there is a discipline problem at a school, whose problem is it? Do we see each teacher as a maverick who will either make it or not in the rough world of classroom discipline? Or do we view a school as a community where all participants are called on to work together in order to create a positive place where learning is central? Is the teacher who "has a discipline problem" suffering, in part, because of the whole system of discipline in the school, as opposed to being personally weak or incompetent?

A reminder is in order. As with all problem-based learning experiences, don't forget to spend some time messing around with the problem before jumping at solutions. What seems enticingly simple at a quick glance may be more complex under the surface.

PROBLEM CONTEXT AND SOLUTION PARAMETERS

Context

You are a third-year teacher at Reston Junior-Senior High School, the only upper-level school in a rural community. You have worked in both the junior and senior divisions of the school, though currently your assignment has you teaching all senior-division courses (grades 9–12). You know all staff members fairly well, and you have a reputation for running an effective classroom. In fact, you've been called upon to serve as one of several "discipline" experts on the peer coaching* committee, which was mandated by the superintendent. In that role, you allow teachers to visit your classroom in order to observe how you manage students.

The school houses 437 students in six grades. The largest set of students is the seventh grade, with ninety-two; the smallest class is grade twelve, with forty-seven. School demographics indicate a majority of white children, with 15 percent Hispanic and 12 percent Native American. More than 70 percent of the students qualify for free or reduced lunch.

The school uses teachers flexibly. Four teachers work exclusively with the lower grades, teaching the "solid" subjects; four teachers work with mixed junior/senior groups (art, music, physical education, special education). The remaining ten teachers work only with senior-division students. A copy of the daily schedule is included in the problem documents.

---

*Peer coaching is a form of ongoing professional development that usually involves observing a colleague teach and then offering neutral or clinical feedback to this person.

Problem

Your principal, Ms. Westlund, recently completed her second round of state-mandated teacher observations and evaluations. In addition to observing all non-tenured teachers for the second time this school year, she managed to get into all tenured teachers' classrooms briefly. The rumor around school was that she did not like what she saw. This rumor has been confirmed by the memo received by every teacher today (see the copy of her memo in the problem documents). Clearly, Ms. Westlund plans to shake up the school.

Are things that bad at RJSHS? You have been content with your own classroom discipline. You don't recall any serious problems in your classroom. Also, you had not heard of any widespread concerns about discipline at the school.

The memo was disturbing to you, and since you were already on the peer coaching committee, you arranged for the committee to get together to determine how you might respond to Ms. Westlund.

Solution Parameters

As indicated in the memo, your group will have an opportunity to present its ideas and recommendations to Ms. Westlund or her assistant principal, Mr. Oesterman. You should understand that there may or may not be questions about your ideas. You may choose to present the ideas in the form of a panel discussion or a presentation by one representative of your group (supported by colleagues) or in some other form. You may include visual aids or handouts in your presentation. The administrators will give you no more than twenty-five minutes of their time—and that includes time for asking questions. Essentially, you will need to decide what you will recommend for your school to do. Also as indicated in Ms. Westlund's memo, each individual will need to write a memo to Ms. Westlund, addressing her requests.

•••••••WORK THE PROBLEM ⟶

PROBLEM DOCUMENTS

A number of documents are included with this packet for your group's use. You will find information about the context here, but remember the importance of going beyond the documents provided. Here are the documents:

4.1 Ms. Westlund's original memo

4.2 Section of a newspaper article on disorder in local schools. This section was a sidebar to a larger piece titled "Standards Move Education in the Right Direction." This sidebar generated more letters to the editor than any other issue in the previous year of publication. Members of the school board reported receiving numerous telephone calls as a result of the piece

4.3 RJSHS daily bell schedule

4.4 RJSHS school code of discipline

4.5 Comparative data on discipline referrals

4.6 Synopsis of several major management systems. These samples provide some indication of the range of options. There are many other approaches to management, so be careful about limiting your exploration to systems on this chart. Several books provide excellent, concise descriptions of various management systems (Cangelosi, 1993; Edwards, 1997; Queen, Blackwelder, & Mallen, 1997)

4.7 A sample evaluation form for presentations

PROBLEM DOCUMENT 4.1   *Ms. Westlund's Original Memo*

RESTON JUNIOR-SENIOR HIGH SCHOOL

Memorandum

Date: February 27, 2003

To: Faculty

From: Ms. Westlund, Principal

RE: RJSHS classroom discipline

I have completed all required observations and evaluations for our current schedule of mandated visitations. While I see a number of excellent things happening in our classes, I am more concerned than ever about the tone of the building and how this faculty is contributing to a problem perceived by the community at large.

As you know from recent news coverage, this community is concerned about the discipline of students in our secondary program. Kids are said to be running wild. Those of you who know me well are aware that I have supported the staff and defended our school publicly and privately. I have not wavered in my support.

However, I was surprised at the number of classrooms that seemed to lack basic control and respect. Students in the classrooms of novice and veteran teachers are not treating the learning situation seriously and they are not treating other persons with the respect they deserve. This is, simply put, unacceptable. I am not interested in blame. I know as well as the rest of you that "the times, they are a changin'." We have to deal with it.

So, here is the plan. Two weeks from today, we will meet as a faculty to determine a course of action. I will no longer tolerate the haphazard and fragmented approach to discipline at this school. We need to commit our whole school to one consistent, workable discipline program. I know that some of you don't think you need this, but our school does! It's a problem we all own.

I am asking two things of you in advance of that meeting. First, if any of you wishes to express an opinion about a schoolwide discipline plan, I would like to hear from you one week from today. We can meet and discuss the issue. This will give me a chance to weigh ideas before our faculty meeting. Second, I want a memo from each faculty member describing how you intend to manage your classroom. I need to know what "system" you use, or what system you think is best for you. Don't tell me you don't need a system or you don't have problems. I will consider these ideas in devising a proposal for our school.

| PROBLEM DOCUMENT 4.2 | *Excerpt from a* **Reston Weekly** *Article on Standards in Education* |

Are Standards *Enough* at Reston?

EDITORIAL STAFF

While the rest of the state is leaping forward with the help of rigorous standards, Reston Junior-Senior High School may be left behind due to the oldest problem in the books: kids' not behavin'. How can any serious learning go on if there is not order in the school? Is it possible for even the brightest, most motivated scholar to master tough standards in an environment where more kids act out than push on?

Visitors to RJSHS in recent months have reported witnessing behaviors that were not part of schools in their experience. "Kids wear hats," reported one mother, who asked not to be identified. "When we were in school, hats were forbidden. There used to be an atmosphere of respect for authority." Another parent, who visited RJSHS as a guest speaker, added this comment: "I won't be going back there. I came as a guest, prepared my lecture carefully. The stu-

dents not only didn't listen, but they literally harassed me. Kids were wearing walkman stereos in class; everybody had gum. I actually had to tell the students to be quiet so I could be heard, and I was a guest! What are those kids learning?"

Ms. Olivia Westlund, principal at RJSHS, conceded that discipline can be a problem at the school. "There's a huge mix of kids here, as you know," Ms. Westlund commented, "and it's a challenge to get them all focused on learning. We realize the unique challenges of rural education, and we are working on climate improvements even now."

Who knows what "climate improvements" might mean? From this writer's desk, it looks as if more educationese is preventing our local school from taking charge, setting up some reasonable discipline and getting on with the business of educating our kids. Does anybody else care?

Junior Division

Period 1:   7:45–9:15
Block SS/LA or M/SCI

9:15–9:30
Advisory and Break

Period 2:   9:35–11:05
Block SS/LA or M/SCI

Lunch: 11:05–11:25

Period 3:   11:25–12:05
Mini-course elective

Period 4:   12:10–1:00

Period 5:   1:05–1:55

Period 6:   2:00–2:55

Senior Division

Period 1:   7:45–8:35

Period 2:   8:40–9:30

Period 3:   9:35–10:25

Period 4:   10:25–11:25

Lunch: 11:25–12:05

Period 5:   12:10–1:00

Period 6:   1:05–1:55

Period 7:   2:00–2:55

Student Discipline

RJSHS is a community of learners. As with all communities, there are expectations for how we can make the community function well. Our theme at RJSHS is SMART. Stay SMART!

Supportive—we are all supportive of every learner

Mature—we must be mature in dealing with each other

Academic—there is one main reason why we are together: academics

Responsibility—take responsibility for your actions

Trust—we can only build community if we trust one another

Certain essentials are needed in a SMART school. These rules are listed below.

1. There is zero tolerance for use or distribution of controlled substances.

2. There is zero tolerance for vandalism, fighting, or harassment.

3. There is zero tolerance for excessive absences or tardies.

4. There is zero tolerance for disrespect, abuse, or insubordination toward faculty and staff.

5. There is zero tolerance for gang activity.

RJSHS will use out-of-school suspension for initial violations, followed by an expulsion hearing with the school board.

PROBLEM DOCUMENT 4.5 *RJSHS Summary Table on Discipline Referrals*

DIVISION	ATTENDANCE-RELATED	FIGHTING	INSUBORDINATION	OTHER	TOTAL
Jr, Fall 2001	87	12	16	44	115
Sr, Fall 2001	143	13	27	50	183
Jr, Sprg 2002	112	17	25	61	154
Sr, Sprg 2002	168	10	43	77	221
Jr, Fall 2002	114	14	18	61	146
Sr, Fall 2002	181	9	41	72	231

PROBLEM DOCUMENT 4.6 *Brief Comparison of Features of Sample Management Systems*

AUTHOR(S)	ASSUMPTIONS	TEACHER'S ROLE	STUDENT'S ROLE	SAMPLE TECHNIQUES
Canter and Canter (1992)	Everyone can control behavior, if expectations, rewards, and consequences are made clear.	Assert control by setting clear expectations and following through on rewards and consequences.	Focus on learning and self-control.	Clearly articulated rules, rewards, and consequences. No excuses for misbehavior.
Emmer et al. (1998)	Misbehavior results when children are not kept engaged and challenged.	Organize an academic, business-like atmosphere.	Focus on academic tasks.	Make organizational decisions well before meeting students; plan activities to keep all learners busy.

AUTHOR(S)	ASSUMPTIONS	TEACHER'S ROLE	STUDENT'S ROLE	SAMPLE TECHNIQUES
Glasser (1990, 1993)	People need to learn to control their own behavior and to become more logical. Misbehavior results from unmet needs.	Leader, not a boss. Facilitate problem-solving among students, helping them to make value judgments.	Learn to accept responsibility and act rationally.	Confront misbehavior with clear description; use of logical consequences, the classroom meeting.
Jones (1987)	Most discipline problems will disappear if there is a more efficient management of time.	Learn to communicate calm control Build positive relationships with students.	Respond to teacher's direction to stay on task.	Set limits with awareness, body position, eye contact, "praise, prompt, and leave."
Kohn (1996)	Behavior does not need to be controlled, but community must be built.	Do not dispense rewards or punishments; instead, assist students in learning to become good citizens.	Participate in creating community by making real decisions.	Actively construct a community of learners.

PROBLEM DOCUMENT 4.7   *Sample Evaluation Form for Presentations*

1. The team demonstrates *consideration of the audience.*   Lo   Med   Hi
- Acknowledges principal's concerns
- Links ideas to memo
- Builds presentation appropriate to purpose

2. The team demonstrates *sensitivity to the context.*   Lo   Med   Hi
- Proposes ideas that do not violate teacher norms
- Makes suggestions that address the range (7–12) and setting (rural) of the students
- Addresses (directly or through questions) implementation

3. The team demonstrates *understanding of management issues.*   Lo   Med   Hi
- Utilizes research in proposal
- Builds an internally consistent (philosophy) proposal
- Applies principles and strategies in defensible ways
- Acknowledges proactive nature of management (as opposed to merely reacting to misbehavior)

·····PROPOSE A SOLUTION ⟶

SOLUTION SUMMARY

Before proceeding to the reflection section of this chapter, write a brief summary of your team's solution here:

Our team defined the "real" problem here as _____

_____

_____

_____

_____

_____

_____

_____

The key features of our solution were _____

_____

_____

_____

_____

_____

_____

_____

My personal view of the problem and solution is _____

_____

_____

_____

_____

_____

_____

_____

TIME FOR REFLECTION

A great many issues arise in contemplating how to address the principal's request for a single classroom management system throughout the school. This reflection section attempts to guide you through some of these issues. Beginning with a general framework, the reflections invite you to think about several categories of management, including the difference between management in a specific classroom and an entire system. We will also examine questions about teacher independence, building a classroom environment, the relationship between discipline and development, and theories and principles of classroom management. Of course, you will find it important to continue your inquiry on this topic well beyond the reflections included here.

Three Components of Classroom Management

Froyen and Iverson (1999) offer an interesting way of conceiving of the task of establishing classroom management. They picture a triangle, the vertices of which represent these three components of management: *content* management, which focuses on organizing activities, space, and instruction; *conduct* management, which focuses on rules and consequences; and *covenant* management, which invites teachers to focus on relationships between the school and home, teacher and student, and students and students. Whatever management system we may be attracted to, this conceptualization of management broadens our thinking so that we don't reduce classroom management to one facet only. The triple focus reminds teachers that management is a part of a complex system of interactions, not a formula with precise and simplistic steps.

Theories, Strategies, and Techniques

Another distinction to keep in mind as we reflect on management issues is among theories, techniques, and strategies. A *theory*, in relation to classroom management, is a broadly-based explanation of how people act. For example, one theory of human interaction says that humans do that which is reinforced by rewards. This is a simplified view of behaviorism, of course, but it gives a certain power to explanations. A different theory might say that humans act to achieve self-fulfillment. Management ideas can be traced back to basic theories about how people function.

In contrast to the idea of a theory of human behavior, we can speak of management techniques. A *technique* is a relatively neutral means of performing an action. For example, some teachers' technique for getting a class to quiet down is to stand at the front of the room and shout, "All right, let's quiet down!" Another teacher's technique to achieve this goal might be to flip the light switch off and on, or to hold up one hand and begin the dreaded one-two-three count with fingers. There is often a relationship between a technique and a theory, but techniques have the capacity to cross over among theories, too.

At a different level, we can speak of *strategies*. Think of how we understand the notion of a "military strategy." In this case, a set of plans come together to achieve a certain goal. The strategy might be to isolate an area by cutting off supplies (a blockade), to patrol the back roads, and to squeeze the enemy with random bombardment. Essentially, the strategy pulls together a set of techniques (blockading, patrolling, bombing) based on a theory. In the same way, classroom management involves building a strategy (or system) that pulls together techniques in a way that fits a theory.

The confusion of many novice teachers comes about because of a narrow focus on only one of these levels—techniques. Too often beginning teachers have gathered techniques from their mentors, their reading, and their experiences, and attempted to bring them together like the shiny collections of packrats plundering the neighborhood. While most of the techniques are worthwhile and potentially effective, what is missing is the notion of strategy: a system of techniques that work together consistently because they draw on the same theory.

Given that broader perspective of the content–conduct–covenant management and the need to align techniques in a strategic way, there are several areas worth reflecting on to bring closure to this experience in understanding the question, "Whose discipline problem is this?"

System Issues: The Broad View of All Components

The Total School.   Fullan and Hargreaves (1991) speak of the "total school" as a way of describing how various factors interact to create an environment that is worth fighting for. They contrast a culture of individualism with a culture of collaboration, arguing that the latter can help to create a school that is not "negative by default," but "positive by design" (p. 37).

Fullan and Hargreaves (1991) are concerned with getting teachers to work together to improve schools. But their notion of complexity and the need for time and careful attention to building a culture also applies to the "total school" from the students' perspective. What if the total school is teaching children that they are not responsible for making good decisions, because there is someone there to decide for them at every turn? What if the total school, as in the Rothstein (1987) example that opened this chapter, is moving children to the place where they begin to "see themselves through the eyes of their caretakers: They were lazy, incompetent, ungrateful, unreliable, ignorant, untalented, untrustworthy persons" (p. 70)?

This is too significant to pass over quickly. Imagine if you were placed in a job where your boss reminds you daily that you aren't very good at what you do. She restricts all your actions by insisting that you get permission for the most routine decisions; she publicly belittles you for your mistakes. After a time, you are elated to learn that you are being transferred to another division of the company. Unfortunately, your next boss is just about as bad. He doesn't belittle you on purpose, but it is clear from his actions that he doesn't think you are very competent. He creates an elaborate set of rules for you to follow and he watches for opportunities to catch you when you make mistakes. He believes that you can learn from your mistakes. So it goes year after year. An occasional supervisor reinforces your intelligence and independence, but most follow the lead of your first boss. After five or six years of this treatment, if you last that long, it's likely you will come to see yourself as incompetent and incapable of making important decisions. The cumulative effect of your bosses will have marked you. Even if you encounter a more trusting boss in your seventh year, it's unlikely that you would be able to shake off your patterns of belief and behavior.

Just so, the cumulative effect of years of control from the outside may limit our students' abilities to take on serious self-control. This illustrates the importance of teachers becoming active in the conversations about what a school system should be like. The system sits like a weight on the noblest of our goals. We need to care for the system.

Teacher Autonomy.   An argument can be made that discipline is a schoolwide issue. Any discipline problem, so this reasoning goes, quickly affects the entire community. A student whose tardiness is tolerated in one classroom will carry the effects into the next classroom; the emotional strain in one place will ooze through to the cafeteria or the hallways or other classrooms in the same building. In contrast, some would argue that discipline is, at its most basic level, always a classroom issue. A given teacher faces a specific group of students in a particular context. That teacher must make decisions that are consistent with her beliefs, decisions that fit her style. Thus, it would seem, the decisions made about management are individual and independent.

Although the main focus of this problem is classroom management, one of the issues raised by the problem is the occupational community in which teachers function. Novices are generally not well equipped for the autonomous and isolated world of teaching. There's a certain irony that such a social occupation—you are always around lots of people—should feel so isolated. This situation has been well documented by numerous researchers (Ashton & Webb, 1986; Doyle & Ponder, 1977–1978; Hargreaves, 1993; Kainan, 1994; Rosenholtz, 1989). Teachers generally operate on their own, decide how to run their classes alone, choose and implement instructional plans by themselves.

While some work is being done to correct this isolation, it is an "occupational reality" that most teachers face. And this autonomy raises two questions that deserve some reflection. First, when is it appropriate to violate the "hands-off" norm of teaching and to offer help, advice, or intervention to a colleague? Second, how can a new teacher continue to grow professionally in such isolation?

Let's consider the first question. Suppose you are working next door to a teacher whose classroom is clearly out of control. The "hands-off" norm says that you leave the situation alone. When I was a beginning teacher, I heard noises coming from a nearby classroom, and I saw a stapler fly across the back of the room. With impressive panache, I marched into the classroom to tell the students to behave while they waited for their teacher to return from wherever she had gone. Before I could utter my threats, I noticed the teacher—she was there! And she apparently was aware of what was going on. I quickly turned and left the room, embarrassed by my gaffe. I did not talk to the teacher. Should I have done so? The "hands-off" norm is a pattern of interaction that says teachers are professionals who handle their classrooms as they choose. Trust them. The teacher whose room I visited so rashly later left the profession, but not before hundreds of students had suffered through her class, with at least one receiving a stab wound during class. And the teacher, herself, experienced years of frustration. Is this really what's best?

From the other side, what about the teacher who wants to grow profession-ally, but worries about this "hands-off" norm? Fortunately, for beginning teach-ers, there is a tolerance for seeking assistance. A beginner should be cautious about who you seek help from and about how you seek that help. Imagine the effect of going to your department head or principal with this statement: "My class is out of control and I need help getting it fixed!" Even if that is true, it's not a productive opening. It betrays a lack of competence and self-confidence, hardly the message you want to deliver to your supervisors. Instead, first consider who to talk to. Most teachers can find colleagues who can create productive environ-ments and who are eager to help novices. After discovering a willing colleague, start off with a better opening line: "I've noticed that your kids always seem to get right to work without your having to yell at them. Can you share some of your ideas with me?" You will find that most of your colleagues will respond positively to that sort of request.

Development?   The school described in this chapter's problem serves a wide range of students—perhaps wider than you have seen in your experience. What implications does this breadth have for answering a question about discipline or classroom management? Is it appropriate to build a management system that gains consistency by sacrificing appropriate treatment?

Children in the early adolescent period face unique issues of development (National Middle School Association, 1995; Stevenson, 1992). Among other things, the young adolescent is likely to be experiencing a radical shift of identification from the family to peer groups. At the same time, this young person is probably wrestling with understanding his or her identity, dealing with what David Elkind (1984) calls a persistent "imaginary audience." These issues are difficult, and they lead to differ-ent sorts of behavior, to forms of acting out that are potentially disruptive.

While all children differ, the students who are finishing their public school years are likely to be much more mature and confident than their middle school counterparts. The question, then, becomes this: Is it possible or desirable to create a management system that "fits" students across such a wide rage of develop-ment? And what if this system were to extend to the elementary schools as well? One might argue that if a management system taps into the way people work—that is, if the *theory* of behavior is universal—this system will work with all chil-dren. The other side would argue that the differences among developmental stages are so significant that no one system can possibly be an appropriate fit. What do you think?

In the Classroom—Content and Conduct Management

Classroom Environment.   While this problem for this chapter focuses our attention on schoolwide management, we need to devote some attention to the classroom level as well. In particular, it is crucial that new teachers recognize the importance of building a positive classroom environment for students, as opposed to simply orchestrating a quiet room.

The connection between the management and instruction aspects of teaching is well documented. Kauchak and Eggen (1998) state this quite forcefully: "*It is virtually impossible to manage a classroom without simultaneous effective instruction, and it is virtually impossible to have effective instruction without effective management*" (p. 332, original emphasis). In other words, a big chunk of the management issues can be taken care of by making sure the class is engaged in some worthwhile task. Does this mean class has to be "fun"? Can a professional make a distinction between time spent in *diverting* activities and time spent in *engaging* activities?

One way to address this question is to consider the outcome of activities. If students are merely filling time in entertaining ways, this is probably mere diversion. Admittedly, a teacher is likely to encounter fewer discipline problems in that situation than when kids are bored. However, it is more defensible for teachers to create activities that are both engaging and worthwhile. The positive classroom environment has at its base a strong instructional focus (Tomlinson, 1999).

Some writers have even seen management as an appropriate realm for incorporating the theory of multiple intelligences (MI) to assist with creating a positive classroom environment (Gibson & Govendo, 1999). Having thought through the use of space and collected varied and engaging activities, the teacher will be able to promote among the students a sense of autonomy and empowerment. Of course, there may be a danger here, in that the theory of multiple intelligences may have to be stretched to make it fit classroom management. For example, Gibson and Govendo cite the example of the teacher who stands at the door to greet students with a smile and handshake as a case of employing "bodily-kinesthetic" intelligence. Is this a case of taking a sensible means of establishing relationships with students and attempting to "dignify" it by tagging it with MI labels? Perhaps the more important point is that the environment can be made a positive experience by providing comfortable space and a warm tone.

Theories and Principles of Classroom Management

At this point, you should have investigated a variety of systems for managing a classroom. Clearly, there are too many for any one teacher to learn them all. Moreover, there is no point in learning them all. You may have decided that the theory a given system relies on just doesn't match your beliefs about good education. For example, you may have seen virtues in a system like Assertive Discipline (Canter & Canter, 1992), which lays out a clear plan for establishing control. But the basic assumptions of this perspective, including the idea of rewarding and punishing, may not match your views. If you are not convinced of the basis, it's probably a good idea not to adopt the approach. Likewise, you may have seen the Glasser

(1990) or Kohn (1996) approaches as naively optimistic about human interaction. One surely does not want to institute Glasser's classroom meetings as a technique in a context governed by a reward-and-punish view of human action.

Sometimes people express scorn for the diversity of theories. "That's all theoretical stuff," you might hear. "We want what works! Who cares about the theories?" This paraphrased complaint dismisses important differences, and it assumes that "what works" is readily apparent. It is not.

The conscientious teacher must be prepared to look beneath the techniques of management in order to assess the effects of management. Orderly classrooms where no one learns are no better, from an instructional point of view, than disorderly classrooms where no one learns. We need to ask ourselves whether the theories and principles we are bringing to life in our classrooms are having the desired effect. That is, are kids learning?

"Being" Issues—Covenant Management

Playing Roles.   Beginning teachers face a puzzling situation in learning to relate to their students initially. The idealism teachers typically bring to their first job is a wonderful asset. Too often, it is a short-lived asset. One factor in the demise of idealism is the pressure to fit the teacher role.

Consider the dilemma of the beginning high school teacher. She may be 22 years old, barely older than her students. In many cases, she may look younger than her students. Yet she has the full weight of responsibility for the classroom, with a little institutional authority. At the same time, she has the desire to create positive relationships with her students, and the line between being a friend and being the authority is a difficult one for the novice to draw.

Thus, in terms of covenant management—the idea of relating well to students—all teachers face a difficult balancing act. What is the proper balance? How can a teacher learn to build positive relationships in the context of responsibility for the classroom? How can the teacher be supportive and friendly without having to be a friend?

Froyen and Iverson (1999) offer some guidance through the idea of roles. Teachers must come to understand the expectations placed on them by virtue of their participation in the public institution of schooling. That is, the role a teacher plays in the system is not simply an expression of the teacher's personality. There is an established view of what is appropriate in the adult–child relationship in the culture that created the school. However, there is also a personal dimension to this relating. Teachers and classes build a history together, and each group differs. The teacher can express a caring attitude toward students, even while keeping the class focused on competent learning (Noddings, 1995). Noddings calls for us to relax the impulse to control others, to allow more autonomy for both students and teachers in decision making.

A Caution about Judging that First Year.   Whether you are facing a first year of teaching or in a position to help someone else who is, a caution is in order. The most anxiety-producing dimension of teaching, at least at the beginning of a career, is keeping control of a class. You want to make sure that your learning environment is positive and safe. However, be careful about adopting the perspective that all judgments about your effectiveness are rooted in this question of discipline. If you become too obsessed with this question, you might lose sight of that far more important issue: student learning. There will be many challenges in your first year of teaching. Give yourself some space to learn.

DISCUSSION QUESTIONS

1. How does a school decide on large system-wide issues? Are any voices lost in such decision making?

2. What are some distinctly different management systems? What fundamentally different views of education do they draw on?

3. What are the implications and consequences of adopting particular systems or approaches to classroom management across the school?

4. What makes for effective rules and procedures in a classroom? Does this vary by the type of classroom (e.g., elementary versus secondary; math versus music)? How does one remain sensitive to individual differences and still maintain "fairness"?

5. What is the extent of the power of a school administrator in determining classroom practices?

6. What "blame" does a school as an institution deserve for the way students behave?

7. What difference does it make for discipline matters that this school is a rural school?

8. Considering the PBL process, what did you learn about working in groups through this experience?

FURTHER READING

Cangelosi, J. S. (1993). *Classroom management strategies: Gaining and maintaining students' cooperation* (2nd ed.). New York: Longman.
Of the many general management texts, Cangelosi's is one of the most readable. He includes a wealth of examples and scenarios for the reader to consider, and he gives fair play to many different approaches to discipline.

Koenig, L. (2000). *Smart discipline for the classroom: Respect and cooperation restored* (3rd ed.). Thousand Oaks, CA: Corwin.
Koenig's book provides an interesting perspective in light of the discussion above about theories, techniques, and strategies. He starts by providing reasons why teachers should reconsider disciplining the way they were treated as young people. Then he provides a progression of strategies, from those that don't work through general strategies and on to strategies for managing specialized and difficult cases. Koenig's book is reader friendly, providing the beginning teacher with a rich pool of ideas at the level of techniques.

Kohn, A. (1996). *Beyond discipline: From compliance to community*. Alexandria, VA: Association for Supervision and Curriculum Development.
A powerful book to contemplate what teachers should do in order to motivate students and manage classrooms. In particular, Kohn raises questions about the role of rewards in

the sort of teaching and management systems we create. He makes us ponder whether treating our students the way you treat pets is a good idea. In a statement that has double meaning for the kinds of classrooms we create, Kohn writes, "Rewards usually improve performance only at extremely simple—indeed, mindless—task, and even then they improve only quantitative performance" (p. 46).

MacDonald, R. E. (1991). *A handbook of basic skills and strategies for beginning teachers: Facing the challenge of teaching in today's schools.* New York: Longman.

MacDonald's handbook has a chapter in it on a special form of teacher survival: "Learning to Work Creatively within the System" (pp. 23–38). This chapter does not provide a manual for management (though he does have a chapter on that, too). However, it is an excellent examination of what it means for teachers to participate in the larger system. Beginning teachers focus on a form of survival that is typically centered on just making it through each day with their classes. They have little time to look elsewhere, and as a result, they may find their creativity stifled by the organization of schooling. MacDonald helps teachers see the big picture, to "see the system for what it is and have the personal strength to resist being overpowered by it" (p. 27).

Tomlinson, C. A. (1999). Mapping a route toward differentiated instruction. *Educational Leadership, 57*(1), 12–16.

In her brief article, Carol Tomlinson says very little about classroom management. However, her description of three different teachers' work is well worth reflecting on from the perspective of seeing management as connected with instruction. Tomlinson describes three teachers. One is teaching important material, but in a way that is devastatingly boring. The second creates an exciting, action-packed classroom, but without any sense of purpose. And the third combines the best of both predecessors: a classroom that is engaging, but directed toward learning. Reading the article helps keep the focus on the learning environment we create for our students.

WEB SITES

MiddleWeb: Exploring Middle School Reform
www.middleweb.com/index.html
A terrific resource for middle school issues. The site is searchable, so entering the phrase "classroom management" will get you a host of up-to-date ideas.

Teachnet.com: Smart Tools for Busy Teachers
www.teachnet.com/how-to/manage
This particular section looks at a variety of ideas for how to handle the classroom management question.

National Middle School Association
www.nmsa.org
This site has links to research, resources, and practice issues.

REFERENCES

Ashton, P. T., & Webb, R. B. (1986). *Making a difference: Teachers' sense of efficacy and student achievement.* New York: Longman.

Cangelosi, J. S. (1993). *Classroom management strategies: Gaining and maintaining students' cooperation* (2nd ed.). New York: Longman.

Canter, L., & Canter, M. (1992). *Assertive discipline: Positive behavior management for today's classroom.* Santa Monica, CA: Lee Canter & Associates.

Doyle, W., & Ponder, G. A. (1977–1978). The practicality ethic in teacher decision-making. *Interchange, 8*(3), 1–12.

Edwards, C. H. (1997). *Classroom discipline & management* (2nd ed.). Upper Saddle River, NJ: Merrill.

Elkind, D. (1984). *All grown up and no place to go: Teenagers in crisis.* Reading, MA: Addison-Wesley.

Emmer, E. T., Evertson, C. M., Clements, B. S., & Worsham, M. E. (1998). *Classroom managment for secondary teachers* (4th ed.). Boston: Allyn & Bacon.

Froyen, L. A., & Iverson, A. M. (1999). *Schoolwide and classroom management: The reflective educator-leader* (3rd ed.). Upper Saddle River, NJ: Merrill.

Fullan, M. G., & Hargreaves, A. (1991). *What's worth fighting for? Working together for your school.* Andover, MA: Regional Laboratory for Educational Improvement of the Northeast and Islands.

Gibson, B. P., & Govendo, B. L. (1999). Encouraging constructive behavior in middle school classrooms: A multiple-intelligences approach. *Intervention in School & Clinic, 35*(1), 16–22.

Glasser, W. (1990). *The quality school: Managing students without coercion.* New York: Harper & Row.

Glasser, W. (1993). *The quality school teacher: A companion volume to The Quality School.* New York: Harper Collins.

Hargreaves, A. (1993). Individualism and individuality: Reinterpreting the teacher culture. *International Journal of Educational Research, 19*(3), 227–246.

Jackson, P. W. (1968/1990). *Life in classrooms.* New York: Teachers College Press.

Jones, F. H. (1987). *Positive classroom discipline.* New York: McGraw-Hill.

Kainan, A. (1994). *The staffroom: Observing the professional culture.* Brookfield, VT: Avebury Ashgate.

Kauchak, D. P., & Eggen, P. D. (1998). *Learning & teaching: Research-based methods* (3rd ed.). Boston: Allyn & Bacon.

Koenig, L. (2000). *Smart discipline for the classroom: Respect and cooperation restored* (3rd ed.). Thousand Oaks, CA: Corwin.

Kohn, A. (1996). *Beyond discipline: From compliance to community.* Alexandria, VA: Association for Supervision and Curriculum Development.

National Middle School Association. (1995). *This we believe: Developmentally responsive middle level schools.* Columbus, OH: National Middle School Association.

Noddings, N. (1995). A morally defensible mission for schools in the 21st century. *Phi Delta Kappan, 76*(5), 365–368.

Purkey, W. W., & Novak, J. M. (1984). *Inviting school success: A self-concept approach to teaching and learning* (2nd ed.). Belmont, CA: Wadsworth.

Queen, J. A., Blackwelder, B. B., & Mallen, L. P. (1997). *Responsible classroom management for teachers and students.* Upper Saddle River, NJ: Merrill.

Rose, L. C., & Gallup, A. M. (1999). The 31st annual Phi Delta Kappa/Gallup poll of the public's attitudes toward the public schools. *Phi Delta Kappan, 81*(1), 41–56.

Rosenholtz, S. J. (1989). *Teachers' workplace: The social organization of schools.* White Plains, NY: Longman.

Rothstein, W. S. (1987). The ethics of coercion: Social control practices in an urban junior high school. *Urban Education, 22*(1), 53–72.

Stevenson, C. (1992). *Teaching ten to fourteen year olds.* New York: Longman.

Tomlinson, C. A. (1999). *The differentiated classroom: Responding to the needs of all learners.* Alexandria, VA: Association for Supervision and Curriculum Development.

Wang, M. C., Haertel, G. D., & Walberg, H. J. (1993). Toward a knowledge base for school learning. *Review of Educational Research, 63*, 249–294.

CHAPTER FIVE

CHANGE THIS GRADE!

INTRODUCTION AND PROBLEM BACKGROUND

Grading students is one of the occupational challenges of teaching that can create some of teachers' most disturbing self-doubts. There is an almost inevitable role conflict in the act of grading: Teachers who have worked hard to cast themselves as advocates and supporters of students now find themselves in the position of judges. To make matters worse, few districts provide teachers with any meaningful guidance on how to grade or have grading standards for the district (Austin & McCann, 1992). The assigning of grades is a sort of "sacred ground" for teachers (Thomas, 1986), where they work alone and with complete authority.

But what happens when the grading policies become public? In a sense, grading policies are always public because students receive grades, share grades with their friends, and report grades to their families. Sometimes these policies can be embarrassing to the teachers and to the schools. Consider the following policy statement about grading:

> Grades are (100 to 90)% is an A, (89 to 80)% is a B, (79 to 65)% is a C, (64 to 50)% is a D, below 50% is an F on the tests. If daily work is in, then (100 to 85)% is an A, (84 to 75)% is a B, (74 to 50)% is an earned C. I will also *give* a C to any student who gets all the daily work in, acceptable and on time, if the student has at least a 35% average and creates no problems for the class. You can get a D or F if the daily work is not in. D comes when a student has a passing average (50% or better) and too many missing daily papers (more than 4) or *all* the daily papers in. F comes if below a passing average and daily papers missing. When absent 2 or more days, you have twice the time you are absent to *makeup* the work missed because of absence.
>
> The first grading period I am lenient and will give a "C" to almost anyone with an average of 30% or more unless a B or better is earned but daily work missing must be made up before the end of the second grade period to receive any grade above a D. (Stiggins, Frisbie, & Griswold, 1989, pp. 10–11, original emphasis)

Even making sense of the statement is a challenge (perhaps an impossibility), but viewing it as evidence of teachers' professionalism is frightening.

Many teachers enter the profession with lots of experience of being graded, but almost no experience or training in giving grades (Airasian, 1996; Frary, Cross, & Weber, 1993). Indeed, for many teachers, the first time he or she thinks about formulating grades is about thirty seconds before beginning that number-crunching, checkmark-averaging, and letter-guessing exercise we know as calculating grades. It can seem pretty mysterious, not only from the students' perspective but also from the teachers' perspective.

Once grades are finalized, they are not as final as they may seem. Grades can be appealed in most districts, and the courts can be involved in the process, too. Yes, a teacher can be sued because of the grade given to a student! The problem addressed in this chapter invites you to investigate grading policies from the perspective of a grade appeal. Of course, the problem may take you beyond simply ruling on a grading policy. There are other issues here, issues of race and culture, issues of how a teacher teaches, issues of trends in education. Remember to seek the complexities of the problem before you simplify it and lock in on a solution.

PROBLEM CONTEXT AND SOLUTION PARAMETERS

Context

You are a part of the Clancy High School faculty. Your school is one of three high schools in the school district; yours is the smallest of the schools, serving 950 students in grades nine through twelve. Most of your student clientele is drawn from the Marvel Hills neighborhood, an affluent section of the community. You do, however, have students bused to the school from two low-income neighborhoods, Reston and Oak Meadows.

The school board for the Clancy Unified School District instituted a policy a few years ago that has come to be known as "No pass, no play." This policy (included here) was designed to address the problem of students continuing to participate on athletic teams despite poor performance in the classroom. The policy was aimed primarily at Thompson High and Mountainview High, the other two schools, which had experienced more frequent violations of the "spirit" of what high school is intended to do. Your school has traditionally been proud of the strong classroom performance of its athletes, though the athletic program has the worst reputation in the city.

Problem

One of Clancy's best athletes is Darrin Washington. Darrin is a solid football player, but his real strength is basketball. His coach calls Darrin "the most gifted player I've had in seventeen years of coaching." Darrin, however, has learned he is getting an F in his English class and therefore will not be able to participate in the basketball season. According to district policy, he has a right to appeal this grade, and Darrin has indicated he will do so.

The principal at CHS, Mr. Jennings, believes in a "collegial" environment and shared decision making. He is planning to appoint a committee of teachers to serve with the administrative and parent representatives on the appeal committee, but before he does so, he wants to discuss the issue in a full faculty meeting.

In preparation for this meeting he has distributed some district documents and general information about the grade appeal (he has been careful not to violate the student's privacy, so particular comments and scores have not been given to anyone but the appeal committee members). He has asked subcommittees to discuss some of the general issues before the full faculty meeting. In particular, he wants to address the following issues:

- What is a fair appeal process?
- Is the district policy equitable and effective?
- How "public" should teachers' grading systems be?
- At what point do we intervene to assist teachers in developing grading systems?
- What kinds of information ought to be included in the grading we do at CHS?

To complicate matters, the teacher who has given Darrin the low mark is a friend of yours and a colleague you regard as committed, fair, and highly professional. Though the "official" discussion of this issue has been about "a student" and "a teacher," the rumor mill is in full action, and virtually everyone knows which teacher and which student is being discussed. Your own sense of loyalty is strong.

You will work with your subcommittee to identify the key issues that need to be addressed at CHS and to formulate your initial positions on the issues raised by Mr. Jennings. What questions does your committee feel need to be addressed that were not raised by the principal?

After your group completes its work on the problem, you will participate in the faculty meeting designed to address this topic. You will be asked to make a judgment about the grade appeal and to present this to Mr. Jennings in writing.

Solution Parameters

The products resulting from this problem will consist of two parts. First, you will participate as a staff member in the faculty meeting designed to address the issues Mr. Jennings has raised. You will be expected to be an active participant. That is, you will be given opportunities to make a case, to present countervailing positions, and to question your colleagues. An observer will be assisting with the ratings of discussion participants.

Your primary product will be a written response to the problem, discussion, and appeal. You will individually write a memo to Mr. Jennings (two to three pages long) in which you will critically examine the key components of this issue. Is the district policy defensible? Does Darrin have a legitimate appeal? Is Ms. Torrence's grading fair? You will need to take and defend a position regarding the grade appeal question, though you are free to address the issue at more general levels if you wish. As always, you should support your position with strong reasoning and evidence. Your response should be clear and well articulated.

········**WORK THE PROBLEM**➤

PROBLEM DOCUMENTS

The following documents are included for your group's use.

5.1 Mr. Jenning's memo to the faculty

5.2 Ms. Torrence's grading policy (from course syllabus)

5.3 Ms. Torrence's statement of a rationale for the grade, including a list of Darrin's scores

5.4 Student's letter of appeal

5.5 Ms. Torrence's portfolio scoring rubric

5.6 Darrin's scores on the portfolio

5.7 Editorial from the local newspaper

5.8 District policies on grade appeals and academic eligibility for athletic participation

---

PROBLEM DOCUMENT 5.1   *Mr. Jenning's Memo to the Faculty*

Clancy High School

Memorandum

To   CHS Faculty

From   Mr. Jennings

Date   1/16/03

RE   Student grade appeal, "no pass, no play"

I am aware that rumors have been flying around the school about a potential misapplication of the "no pass, no play" rule. I simply want to inform you all of the process we are going through to resolve this issue, and to solicit feedback for our next faculty meeting.

First, as professionals, we all must emphasize the importance of the confidentiality and right to privacy of the persons involved. I will not mention names here, and I encourage all faculty members to avoid discussing this issue outside of school. Second, I also wish to emphasize the importance of following procedures carefully and completely.

Given that, here is a brief summary of the timeline involved in this case:

> Mid October: first 9 weeks' grades came out, with student earning D
>
> Mid November: second 9 weeks' midterm reports came out, with student notified that he/she "was in danger of failing"
>
> Mid November: extracurricular practice begins

December: exhibition games begin

Late December: final grades reported, and student ruled ineligible

Late December: student initiates appeal process, speaking first to teacher

Early January: parent/teacher meeting scheduled (parent unable to attend)

Early January: student appeals to principal

I have asked a number of your colleagues to join a group of two parents and one student in ruling on this appeal. However, I am concerned that the effects of this case may be damaging to the entire school. Therefore, I would like to discuss the issues raised here in our next faculty meeting. In preparation for that, I am asking department subgroups and teams to meet and discuss the following questions:

- What is a fair appeal process?
- Is our district policy equitable and effective? (Recognizing that we are obligated to follow current policy, though we may offer suggestions for changes.)
- How "public" should teachers' grading systems be?
- At what point do we intervene to assist teachers in developing grading systems?
- What kinds of information ought to be included in the grading we do at CHS?

Our faculty meeting will be a discussion of these issues, with committee members having a chance to participate just the same as everyone else. Following our discussion, each committee member will provide me with recommendations in writing.

This is a serious time for CHS, and I urge you to take your charge seriously.

PROBLEM DOCUMENT 5.2   *Ms. Torrence's Grading Policy*

Grading System, English 11

Ms. Torrence

Clancy High School

I believe that no student should be judged by limited lenses. I think that every student deserves the opportunity to prove herself or himself successful in a number of ways. No one should be boxed in by a single measure of success.

In fact, recent evidence is demonstrating that people learn in a variety of ways; people have a variety of "intelligences." My class is designed to allow this variety to come forth. Grades will be determined by the following criteria:

Tests (but not normal tests!)	135 points	A = 800–860
Papers (we write a lot!)	225 points	B = 731–799
Intelligence portfolio	400 points	C = 671–730
Participation	100 points	D = 602–670
Total	860 points	F = 0–601

Obviously a big part of your grade is the intelligence portfolio, where you will have the opportunity to demonstrate that you, too, can be smart in a variety of ways. More details about this will follow.

Here are some grade policies you need to watch out for:

- Work is due when it is due. If you turn in a paper or project late, your grade may be penalized.
- If you are absent, get the make-up work from a friend or me. If you are gone when something is due, it is due immediately on your return.
- You can re-write some papers. If in doubt, ask me.
- Make sure that all your work is all yours. Don't turn in papers you have copied from books or friends; give credit to people whose ideas you have used.

PROBLEM DOCUMENT 5.3   *Ms. Torrence's Statement of a Rationale for the Grade*

Darrin Washington Appeal: Teacher Comments

I understand why this student wants to appeal, since sports are so important to him. But I really don't think he has a case. I gave him opportunities to re-write poorly done work, and he chose not to do so. I think the choice is obvious. And he needs to realize there are consequences for his actions, that it isn't a matter of some coach stepping in to rescue the star player who doesn't get his work done.

I think the grades speak for themselves. Here's a summary of what Darrin did this term:

Test one (82 points possible): 59
Test two (52 points possible): 39
Intelligence portfolio (400 points possible): 248
Paper 1 (30 points possible): 25
Paper 2 (35 points possible): 28
Paper 3 (50 points possible): 33
Paper 4 (50 points possible): 0
Paper 5 (60 points possible): 40
Participation (100 points possible): 75

Total: 547 (Passing mark requires 602 points)

Obviously, if Darrin cared at all he would have turned in something for the fourth paper. Even after I graded these, I told Darrin he could do something, but he didn't even answer—just stared at me like I wasn't even a person. I was actually frightened of him. He could have written, especially since this was a personal reaction paper, a chance for him to say how he felt about the stories we had been reading in class.

His worst problem, of course, was in the portfolio of intelligences. For this, the students had an opportunity to show seven kinds of smarts. They just had to show something for each area.

They could put in anything that demonstrated how they related the intelligence to themselves and this class. Fifty points for each intelligence, and another fifty for an overview that brought the whole thing together. You would think that something like this would be perfect for a kid like Darrin, who doesn't do too well on the classic academic stuff. But instead, he just blew it off. As I recall, he made some feeble attempts at a few of the intelligences (and I think I was extra generous on those), but he left out some altogether. And surprisingly, it would be something like kinesthetic intelligence. Weird.

I know he has said some things about my not liking him, but that is obviously the farthest thing from my concern here. Darrin simply needs to buckle down and do some work. He'd pass if he tried, and if the school steps in to assist him because he's the best basketball player, I wonder if he'll ever learn to do real work.

PROBLEM DOCUMENT 5.4   *Student's Letter of Appeal*

Dear Mr. Jennings,

I found out it's OK to try to get a grade changed if you write something, so I'm writing to you. I don't think it's fair what Ms. Torrance is doing, and I'd like to have you see my side of it.

First, I want to say I know I didn't turn in a paper, but there's a reason. I got the feeling by then that it didn't matter whatever I did. I figured she would find something wrong no matter what, and that's why I didn't do it. I should have, but I didn't. I guess sometimes you give up when it not time.

I just don't think she'd do this to a white kid. Shes not going to say that's true, but it seems the only way to figure it. All this stuff she has us do, sometimes it seems crazy, shes got us to try all kinds of strange stuff. Like the portfolio. That's what burns me the most and maybe why I didn't figure I should bother with any more papers, even though I did one later. I mean, it's a english class. She has us doing stuff like dancing to poems. I don't mind reading poems, but its like an insult to have us dance like we can't really understand the words. Or how about writing up an account of our "meditation"? She wants us to go off and sit like really quiet and get some kind of strange ideas that we write about and I just don't think that's right. I could do it, yeah, but why am I going to do that sort of thing?

And I don't think the white kid's maybe mind it or something, but I do. And she'll say, "Darrin, this is culture stuff." I can't put it down right, but she just makes me feel stupid, like "Oh, that's OK, you're just not as smart as the other kids." So she makes the grades, and shes got all the power. I try to say, like, I matched some of my music to the poems she gave us, and it turns out that rap isn't the kind of music you put with poems or something.

I just don't see why I got to be the exact thing she wants. It's like she want to crawl inside my head instead of teaching me something. I know I don't have great grades, but on tests and that I do OK. I think I might a passed on that or something. But all this other stuff, it's like she wants me to act stupid instead of learning about english.

I know I don't put down my ideas as good as some kids, but I don't feel like this is fair. Shes got ways to always make me look bad and it's like she's trying to do that all the time. I can learn the english and I can even read the litarture too. She's got it in for me and maybe blacks, all black kids. Or maybe athletes.

Sincerly,

Darrin Washington

PROBLEM DOCUMENT 5.5 *Ms. Torrence's Portfolio Scoring Rubric*

Ms. Torrence

Intelligence Portfolio Rubric

The portfolio of intelligences will consist of seven sections (one for each intelligence) and an overall score for the portfolio. Each section and the final product will be graded according to the following portfolio rubric.

4 (OUTSTANDING = 50 points)
   The section is characterized by "above and beyond the call of duty" work. Each entry fits well with the purpose (i.e., the intelligence documentation). The creator goes beyond minimal expectations by, for example, providing extra evidence of accomplishing a task. The writing throughout is clear and essentially error free.

3 (GOOD = 45 points)

The section is characterized by "mission accomplished" work throughout. For every point made, the creator includes some relevant evidence. Writing is strong, and no errors confuse the reader, though there may be errors.

2 (ACCEPTABLE = 37 points)

The section is characterized by "search and destroy" work throughout. That is, there is an attempt to document student development, but in the process of searching, some parts are not clearly addressed. The reader leaves with uncertainty about how well the intelligence has been addressed. In addition, the errors in the work "destroy" some of the reader's concentration.

1 (WEAK = 33 points)

The section is characterized by unaware "SOS" work. It needs help. Any given entry may be unconnected to the purpose. Errors in writing are so significant that it comes across like Morse code to someone who doesn't know Morse code. There's some credit for effort, but very weak.

0 (MISSING = 0 points)

Missing in action.

PROBLEM DOCUMENT 5.6 *Darrin's Scores on the Portfolio*

Darrin Washington:	
Overall	33
Linguistic	37
Logical-Mathematical	45
Spatial	45
Bodily-Kinesthetic	0
Musical	45
Interpersonal	37
Intrapersonal	0
Total	242

CLANCY CLARION
Editorial

Rare are the moments when a backbone emerges somewhere in the public schools, but such a moment has occurred in recent days at Clancy High School. Rumors are flying, as is so often the case, and perhaps the sketchy details will form a picture we all can comprehend. For now, it is enough to report and support the idea feeding these rumors.

Most readers will recall that in 1991 our school board ratified a "no pass, no play" rule for Clancy's youth. The spirit of this policy, which conforms to the State Department of Education's more lenient rule, is that learning comes first. Period. No more will high school be a babysitting service for wannabe players awaiting a call from the NBA. No more will high school be a social-club waiting room, where misguided young people erect barriers of ignorance and mockery to the learning of their classmates. The policy said, in no uncertain terms, that we are serious about learning in Clancy!

Nothing much has come of the policy over the years, largely because it has affected students little and athletic programs not at all. But that may be changing. Word on the street is that one school may see serious repercussions to its basketball program due to the policy. And we say great! Let's see just how serious this community is about learning. Let's see if there really is a backbone somewhere in education.

Mind you, we are not interested in interfering with internal matters at the school. That's what we hire good teachers and sharp administrators for. But what we do expect—no, demand—is that the schools answer to the public who pay the bills and elect the leadership for the system. This paper will not go on record as supporting anything that harms students. We will go on record as supporting the policies that help our kids succeed. There is no question that putting the academics back in the driver's seat will help our young people grow into responsible adults.

91–103 *Grade appeal process.*

If a student or parent/guardian desires to appeal a grade awarded for a particular class, the proper procedure is as follows. First, the student and/or guardian initiates a conference with the instructor who awarded the grade. If this does not resolve the issue, the student and/or parent meets with the principal or the principal's designee. At the principal's discretion, a committee of faculty, administrators, and parents may hear the appeal. The decision of this committee is final.

92–58 *Academic eligibility for extracurricular participation.*

Given the goal of Clancy public schools is to promote the academic achievement of all students in conjunction with a vibrant extra-curriculum, all students will be required to meet the following criteria to participate in interscholastic or extracurricular activities:

a. in the previous semester, the student will have received no final grade below *D* in any required course;
b. in the previous semester, the student will have accumulated no more than 10 absences from any course, excepting school-related absences;
c. in the previous semester, the student will have been subject to no disciplinary actions resulting in more than three days' suspension.

••••PROPOSE A SOLUTION ➤

SOLUTION SUMMARY

Before proceeding to the reflection section of this chapter, write a brief summary of your team's solution here:

Our team defined the "real" problem here as _____

_____

_____

_____

_____

_____

_____

_____

The key features of our solution were _____

_____

_____

_____

_____

_____

_____

My personal view of the problem and solution is _____

_____

_____

_____

_____

_____

_____

TIME FOR REFLECTION

Having completed the inquiry into this grade appeal and a "faculty" discussion of the matter, there are numerous issues that deserve attention. First, consider what it means to participate in the broader community of the school faculty. Indeed, the whole notion of community comes into question as we consider teacher autonomy. This section also urges you to think about racism in the schools, what is meant by "extra" curricular activities, trendy teaching, how we make grades for our students, and the impact of district policies.

Participating in Faculty Life

One of the realities teachers face in their occupation is the faculty meeting. Variously praised as democracy in action and condemned as the worst remnant of bureaucratic ineffectiveness, the faculty meeting is a fixture of school life. What did your mock faculty meeting look like? Were there people who refused to contribute and others who refused to stop? Did some teachers react emotionally while others guarded themselves with cynicism and sarcasm? If you saw these characteristics in the meeting, you were probably viewing a fairly typical faculty meeting.

A question that each teacher must face in stepping into the school environment is "How do I participate effectively in faculty life?" Most teacher education programs offer little guidance in this question. How actively does the new teacher take part in meetings, committees, lounge conversations? Clearly, this is an issue that draws partly on the personality and interaction style of each teacher, but it also draws on what we call the "culture of school" (Sarason, 1982). In your discussions with peers, practicing teachers, and instructors, try to find what may be an effective posture for the new teacher to assume. Consider ways that you can allow your own creativity and thoughtfulness to emerge without alienating those around you. Teacher induction has been a notoriously "sink-or-swim" proposition; new teachers should be careful to participate in ways that don't cause their colleagues to throw them rocks instead of life preservers. But even seasoned teachers do well to consider how their participation in faculty life might be viewed by others.

Much of the solution to this balance has little to do with teacher preparation, per se. Instead, it draws on your interpersonal skills (which are one target of the PBL experience!). Carefully consider how your messages are received by others; learn to listen more than you speak.

Teacher Autonomy

In this problem, your group probably raised questions about Ms. Torrence's teaching practices and grading procedures. From what we see in her documents, she appears to have quite a bit of creativity and energy. She clearly has stayed in touch with the professional literature (multiple intelligences, portfolio assessment), and she has been somewhat better than average in terms of articulating what she does (she gives students a description of how she will grade and what the portfolio should look like). Of course, we don't have the opportunity to look inside her classroom and see first-hand what she does with her students. We can only guess.

There is a pattern in teaching known as the "hands-off" norm (Lortie, 1975). Essentially, this behavior pattern is based on a belief that each teacher should be able to make decisions for his or her own classroom, and other teachers should provide the space for this to happen. The grade appeal problem raises a question about such a norm in a profession. What if a teacher's practices negatively impact young people? Do we still keep our hands off?

Other professions, such as medicine, law, or counseling, have boards that review the practices of their members when questions are raised about the performance of these members. If a doctor is taking advantage of her patients, the professional review board can actually revoke that doctor's license. What about teachers? Is it appropriate for a committee of peers to examine Ms. Torrence's practices? Is it appropriate to go beyond simply saying she delivered what she promised and to ask whether what she promised was worthwhile? Should teachers be making judgments about other teachers' work?

Despite the long-term hold of this norm for teacher autonomy, there are hopeful signs for greater teacher collaboration. More than a few researchers, theorists, and advocates are calling for greater joint work at the secondary level (Fullan & Hargreaves, 1991; National Association of Secondary School Principals, 1996; Wasley, 1994). To the extent that you are able to develop working relationships with your colleagues, where the conversation about teaching is a fair topic, you will be able to turn the "hands-off" norm into a "joined hands" norm.

Racism in the Schools

Darrin hints that he may be treated differently because he is African American and his teacher is white. He also hints that he may be treated differently because his teacher is prejudiced against athletes. Once again, it is difficult for us to judge these hinted accusations without having the chance to observe or interview participants. But are his accusations relevant more generally?

Institutional racism is a concept that argues that some elements of schooling are simply set up so that certain groups will always be at a disadvantage. The language of schooling may be more accessible to majority children; the curriculum may be more relevant and appealing to children of the dominant culture. The issue may go beyond racism, to include differences among classes of children. For example, McLeod (1987) concludes that an apparently meritocratic system—you get places because you deserve it—works to guarantee inequality: "In contemporary America, the educational system, by sorting students according to ostensibly meritocratic criteria, plays a crucial role in the legitimation of inequality" (p. 113). For some kids, the system may be stacked against them.

What about the Darrin Washington case? Was race a factor here? What was the impact of Darrin's coming from one of the poor neighborhoods that fed into this otherwise affluent community? Conversely, was the issue of race simply an excuse for Darrin's lack of effort? At what point does a student adopt "failure avoiding" behaviors (Woolfolk, 1998) such as not trying or devaluing performance rather than face the unpleasant possibility that something about his or her core being is deficient? And what about a teacher or school that offers special privileges for the gifted athlete? In too many places, Darrin's case would be judged in a different light if the possibility of a team's lack of success hinged on the outcome.

The idea of institutional racism suggests that many well-meaning individuals who would never perceive themselves as racists are actually supporting racism. All teachers must be careful to look beyond good intentions.

Extracurricular?

Defining what constitutes the curriculum and what is in the "extra" curriculum is not always easy. Walker and Soltis (1997) write that *curriculum* refers "not only to the official list of courses offered by the school—we call that the 'official curriculum'— but also to the purposes, content, activities, and organization of the educational program actually created in schools by teachers, students, and administrators" (p. 1). That definition draws in all experiences of a child at a school. Is a sports program (or a drama program or a journalism program or student government) really *extra*?

And if we see participation in "extra" curriculum as a reward for doing well in other parts of the school experience, what are the consequences of that? Kohn (1993) argues that any time we use rewards to motivate children we are probably damaging their long-term motivation and performance—we are undervaluing what ought to have intrinsic worth. Oosterhof (1999) argues that by making a passing mark the gatekeeper for participation, we are saying that grades are a measure of effort—anyone can try—as opposed to achievement. Why should the child who cannot succeed in the classroom be prohibited from succeeding on the playing field? On the other hand, what is school really for? These questions help us to formulate appropriate and effective personal philosophies about grading.

Trendy Teaching?

Ms. Torrence could be seen as being on the cutting edge of instruction. She was, after all, a veteran teacher who incorporated new ideas into her pedagogy. While some of her colleagues were still probably re-using worn dittos from decades earlier, she went to the literature and drew on such ideas as portfolio assessment and multiple intelligences.

Encouraging innovation is one means to keep education fresh and alive. An inspirational example comes from the 25 percent rule at 3M Corporation, which says that 25 percent of the profits of any division of the company must be from products developed within the last five years (Donnellon, 1996). Accompanying this rule, however, is the 15 percent rule, which calls for 15 percent of a new product division employee's time to be "thinking time" in order to generate new ideas (Skopec & Smith, 1997). That spirit of innovation would serve us well in education. What if we gave teachers plenty of time to think and expected new ideas to come of this?

On the other hand, there is no shortage of recommended changes for teachers to adopt. What should be our perspective as professionals? What evidence do we require in order to incorporate "multiple intelligences" or "brain-based learning" or "problem-based learning" into our teaching practices? Ms. Torrence may or may not have instituted "multiple intelligences" properly (see Gardner, 1995), but we need to go to a level of thoughtfulness that is deeper than simply grabbing the slogan of the day. So how do teachers decide to innovate? Where can they find support to make innovations that are productive for themselves and their students? Part of the answer lies in teachers learning to make professional development and professional conversation a central part of their career goals.

Making the Grade

Perhaps the most prominent issue in this problem is a teacher's responsibility to assign grades in a fair and defensible manner. Too often teachers are satisfied with a complex set of numbers to justify a mark, when in reality, those numbers may disguise more than they reveal. Grades may be markers of student *learning,* or they may be markers of student *compliance* (Stiggins, 1995).

We all have horror stories of grades we or our friends or relatives received that were egregiously unfair. Yet in almost every case, the teacher did not set out to be unfair, vindictive, or petty. It is more likely the case that the teacher was a prisoner of a numbers system with little thought behind it and little awareness of its consequences. Grading is serious business, but it tends to be private business, and the misconceptions and poor practices we may have adopted rarely receive deliberate, thoughtful attention.

What, then, to do about this? Teachers need first to have a strong grounding in how to make grades that reflect both their own values and their students' achievement, and it would seem that few teachers receive adequate preparation for this in their own education (Stiggins, 1995). A number of texts provide such guidance. However, initial thoughtfulness takes us only so far. Perhaps a more productive and responsive approach would involve teachers sharing their grading systems and samples of their grading practices with one another. In serious professional conversation about grading practices, teachers can embody the sort of reflective practice that promises to help us continue to improve and to treat our students fairly.

The difficulty of grading can never be minimized. But how do we, as professionals, help each other to make grading practices supportive of students as well as fair and informative? What would you say to Ms. Torrence about her grading system?

District Policies?

A final point for reflection is the relationship between a teacher's daily work and the policies that govern this work. How do such policies get in place? What is the governance model for public schools in America? Is it legal and ethical for a school board to tell me how I have to grade my students? Even to overturn my grades?

There is a sort of innocence on the part of many beginning teachers. "I will do my job in my classroom," they think, "and I'll be fine." What many such teachers do not realize is that the legal responsibility for what goes on in that classroom is only partially the teacher's. Somewhere outside of that classroom, outside of that school, maybe even outside of that city, there is a group of people with the ultimate authority for what happens in a school. What is the structure of school governance in your state? Does the state itself have authority over textbooks and curriculum and even grading? Is there a locally elected school board that holds this authority? And what impact does the presence of such bodies have on the practices of teachers? Awareness of who is in charge of such decisions is an important quality of a professional.

In the grade appeal process described in this problem, the school board had passed a policy that may or may not have been effective in terms of its intended purpose. How do such policies get approved? When they turn out to be counterproductive, how do such policies get changed? What is the teacher's role in this process?

DISCUSSION QUESTIONS

1. How can teachers—especially beginning teachers—learn from their colleagues about the process of grading? What ways can beginners find to develop support groups?

2. In adopting new ideas and practices, how do you make sure that the students' best interests are honored? That is, when is the risk of trying something new worth taking? How soon does a teacher give up on a new idea? How do you use colleagues to help you maintain a spirit of innovation and good judgment about what works?

3. What position should a teacher take when the school or district policies seem to be damaging to students or the educational process? Is there a conflict between the ethics of teaching and the obligations of working for a given employer?

4. What might you learn about relating to your students from the experience of Ms. Torrence? In particular, did she appear to have difficulties relating to specific groups of students?

5. Is institutional racism a problem in schools? Do schools provide unfair advantages or obstacles for athletes or other specialized groups?

6. Considering the PBL process, what did you learn about determining the relevance of different and sometimes competing information? How effective were you at filtering information?

FURTHER READING

Most texts on assessment or evaluation of learning have chapters on how to grade your students (Airasian, 1996; Linn & Gronlund, 1995; McMillan, 1997; Popham, 1999; Stiggins, 1997), and any of these can be quite helpful in being systematic about grading.

Armstrong, T. (1994). *Multiple intelligences in the classroom.* Alexandria, VA: Association for Super-vision and Curriculum Development.
There are numerous works that describe how to implement "multiple intelligences" in the classroom. Among these, Armstrong's (1994) provides a helpful scheme for applying the theory. Fogarty's (1997) provides a number of teaching models that can be adapted to the theory. In every case where "multiple intelligences" are invoked, we do well to remember Gardner's (1995) cautions about misusing the theory.

Buss, D. C. (1998). The student activity program: Its place in the secondary school. In P. S. Hle-bowitsh & W. G. Wraga (Eds.), *Annual review of research for school leaders 1998* (pp. 81–118). New York: Simon & Schuster Macmillan.
The place of the "extra" curriculum is a topic worth investigating further, and many teach-ers have little more to go on than their own experience. Buss has written an excellent chap-ter to introduce the issues.

Hanssen, E. (1998). A white teacher reflects on institutional racism. *Phi Delta Kappan, 79*(9), 694–698.
A short piece that helps teachers see the world of teaching through a different lens, Hanssen's reflection on institutional racism makes for powerful reading. She examines subtle, but pervasive, forms of racism in the curriculum, the faculty, and the ethos of the school. "We need to remember," she writes, "that institutional racism typically isn't ugly. Rather than being expressed through racial slurs, it tends to be wrapped in noble procla-mations of tradition, fairness, and high standards. Rather than being a rare incident, it is woven into the fabric of our historically racist society" (p. 698).

Kohn, A. (1993). *Punished by rewards: The trouble with gold stars, incentive plans, A's, praise, and other bribes.* Boston: Houghton Mifflin.
Kohn raises serious questions about the role of grades in the students' lives, particularly at the level of long-term consequences for learning. He suggests that what seems to make sense to motivate learners may have the exact opposite effect. In a shorter piece (Kohn, 1994), he urges teachers to rethink the grading issue as a matter of *why do it* instead of *how to do it.*

MacDonald, R. E. (1991). *A handbook of basic skills and strategies for beginning teachers: Facing the chal-lenge of teaching in today's schools.* New York: Longman.
MacDonald has an inspirational chapter on "learning to work creatively with the system." This chapter invites student teachers and beginning teachers to understand components of a system that sometimes doesn't work in their interest, and to take advantage of the system for personal growth. Well worth reading.

McLeod, J. (1987). *Ain't no makin it: Leveled aspirations in a low income neighborhood.* Boulder, CO: Westview.
McLeod has a devastating portrait of how the system works against children from lower classes and racial minorities. His provocative title is the first step in seeing the world from the perspective of young people who can see no opportunities for themselves in the sys-tem. In a similar manner, Kozol (1991) provides a more direct view of what goes on in par-ticular schools, again especially for the poor and minority groups. His view is a healthy perspective for teachers to consider.

Sarason, S. B. (1982). *The culture of school and the problem of change* (2nd ed.). Boston: Allyn & Bacon.
Sarason's description of school culture is an insightful exploration of what schools are like. In particular, he challenges us to consider the "universe of alternatives," rather that simply accepting things as they are. He urges us to observe schools the way someone totally unfa-miliar with the institution might see them. This helps us to see what may be odd in the midst of what we take for granted.

WEB SITES

National Council of Teachers of English
www.ncte.org/teach2000/gp.shtml
This site offers support for new and experienced teachers. It is especially helpful in considering the grading of papers.

National Association of Secondary School Principals
www.nassp.org/services/legal_ferpa.htm
This site presents common grading practices that are prohibited by FERPA. These are important points to think about as you make grades.

REFERENCES

Airasian, P. W. (1996). *Assessment in the classroom.* New York: McGraw-Hill.

Armstrong, T. (1994). *Multiple intelligences in the classroom.* Alexandria, VA: Association for Supervision and Curriculum Development.

Austin, S., & McCann, R. (1992). *"Here's another arbitrary grade for your collection": A statewide study of grading policies.* Paper presented at the Annual Meeting of the American Educational Research Association, San Francisco, CA, April 20–24. (ERIC Document Reproduction Service No. ED 343944).

Buss, D. C. (1998). The student activity program: Its place in the secondary school. In P. S. Hlebowitsh & W. G. Wraga (Eds.), *Annual review of research for school leaders 1998* (pp. 81–118). New York: Simon & Schuster Macmillan.

Donnellon, A. (1996). *Team talk: The power of language in team dynamics.* Boston: Harvard Business School.

Fogarty, R. (1997). *Problem-based learning and other curriculum models for the multiple intelligences classroom.* Arlington Heights, IL: IRI Skylight Training and Publishing.

Frary, R. B., Cross, L. H., & Weber, L. J. (1993). Testing and grading practices and opinions of secondary teachers of academic subjects: Implications for instruction in measurement. *Educational Measurement: Issues and Practice, 12*(3), 23–30.

Fullan, M. G., & Hargreaves, A. (1991). *What's worth fighting for? Working together for your school.* Andover, MA: Regional Laboratory for Educational Improvement of the Northeast and Islands.

Gardner, H. (1995). Reflections on multiple intelligences: Myths and messages. *Phi Delta Kappan, 77*(3), 200–209.

Hanssen, E. (1998). A white teacher reflects on institutional racism. *Phi Delta Kappan, 79*(9), 694–698.

Kohn, A. (1993). *Punished by rewards: The trouble with gold stars, incentive plans, A's, praise, and other bribes.* Boston: Houghton Mifflin.

Kohn, A. (1994). Grading: The issue is not how but why. *Educational Leadership, 52*(2), 38–41.

Kozol, J. (1991). *Savage inequalities: Children in America's schools.* New York: Trumpet Club.

Linn, R. L., & Gronlund, N. E. (1995). *Measurement and assessment in teaching* (7th ed.). Englewood Cliffs, NJ: Merrill.

Lortie, D. C. (1975). *Schoolteacher: A sociological study.* Chicago: University of Chicago.

McLeod, J. (1987). *Ain't no makin it: Leveled aspirations in a low income neighborhood.* Boulder, CO: Westview.

McMillan, J. H. (1997). *Classroom assessment: Principles and practice for effective instruction.* Boston: Allyn & Bacon.

National Association of Secondary School Principals. (1996). *Breaking ranks: Changing an American institution: A report of the National Association of Secondary School Principals in partnership with* the Carnegie Foundation for the Advancement of Teaching on the high school of the 21st century. Reston, VA: Author.

Oosterhof, A. (1999). *Developing and using classroom assessments* (2nd ed.). Upper Saddle River, NJ: Merrill.

Popham, W. J. (1999). *Classroom assessment: What teachers need to know* (2nd ed.). Boston: Allyn & Bacon.

Sarason, S. B. (1982). *The culture of school and the problem of change* (2nd ed.). Boston: Allyn & Bacon.

Skopec, E., & Smith, D. M. (1997). *How to use team building to foster innovation throughout your organization.* Chicago, IL: Contemporary Books.

Stiggins, R. J. (1995). Assessment literacy for the 21st century. *Phi Delta Kappan, 77*(3), 238–245.

Stiggins, R. J. (1997). *Student-centered classroom assessment* (2nd ed.). Upper Saddle River, NJ: Merrill.

Stiggins, R. J., Frisbie, D. A., & Griswold, P. A. (1989). Inside high school grading practices: Building a research agenda. *Educational Measurement: Issues and Practice, 8*(2), 5–14.

Thomas, W. C. (1986). Grading—Why are school policies necessary? What are the issues? *NASSP Bulletin, 70*(487), 23–26.

Walker, D. F., & Soltis, J. F. (1997). *Curriculum and aims* (3rd ed.). New York: Teachers College.

Wasley, P. A. (1994). *Stirring the chalkdust: Tales of teachers changing classroom practice.* New York: Teachers College.

Woolfolk, A. E. (1998). *Educational psychology* (7th ed.). Boston: Allyn & Bacon.

CHAPTER SIX

AN AFROCENTRIC CURRICULUM?

INTRODUCTION AND PROBLEM BACKGROUND

> "[I]n the days after King's assassination, greatly moved by the death of one I had admired so much, I lobbied for a course in black history in a school 90 per cent white. At that time, a black-history course was as common as a course in necrophilia."
>
> (Conroy, 1972, p. 13)

The question Conroy raised as a high school teacher is perhaps the classic question of curriculum: What should we teach? It's been raised in many forms—*What* knowledge is of most worth? *Whose* knowledge is of most worth? (Beyer & Apple, 1988)—with many different answers. Some have seen the curriculum as a device used by groups to control students or keep them in their place in society (Anyon, 1981; McNeil, 1986). Some have seen the curriculum as the logical response to the way knowledge naturally occurs (Phenix, 1964). However it is phrased, the answer to "What should we teach?" is far from a simple, universally agreed-upon principle. The curriculum is a contentious issue.

And who is contending? In part, there are groups of professional educators in the fray. Teachers of different subjects have their views of what the curriculum should be; administrators have their view; school board members have theirs. Parents have a view of what the curriculum should be (usually what it was for them)—and different parent groups will advocate for different forms of curriculum. Business leaders and politicians have strong views about what kind of knowledge the schools should pass along to children. Given the chance, students might even have something to say. All these groups are known as "stakeholders" in education. They all have some end in mind for the curriculum that children experience, and they all appear willing to battle for their views.

One common notion is that the curriculum is a neutral matter, unaffected by politics, economies, or other factors. It's just school: reading, writing, arithmetic and the rest sit like boulders in the countryside, unbiased and disinterested. But that notion is challenged somewhat in this particular PBL experience. In the face of apparent neutrality, this problem gives voice to stakeholders who challenge the idea that the curriculum doesn't "take sides."

As Vann and Kunjufu (1993) note, the lessons taught in schools often come to us indirectly: "Schools are powerful institutions. They teach, socialize, and indoctrinate. They can dispel myths or perpetuate them. If you have been constantly taught that your ancestors were well-educated, cultured innovators, how would you feel about the descendants of slaves? If you have been taught that your ancestors were illiterate, impoverished sharecroppers, how would you feel about yourself?" (p. 491).

This PBL experience will allow you to dig around a bit in the world of curriculum. You will be invited to think about the organization of subject matters, the focus of subjects, and perhaps even who might be teaching those subjects. As always, I invite you to approach the topic in a fresh way, as free as possible of your previous opinions in this matter.

PROBLEM CONTEXT AND SOLUTION PARAMETERS

Context

The community of Layton, California, is in some turmoil. McLarker High School, the only high school in this community of 40,000, has experienced a fairly rapid demographic shift over the past decade. Where once the school served a predominantly white community, the school now has fewer white students than minority students. At the same time, there has been little change in the teaching staff, which is characterized as a well-educated, stable community of professionals.

Over the past few years, a steady pattern has emerged. The white students tend to be fairly successful in their graduation rates, while minority students, particularly the African-American students, experience dropout rates more than twice those of their white counterparts. It seems that this development came about slowly, almost imperceptibly. Thus the school staff did not expect the sort of criticism that arose from one segment of the population.

Problem

An ad hoc committee of parents has begun actively to lobby the school board for a curriculum "more sensitive to the needs of all McLarker's students." In particular, the committee argues, McLarker High has been doing a terrible job serving the African-American students. The curriculum changes should address this issue.

This proposal is not without controversy, even among the African-American community. Some parents argue that the curriculum is fine, but that the teachers are simply biased against their children. Others contend the curriculum is irrelevant to too many students. Still others see the curriculum as irrelevant to all students, regardless of their race.

Not wanting to be solely responsible for addressing this issue, Superintendent Adkins created a committee of educators to look into the proposal made by the ad hoc committee. You are a member of this committee of fellow teachers.

Solution Parameters

Your team must make a recommendation to the school board regarding the request of the parent committee (the memo with the request is included). Your particular charge is to explore the issue from the perspective of *professional educators.* In other words, a survey of local opinions would be of little importance to your report, whereas a synopsis of leading authorities' positions would be quite valuable. Specifically, your response must include the following components in an oral presentation to the school board:

1. A brief statement of your curriculum philosophy and design principles
2. An answer to the Afrocentric curriculum question that addresses the parents' concerns (e.g., support, oppose, adapt)
3. Curricular and/or teaching recommendations you see as appropriate to the situation (and this could mean no changes in current practice)

The oral presentation will be made to the Layton School Board. You will have approximately fifteen minutes to speak to the board, followed by a question-and-answer session lasting approximately ten minutes. You may choose to include visual aids (such as Power Point slides) or documents to support your position.

········WORK THE PROBLEM ⟶

PROBLEM DOCUMENTS

The following documents are provided for your examination in formulating a decision about the Afrocentric curriculum (but remember, you will need to go beyond these particular documents to solve the problem):

6.1 Memo from the ad hoc parent committee on equity issues in the Layton school district

6.2 Principal Oliver's response to the committee (a guide for the task force)

6.3 McLarker High School enrollment figures

6.4 Population trend analysis from the Layton Chamber of Commerce

6.5 Role-playing guidelines for presentations to the Layton School Board

---

PROBLEM DOCUMENT 6.1 *Memo from the Ad Hoc Parent Committee*

MEMO

To   Ms. Oliver, Principal MHS

From Equity in Schooling Parent Committee

Date 9/24/03

RE   Curriculum Relevance

As representatives of what we see as the neglected portion of our students, we call upon you to exert all your influence on behalf of the most at-risk students in our high school. The statistics speak for themselves:

- Of 2,450 students, 682 are African Americans (28%).
- Of those 682 students, 434 are freshmen and sophomores (64%).
- The white dropout rate at MHS is currently 14.1%; the African American dropout rate is 43%.
- African-American students comprise 28% of the school population and 52% of the lower-track classes. Meanwhile, African-American students make up less than 5% of the advanced placement classes.
- There are currently no courses in the MHS curriculum that specifically focus on the African-American experience. While some instructors (a group that is over 80% white) claim to address African-American issues, this is not enough. The last major revision of the curriculum occurred before the shift in Layton population patterns.

As Duane E. Campbell has written, "Many African American families have experienced school as a place where their child is measured, tested, and found to be inadequate. Hard work in school does not always lead to success. In spite of the nation's formal commitment to democracy in schools, the experience of a lower class, African American child is likely to be significantly different from the ideal. School may be a frightening, cold, intrusion into the child's life. Or it might even be a zone of safety from the violence in many neighborhoods" (1996, p. 29).

Therefore, we are asking that the Curriculum Committee initiate an Afrocentric curriculum to address the way this school is short-changing our children. Specifically, we wish to see a focus study that includes African art, African music, African literature, African history, and African society courses. In addition, we would like the science and math departments to address this issue through African-oriented courses, segments or units.

We understand the difficulty of initiating change quickly, and we expect this to be a matter for next year's offerings. However, the urgency of the matter dictates your immediate attention to the matter. Too many of our children are failing in this system. *Or, perhaps more accurately, this system is failing too many of our children!*

PROBLEM DOCUMENT 6.2   *Principal Oliver's Response to the Committee*

McLARKER HIGH SCHOOL

LAYTON, CALIFORNIA

10/2/03

To the Task Force Members:

I appreciate your willingness to serve McLarker High School by looking into the complaints lodged by the ad hoc committee on equity. Superintendent Adkins was wise in her selection of qualified and committed professionals to look into the problem.

Since the superintendent chose to have educators from throughout the system investigate this problem, there will be many among you who know little or nothing about our school. To help you with your deliberations, I wanted to provide a background sheet of information.

First, you should realize that McLarker is an excellent school. We have a tradition of achievement that would stand against any school you might choose. I, too, believe that any school can do more, become better. But you must understand that this is not a bad school, not a school hostile to children or to learning. Despite some of the claims of the ad hoc committee, you should be aware that our African-American students are scoring at nearly the state average for their group on California's assessments. I invite you to examine that information carefully as you consider how to respond to this request.

Second, you should also realize that McLarker's teachers are as professional a bunch as you will find anywhere. We have very experienced teachers with a great deal of advanced training. I would challenge you to find any school in the country that has more experimentation with instructional methods going on. I am confident that the best in pedagogical innovations make their way into MHS, and if there is anything that can be done to ensure the success of students of color, it is something we are doing here. True, only a small minority of teachers are themselves persons of color, but we actively seek teachers of color at every hiring opportunity. In short, we are aware of our limitations and dedicated to making the place better.

I do not mean to influence your investigation. I simply think it is important for you to understand the true nature of this institution of learning before the temptation to dismantle it grows too strong. I fully support Superintendent Adkins and her empowering your committee. I look forward to working closely with you in your investigation.

Allison Oliver

Allison Oliver, Principal

| PROBLEM DOCUMENT 6.3 | *McLarker High School Enrollment Figures* |

YEAR	TOTAL	AFRICAN AMERICAN	ASIAN	CAUCASIAN	HISPANIC	NATIVE AMERICAN	OTHER
2002–03	2461	682	470	921	350	27	11
2001–02	2283	650	360	911	323	31	8
2000–01	2165	627	282	875	341	25	15
1999–00	2006	572	171	890	336	26	11
1998–99	1918	585	130	847	322	18	16

The Commerce Connection
Layton Chamber of Commerce

Population Trend Analysis for Potential Employers

In recent years, the business climate for Layton has been enjoying exceptional success. Not only is this community of prime interest for its superb climate and ideal location (within two hours of what most people consider to be the best airport in the nation), it is also a community with a talented and diverse workforce ready to serve a variety of industries. In the past decade alone, some of the accomplishments of the Layton commerce community include:

- Development of a major telemarketing center
- Opening of two outlet malls
- Creation from the ground up of a nation-wide provider of exotic plants
- Founding of a research division for a major medical technology firm
- Opening of a distribution center for a national drugstore chain
- Preliminary steps for a software development firm.

To sustain this sort of development, the climate for new construction in Layton has been unparalleled in the region. Population grew from just 23,000 a decade ago to over 40,000 today. Embedded in that population growth is a storehouse of employee riches awaiting potential employers:

- Traditional suburbanite families, with emphasis on education, continue to make up the bulk of the City.
- Growth in the Asian sector—a national resource for computer industries—has exploded over the past decade, with double-digit increases in the community each year.
- Cultural sensitivity in the City has made this a welcoming place for many immigrants from Central America.
- A continuing source of riches is the solid working-class community.

According to an analysis conducted by the Chamber, the trend of diversification promises to continue over the next decade. Layton's population should exceed 100,000 within 12 years. Most of the population growth is likely to sustain the favorable climate for economic development that the community has profited from for the past ten years. Look for the new face of Layton to be just as varied and supportive as the current face of the city!

Role-Playing Guidelines for Presentations to the Layton School Board

Instructions for Role-Playing Board Presentations

In order to give the presentations to the board a greater sense of realism, it is important to have participants role-play board members. One difficulty in such role-playing is that a person's beliefs, biases, and insecurities interfere with the exploration of ideas. Therefore, a number of board member profiles are provided here. Having participants play these roles in listening to, judging, and questioning presentations will help to recreate the conditions of an actual school board wrestling with such problems.

Guides:

The presentation you are about to see is the result of a group of future teachers assuming roles to solve a problem related to curriculum. The essence of the problem is that a group of parents has called for curricular change because some students in the school district may not be served well by the curriculum and/or instructional practices of the school. Committees of teachers will present their recommendations to the school board. The role you will play is as follows:

Concerned Parent

Your child has been adequately challenged and instructed in the present system, so you are puzzled by the need to change. You may be given an opportunity to ask questions about the proposed solution or to express your opinion.

Chair of the School Board

Your job is to conduct the meeting. You will hear from two or more committees on the question before you. After each group presents, you will conduct a question and answer session. Be sure to include parents, if any are present, in the questioning.

Board Member

You have been elected by a constituency you perceive as largely African American. You strongly support a change in curriculum, and you generally see attempts to preserve the status quo as continuing oppression. You feel a powerful allegiance to your constituency.

Board Member

You ally yourself with the traditionalists when it comes to school issues. You are *very* skeptical of any change because you are convinced that traditional education has served all children well. You want hard evidence for any changes, and your theme is that basic education is the pathway to success regardless of one's ethnic or cultural background.

Board Member

You are the newest member of the board, and you generally try to position yourself wherever you see the Chair leaning. You pride yourself in asking insightful questions. Also, as a minority member, you feel you represent *all* minority groups.

⸱⸱⸱⸱PROPOSE A SOLUTION ⟶

SOLUTION SUMMARY

Before proceeding to the reflection section of this chapter, write a brief summary of your team's solution here:

Our team defined the "real" problem here as _____

_____

_____

_____

_____

_____

_____

_____

The key features of our solution were _____

_____

_____

_____

_____

_____

_____

_____

My personal view of the problem and solution is _____

_____

_____

_____

_____

_____

_____

_____

TIME FOR REFLECTION

This PBL experience probably raised a number of issues for you. In this section, I invite you to reflect on what you've discovered about the curriculum decision-making process, including the philosophy behind such organization, the stakeholders who participate in decisions, and the implications of how curricular decisions affect students. The reflections consider the practice of tracking, particularly in light of racial implications. Related to this question, what do teaching techniques have to do with reaching different cultural groups? Finally, the reflection asks you to think about how a teacher relates to the governing board that generally has the power to make decisions about curriculum.

Building a Curriculum

As a student making your way through school, you probably gave little thought to how a curriculum is put together. You probably did as you were asked, studied the topics as they were presented, and answered a lot of questions at the ends of the chapters. In most cases, the construction of the curriculum amounts to selecting a textbook and building a course around it. For conscientious professionals, there may be some soul-searching and debate prior to the textbook selection. Occasionally, a group of educators will decide there simply is no textbook that can do what they want done, so they forego that anchor of the American school day and proceed without it. That, however, is the exception.

In his examination of the role of textbooks, Michael Apple (1988) makes a case that publishers simply have too much power in determining what will be studied in schools. He raises the perennial question of curriculum organization, "What knowledge is of most worth?" but he twists it slightly to "Whose knowledge is of most worth?" Apple's discussion raises the possibility that the curriculum, as filtered through the textbooks, is not some neutral collection of knowledge, but a politically-charged tool with specific goals that are not readily apparent even to the teachers who teach the curriculum (Apple, 1990).

Jean Anyon (1981), who examined how children in different social classes experienced the curriculum, presents another view of this politicized role for curriculum. Anyon found not only that the children from different classes received different text resources, but also that the expectations of their teachers were dramatically different according to social class. The children developed significantly different views on the creation and use of knowledge, depending on the social class to which they belonged.

Both of these authors question the commonly held assumption that the curriculum is simply an organization of knowledge, without regard to the politics or values that undergird it. In his classic explanation of how a curriculum is built, Ralph Tyler (1949) offered a view of the construction of curriculum that appears to conform to this notion of the neutrality of knowledge. Tyler argued that a school community creates a curriculum through a relatively straightforward process. First, ideas about what should be taught are drawn from three sources: the students, the subject matter, and society. Second, the resulting ideas are screened through two "filters": what we know about the process of learning and a philosophy of education. Finally, curriculum is built around four key questions:

1. What are worthwhile educational objectives?
2. What activities will allow us to accomplish these objectives?
3. How should we organize the activities?
4. How will we know if we've accomplished the activities?

Other writers have presented similar schemes that position curriculum development as a technical process. In contrast, Paolo Freire (1990), a Brazilian teacher and activist, put the political element of curriculum at the heart of the process for constructing curriculum. In Freire's view, curriculum is a means to give power to oppressed people by allowing them to identify, name, and begin to resist their oppressors. Freire opposes the "banking" conception of schooling, where learners simply acquire greater deposits of neutral facts. Instead, he views curriculum as a means to liberate people.

In the context of this problem, there are two perspectives worth considering as you contemplate the building of a curriculum. First, what is the perspective implied by the parents' request and the context of a school board's responsibility for the curriculum? That is, in the organizational reality of schools, what does it mean to make curricular decisions? Do the interests of particular groups come into play here or is this a matter of selecting knowledge in a more neutral fashion? Second, as a group coming to decisions about the problem itself, how did you find your team operating? That is, what was your process of decision making in relation to curriculum?

Stakeholders in Curriculum Decision Making

In considering the decisions made about curriculum, the idea of "stakeholders" comes into play. A stakeholder is anyone who has a specialized interest in the nature of a decision. For example, in deciding to restrict the use of a piece of public land, a number of groups have interests in the outcome, including the current users of the land, people whose income may be derived from that land, advocates for wildlife habitat, neighbors to the region, and so on. In decisions about curriculum, stakeholders would include those who teach, those whose children are taught, the children themselves, those who produce materials, test-makers, and so on.

It becomes important for teachers to recognize this feature of curriculum so that the debates are framed properly. Posner (1988) makes a distinction between curriculum technique and curriculum conscience—an important distinction for the educator to consider. A curriculum "technician" would be concerned only with technical matters of what *works* best, without regard to what *is* best. That's the work of curriculum conscience. An awareness of the multiple stakeholders in education helps us understand the complexity of determining what is best.

Eisner's (1985) ideas about different views of curriculum help to highlight this idea of stakeholders. Eisner distinguishes among several levels of curriculum. The articulated, documented curriculum is what he refers to as the "explicit" curriculum.

The things students learn without being taught intentionally constitute the "implicit" curriculum. Such implicit lessons might include things like the importance of waiting your turn, promptness, or what is really valued in the culture. In her book on multicultural education, Hernandez (1989) emphasizes the power of this "hidden" curriculum in the lessons minority children learn in school. For example, she describes how speaking with an accent can lead to students' being discriminated against. She also addresses different response modes among differing cultural groups and how one mode may be disadvantaged in the schools. Eisner also writes of the "null" curriculum, that which is simply ignored by the schools. Others use different curricular labels, such as the "official" curriculum, the "hidden" curriculum, the "lived" curriculum. Whatever the label, it becomes clear that taking the perspective of any particular stakeholder group brings out a different view of a given school experience. When African studies are not mentioned in the curriculum, this area would be in what Eisner calls the null curriculum. When African-American students are taught that their heritage is one of slavery, the explicit curriculum sends a powerful message. When African-American young people are monitored more carefully than others, the "implicit" curriculum tells them that they are not to be trusted.

Indeed, curriculum decisions cannot escape the influence of stakeholders. As Walker and Soltis (1997) argue, "judgments about the merits of curriculum are many-valued, multifaceted, context-dependent, and relative to larger social, philosophical, and educational viewpoints" (p. 9). It seems there is no easy way out of this, which makes it all the more crucial that teachers are able to articulate the purposes behind their curricular choices.

Tracking

A second issue raised in the course of this problem—explicitly, from the parents' perspective—was the practice of tracking students into different curricular experiences by virtue of their "abilities." What are the implications of tracking students into different courses?

In general, teachers prefer to teach relatively homogenous groups of students. The basis for this is quite practical. If you have a classroom where you can predict the learning needs of students and where you can design learning experiences that all students can readily accomplish, the planning and instructional tasks of the teacher are far less complex. For example, if the teacher is able to call on all students to do a syntactic analysis of their sentences to determine the effects of rearranging the placement of prepositional phrases, the teacher can push all students forward. But imagine if the teacher has three students who are ready to analyze their sentences, twenty students who are fairly sure of the sentence and the prepositions but uncertain of how to rearrange them, and five students who do not know how to write a sentence. Teaching this group is much more challenging than the class that is uniform in abilities and understandings.

Clearly, there are certain subjects where the effects of a widely dispersed ability range of students cause more difficulty than in other subjects. While history teachers are less likely to face frustrating gaps in skills, math teachers often complain of the impossibility of teaching mixed-ability groups. The rationale for specialized courses is founded on addressing the real differences among students. Remedial reading classes are a way to help students get their abilities—crucial survival abilities—to the level where they can succeed. Advanced placement courses in history, English, or physics are designed not only to keep academically able students engaged in schooling, but also to give them a head start on and a reason to pursue opportunities in higher education. Thus, it would seem from a pragmatic perspective that tracking is simply a logical response to the variations in students' prior knowledge. Why should this be an issue?

Tracking and Race in Schools

The "issue" arises when one examines the way that tracking has been implemented in schools. The various tracks in most secondary schools have become a *de facto* means of segregating races and classes of students. Statistically, the complaint made by the task force in this problem is consistent with national experience: higher tracks tend to be populated by white children from higher SES (socioeconomic status) families; lower tracks tend to be populated by children of color and children from poor families (Wheelock, 1992).

Of course, to observe that more students of color are present in the lower track at a school may not be to note an injustice in the school. Some would argue that the disproportionate number of minorities in lower tracks merely reflects the culture in which we live. That is, tracking in the schools does not *cause* these students to fall behind their peers; tracking is the *natural manifestation* of the way our society is organized. Children of minority backgrounds do face fewer opportunities than their peers face and therefore the schools must adapt to this reality in order to meet the needs of all children. What do you think? Is tracking a means of perpetuating the inequities of our society? Or is tracking a means of redressing such inequities by allowing disadvantaged children the additional assistance needed to catch up with their peers?

The debate about the *intentions* of tracking may not be as significant as an examination of the *effects* of tracking. What did your research reveal about the schools where tracking is practiced? Is it possible that the educational purposes for tracking could be accomplished without the social consequences of segregation?

Teaching Techniques and Culture

In her essay on effective teaching practices in multicultural classrooms, Geneva Gay (1992) argues that instructional techniques should honor the goals and concepts of multicultural education and that they should be part of a systematic plan to infuse multiculturalism in the schools. She addresses several specific recommendations for teachers to use in their instruction. Among her ideas: consider reducing the dominance of teacher talk in the classroom, expand examples to use culturally-sensitive models (e.g., ethnic protest poetry), and build more cooperative classroom environments. She writes, "The ultimate answer to creating effective instructional practices for multicultural classrooms is empowering teachers to make better decisions for themselves within their own teaching contexts" (p. 54).

This clearly does not address an Afrocentric perspective per se. Her comments are sufficiently open that one might be able to draw on them, but it is unlikely we could construct an actual plan from them. The question of instruction and culture seems to remain: Is there a particular "technique" that is best for particular groups? Is there a technique of instruction that would allow greater success for African-American (or any other group) students?

To answer that question risks stereotyping and overgeneralizations; most writers avoid the level of detail that would suggest a particular technique, relying instead on principles of sensitivity and a general condemnation of traditional, teacher-dominated pedagogy. We do know, however, that different cultural groups rely on different patterns for the learning of their children. In some groups, children begin very early to mix with adult society, often without the restriction of having to act like adults. In some groups, listening quietly to elders is an essential part of learning. Where does this leave the well-intentioned teacher? Are there too many options, so that we are driven back to the "neutrality" of the way things have always been done?

Probably not. What is most important is to develop the awareness that embedded within instructional strategies are unspoken assumptions about how people learn. And people learn in different ways, with important patterns found in cultural groups. Committed teachers learn to recognize that their teaching techniques affect different groups in different ways, and they seek what will build on the prior experiences of all their students. Committed teachers learn about the communities in which they work, so that they can build on the strengths and wonders of those communities. Perhaps most important of all, committed teachers learn that just because students don't mirror the teachers' techniques and beliefs, that does not mean the students are not learning.

Dealing with School Boards

The context of the solution for this problem involved making a presentation to a school board. For most public schools, it is the school board, elected by local communities, that holds the decision-making power over schools. This authority includes setting policies, hiring and firing personnel, deciding about textbooks and curricula and all matters of budget, such as setting salaries for teachers and administrators. Clearly, this is a powerful force in the professional lives of teachers. How do teachers relate to such boards?

For the most part, especially in larger districts, the relationship with the board is distant for typical teachers. On occasion, teachers are invited to address the board or appear before it for an award or recognition. On even rarer occasions, teachers are called before the board to explain their actions or to face disciplinary action. However, the day-to-day functioning of the school board calls for citizen participation. As the board weighs alternatives, citizens—including teachers—have the right to express opinions. When professional educators appear before the school board, they are under greater pressure than community members are to represent themselves well. A school board member is likely to want hard evidence from teachers who address the board, evidence that demonstrates professionalism in the inquiry and presentation of the teacher. Anecdotal evidence and opinions unconnected to the vast research base in education are unlikely to represent teachers well—even if these forms of discourse are popular approaches for the board members themselves! At the same time, stories and accounts involving the children of the district itself tend to have tremendous rhetorical power with the board.

One important point to consider in dealing with school boards is that members who were elected by small and specific constituencies often constitute the boards. The service associated with board memberships is demanding, and it draws a certain kind of individual. Certainly there are many altruistic, committed board members. There are also board members who have been elected by groups that are critical of, sometimes hostile toward, public education. While this may seem ironic and unpleasant, it is a realistic possibility. As a teacher, you must remember that you work for this board, in that it represents the "public" in public schooling. Antagonizing the board is likely to be futile at best, self-destructive at worst. So consider how you might address a school board in the most professional manner possible. As you use solid evidence—research findings and real examples—you are likely to be effective. Beware of becoming entangled in the political in-fighting that so often occurs with such boards, particularly in smaller communities.

DISCUSSION QUESTIONS

1. Given the conflicts that arise among stakeholders in school decisions, how can a teacher maintain a position that has space both for his or her opinions and for the respect due to all the stakeholders? How does a school help balance the demands and expectations of competing stakeholders?

2. How does the challenge to tracking implied by the ad hoc committee mesh with your view of your own area of the curriculum? What trade-offs do you see in taking a position for or against tracking?

3. What role does the beginning teacher take in relationship to the building of a curriculum? Does one have to earn the respect of colleagues before venturing ideas, or does one offer new ideas right away, based on recent educational experiences? And as a teacher gains experience, is there an obligation to participate in curricular decision making?

4. How does a person's view of what constitutes the curriculum affect that person's teaching—both at the level of deciding what to teach and at the level of deciding how to teach? Consider the implications of viewing the curriculum from the perspective of Freire versus Tyler.

5. What do you see as the relationship between the curriculum and cultures?

6. Considering the PBL process, what did you learn about your patterns of problem solving? For example, do you find a desire to move to a solution quickly, or are you comfortable playing with the details for a time? How would you describe your problem-solving approach?

FURTHER READING

Beals, M. P. (1994). *Warriors don't cry: A searing memoir of the battle to integrate Little Rock's Central High*. New York: Washington Square Press.
This particular book moves quite a distance from the question of Afrocentrism in the curriculum. Instead, Melba Pattillo Beals writes an account of her experience as a member of the "Little Rock Nine," the children who were the first African-American students in Central High in Little Rock, Arkansas. She tells how she and her friends, eager to have a chance at attending school whatever the curriculum, paid for integration with their innocence.
Although the book tells of an event long ago (1957), it is a powerful tool for building empathy for the experience of being rejected for one's race. Beals writes that "During those years when we desperately needed approval from our peers, we were victims of the most harsh rejection imaginable" (p. 2). Furthermore, she sees the struggle she faced in Little Rock as an ongoing national struggle: "Today, thirty-six years after the Central High crisis, school integration is still not a reality, and we use children as tender warriors on the battlefield to achieve racial equality" (p. 310).

Beane, J. A. (1997). *Curriculum integration: Designing the core of democratic education*. New York: Teachers College.
James Beane has been a consistent advocate for "curriculum integration," and this book provides a clear case for the practice. Beane questions organizing the school experience around high-status subject areas to the neglect of the important questions students actually have (see especially Chapter 3). Instead, he argues that curriculum should be built around the intersection of student questions about themselves and about society. It is important that students encounter knowledge in use, applied to the real-life situations they face. His notion of local control suggests that communities like Layton would not likely ignore issues of culture in their midst.

Hanssen, E. (1998). A white teacher reflects on institutional racism. *Phi Delta Kappan, 79*(9), 694–698.
Hanssen's brief, personal account doesn't portray a system of racism with dramatic, violent attacks on individuals. Instead, she helps us to see the subtle and persistent elements of racism. Her insights help us see the taken-for-granted parts of a system that assumes a rightness about the way things are and frowns on the questions raised. It's quite a task—something like a fish trying to convince his fellows that the water is dirty when they're still saying, "what water"? The work helps us see what is meant by "hidden" curriculum.

Sizer, T. H. (1992). *Horace's school: Redesigning the American high school*. Boston: Houghton Mifflin.
Sizer takes the reader through a committee's deliberations on reforming a high school. His book gives a different view of how curriculum decisions might be made, with participation from teachers, administrators, students, parents, and community members (a large range of stakeholders). The interconnections among curriculum and instruction and assessment become clear. In addition, he allows his teachers to dig up the high school's "dirty little secret," a question of race that relates well to the areas of focus in this problem.

WEB SITES

Association for Supervision and Curriculum Development
www.ascd.org/readingroom/books/glatthorn94book.html
Excerpts from Allan A. Glatthorn's 1994 book on developing curriculum.

Black Alliance for Educational Options
www.baeo.org/options/home_school.jsp
Includes interesting links to look at Afrocentric curriculum in home schooling.

Coalition of Essential Schools, Horace *on Developing Curriculum in Essential Schools*
www.essentialschools.org/pubs/horace/12/v12n04.html
An on-line publication of the CES.

Molefi Kete Asante
www.valdosta.edu/~cawalker/afrocentric.htm
A paper on Afrocentric curriculum.

A New Look at Afrocentric Curriculum
www.nbufront.org/html/FRONTalView/ArticlesPapers/AfroCentricCurriculm.html
A paper by Samuel A. Iyewarun.

REFERENCES

Anyon, J. (1981). Social class and school knowledge. *Curriculum inquiry, 11*(1), 3–42.

Apple, M. W. (1988). *Teachers and texts: A political economy of class and gender relations in education.* London: Routledge.

Apple, M. W. (1990). *Ideology and curriculum* (2nd ed.). New York: Routledge.

Beals, M. P. (1994). *Warriors don't cry: A searing memoir of the battle to integrate Little Rock's Central High.* New York: Washington Square Press.

Beane, J. A. (1997). *Curriculum integration: Designing the core of democratic education.* New York: Teachers College.

Beyer, L. E., & Apple, M. W. (1988). Values and politics in the curriculum. In L. E. Beyer & M. W. Apple (Eds.), *The curriculum: Problems, politics, and possibilities* (pp. pp. 3–16). Albany: State University of New York.

Conroy, P. (1972). *The water is wide.* Boston: Houghton Mifflin.

Eisner, E. W. (1985). *The educational imagination: On the design and evaluation of school programs* (2nd ed.). New York: Macmillan.

Freire, P. (1990). *Pedagogy of the oppressed* (M. B. Ramos, Trans.). New York: Continuum.

Gay, G. (1992). Effective teaching practices for multicultural classrooms. In C. Diaz (Ed.), *Multicultural education for the 21st century* (pp. 38–56). Washington, DC: National Education Association.

Hanssen, E. (1998). A white teacher reflects on institutional racism. *Phi Delta Kappan, 79*(9), 694–698.

Hernandez, H. (1989). *Multicultural education: A teacher's guide to content and process.* New York: Merrill.

McNeil, L. M. (1986). *Contradictions of control: School structure and school knowledge.* London: Routledge & Kegan Paul.

Phenix, P. H. (1964). *Realms of meaning: A philosophy of the curriculum for general education.* New York: McGraw-Hill.

Posner, G. J. (1988). Models of curriculum planning. In L. E. Beyer & M. W. Apple (Eds.), *The curriculum: Problems, politics, and possibilities* (pp. 77–97). Albany: State University of New York.

Sizer, T. R. (1992). *Horace's school: Redesigning the American high school.* Boston: Houghton Mifflin.

Tyler, R. W. (1949). *Basic principles of curriculum and instruction.* Chicago: University of Chicago.

Vann, K. R., & Kunjufu, J. (1993). The importance of an Afrocentric, multicultural curriculum. *Phi Delta Kappan, 74*(6), 490–491.

Walker, D. F., & Soltis, J. F. (1997). *Curriculum and aims* (3rd ed.). New York: Teachers College.

Wheelock, A. (1992). *Crossing the tracks: How "untracking" can save America's schools.* New York: The New Press.

■ ■ ■ ■ ■

CHAPTER SEVEN

TO TEAM OR NOT TO TEAM?

INTRODUCTION AND PROBLEM BACKGROUND

In addition to the many professional educators who make decisions about schools, curriculum, and policies, there are many non-educators who influence the decisions about schooling. Legislators and politicians set the basic budgets, direction, and limits of schools. Locally elected school board members create the policies that govern curriculum and the daily lives of students and teachers. Textbook publishers, often far removed from the particular educational context and values of the community, determine what focus a particular subject is likely to take. And a host of educational consultants work their magic at every level of the schooling enterprise.

This problem gives you the opportunity to look at the world of schooling from the perspective of a consultant to educational institutions. You might ask what is the value of taking such a perspective. There are several important reasons for playing this role in thinking about the problem presented here. First, teachers do well to practice the habit of seeing their world as outsiders might see it. Both for the purposes of self-improvement and enhancing public relations, teachers need to develop the capacity to step outside their immediate concerns as teachers of particular children and subjects in order to see the bigger picture. Second, taking a role more dramatically removed from that of the classroom teacher serves as a powerful reminder that problems are always identified, defined, and addressed from particular perspectives. That is, there is no detached and neutral position from which a problem can be solved. In the social world that schools inhabit, problems look different from different positions. When we forget this fact, we are in danger of losing the empathy that makes us effective.

A third reason for viewing the world from a consultant's perspective is more practical. In your career as an educator, you will almost certainly encounter consultants who offer services or goods to your school. That textbook company representative will one day show up outside your door hawking a solution to your problems. To help you succeed, the school leadership will sooner or later bring in "experts"—who may or may not have worked in schools. Having thought like a consultant at one time in your professional development or preparation to teach may serve you well in relating to such individuals.

Finally, the consultant role allows a spirit of playfulness in taking on this problem. The basic question could certainly be tackled in the capacity of teachers making the actual decision. The consultant role lets you play with another identity in another move outside a typical comfort zone.

The focus of this PBL experience draws on fairly recent developments in the organization of schools. From the late 1960s through the early 1990s, most junior high schools were transformed from institutions built around a mini-high school model to institutions founded on what is called a middle school model. While some observers have argued that the transformation was largely superficial and ineffective (Dickinson, 2001), it was certainly dramatic. A major element of that transformation was the reorganization of teachers from departmental structures to interdisciplinary teams (Erb, 1997). *Turning Points* (1989), a publication of the Carnegie Council's Task Force on Adolescent Development, articulated a clear vision for the importance of such teams. Critics have pointed out that the teams often do not carry out the vision of *Turning Points,* but for the most part, middle schools have not been averse to organizing teachers into cross-subject teams.

In 1996, the Carnegie Foundation issued another important position paper, titled *Breaking Ranks* (National Association of Secondary School Principals, 1996). This report focuses on changes needed at the high school level, though it has many similarities to *Turning Points* (which was revised and reissued in 2000). *Breaking Ranks* builds a vision of high schools with smaller communities of learners, greater connections among school subjects, and a more robust collaboration among teachers—even calling for reorganizing the traditional department to support more integrated curriculum (p. 45). Many elements of the *Breaking Ranks* report are similar to recommendations proffered by Theodore Sizer (1992) in his common principles for the Coalition of Essential Schools.

Whereas teachers of junior high aged students have been generally favorable toward restructuring their schools into teams, high school teachers have been more resistant. Part of the issue may relate to the subject matter identities of high school teachers, which are presumably more firmly established than that of their middle school counterparts. Ball and Lacey (1980) examined subject area departments, concluding that the alliances created in the departments were powerful and political. Often we assume that it is the particular demands of knowledge in the subject areas—what is called *epistemology*—that determine departmental positions. In contrast, Ball and Lacey found that departmental structures served sociological functions of preserving the positions and status of the members.

The implications of the findings of Ball and Lacey (1980) line up well with the general resistance of high school teachers to organizing in some manner other than along subject lines. The subject department preserves a place for teachers and perhaps an organized voice for their concerns. The possibility of relinquishing this for interdisciplinary teams is a risk. Of course, it isn't necessarily clear to high school teachers that organizing in teams will benefit them or their students.

This PBL experience invites you to think about the risks, benefits, and possibilities of reorganizing the traditional high school. It invites you to think about what teachers from different subject areas might bring to their work if they were to work more closely with colleagues from other subject areas. Furthermore, this experience invites you to think about working conditions in a school from the vantage of someone not associated with schools at all.

PROBLEM CONTEXT AND SOLUTION PARAMETERS

Context

You have recently joined the firm Creative Consultants, International (CCI). Your company has a rich tradition of providing nonprofit organizations, health providers, government entities, and schools with solutions to a variety of problems related to how these entities organize their work. The company builds its success on the principle that every idea generates more ideas.

The work of CCI is conducted by teams of consultants. Each team builds its own vision and operating procedures. Using a cross-functional strategy, managers try to assemble teams that have a diversity of membership: different skills, knowledge areas, and personalities are crucial to each team's success. However, once these disparate personalities are brought together, CCI teams learn to commit themselves to the common purpose or task assigned to the team.

Problem and Solution Parameters

Your team has been charged with investigating the possibility of instituting a teaming program in Watertown High School. The school has a reputation for being a good place, the sort of school that prompts people to comment "If it ain't broke, don't fix it." Yet there are teachers and community members who are dissatisfied with the lack of progress in the school. The issuing of *Breaking Ranks* provided impetus for these people to call for reform of this above-average high school.

The topic is of special interest to you, because you have seen the impact of teams on business practices, including the work of CCI. What you don't know is whether such teams would bring comparable benefits to teachers. Your team's task is to make a recommendation to the Watertown School Board regarding the following issues:

- Whether or not to institute teaming
- What the general steps in the process of instituting teaming should be
- Specific cautions and trouble shooting
- Models that would be appropriate for this school

Of course, should you decide that teaming is not appropriate, it would be important for your team to offer a clear justification for your position and recommendations for enhancing success in the school with its current organizational structure (or some other alternative). Based on your inquiry into the conditions and expectations of high schools, you may decide that teaming is not a good fit.

········WORK THE PROBLEM ──➤

PROBLEM DOCUMENTS

In order to assist you with your inquiry in this matter, the following documents have been provided for your examination (remember the principle of PBL—there is probably more than you need here, but certainly not enough):

7.1 Memo documenting the contractual agreement with Watertown Schools

7.2 Demographic fact sheet on the high school

7.3 Indicators of school culture, compiled by the school counseling staff

7.4 Statistical reports on the high school

7.5 Memo of opposition from Advanced Placement teachers at the school

7.6 Memo of support from minority teachers in the high school

7.7 A summary of the recommendations from *Breaking Ranks*

PROBLEM DOCUMENT 7.1   *Memo Documenting the Contractual Agreement with Watertown Schools*

CREATIVE CONSULTANTS INTERNATIONAL

> **Task Charge #475**

To: CCI Probationary Teams
From: Director Jones
Date: 10/15/03
RE: Watertown Contract (#475–196)

As you are well aware, your probationary status with the company is nearing a decision point. Each member of your team has had the opportunity to work with seasoned professionals at CCI for a time. You have had significant, if limited, work in the newly-formed probationary teams. This contract is your opportunity to move forward to regular status as a consultant team at CCI. In keeping with company philosophy, the decision about your status will be made for the entire team rather than for individuals.

Your charge is to provide a proposal to the Watertown School Board on the issue of whether or not they should reorganize the high school into cross-disciplinary teams of teachers. Their current structure, in keeping with strongly established patterns throughout the country, is a departmental structure. That is, teachers in similar subject areas are grouped for purposes of decision making about curriculum, resources, certain policies, and above all, for the convenience of the administration in communicating with the staff.

One of the school board members recently encountered a national report (summary of which is included with your document package) suggesting that schools may serve students more effectively if teachers work as members of cross-disciplinary teams. While this school board member was unable to convince the board to officially adopt the new structure, this member persuaded the board to hire professional analysts—us—to give a recommendation.

You will find that presenting a recommendation to a school board is somewhat different from the work your team has conducted in the past. It would be well worth your time to investigate effective tactics for such a presentation; however, at the very least, be aware of the following issues:

1. The bottom line to which we are accustomed (profit) will be more ambiguous to the school board.
2. The formality of the presentation situation will likely be extreme.
3. The competing stakeholders to whom you must appeal may raise other complexities. That is, while our hiring mandate arises from the Board, there will be other constituencies who will have impact on the results. It is wise to consider constituencies broadly.

PROBLEM DOCUMENT 7.2 *Demographic Fact Sheet on WHS*

| | Fact Sheet #475-001 |

Watertown High School Data

Demographics: Watertown High School serves five neighborhoods in the greater San Lupos area. Three of the neighborhoods comprise primarily middle-class homes with few reduced-lunch clients. One neighborhood consists of large executive homes, though nearly half of the students from these households attend the private academy, Whitside East. The remaining neighborhood, South Rancho, is the largest of the five and is home to many immigrant families, blue-collar workers, and unemployed people.

Student data:

Grade	Male	Female	Asian	African American	Caucasian	Hispanic
9	216	199	86	83	122	124
10	202	192	83	77	125	109
11	189	210	75	72	140	112
12	177	163	80	48	143	69
(1,548)	784	764	324	280	530	414

Students receiving free or reduced lunch: 38%

Faculty data:

Full-time	m	f	Part-time	m	f
	50	37		4	8

Scheduling information: Semester system, block schedule.

Period 1	7:40–9:05	Period 3b	11:20–12:45
Period 2	9:15–10:40	Period 4	12:55–2:20
Period 3a	10:50–12:15		

Teachers instruct for three of the four periods. Department heads instruct for two periods, with one period provided for administrative activities.

School is characterized by a strong departmental structure: little communication or interchange occurs among faculty members from different departments. Monthly faculty meetings are well attended (required—the assistant principal takes attendance). Faculty members tend to sit in their departmentalized groupings. Reports indicate that social functions continue to reflect a preference for departmental association, though the data are quite limited in this regard.

PROBLEM DOCUMENT 7.3   *Indicators of School Culture, Compiled by WHS Counseling Staff*

Fact Sheet #475-002

The following are indicators of school culture compiled for CCI by Watertown High School counseling staff.

A. Discipline referrals by grade and sex:

	99–00		00–01		01–02	
	m	f	m	f	m	f
9	392	205	412	202	455	255
10	255	225	287	191	300	250
11	195	150	198	174	181	180
12	133	65	115	100	156	140

B. Watertown Gang Task Force recommended a revised dress code for the school in the fall of 2001 to eliminate "colors" conflicts. After serious and heated debate, the faculty chose not to adopt the new code. One vice principal resigned in protest and is currently opening a charter school. It is anticipated that a number of the faculty members will seek teaching jobs in the new charter school as the positions become available.

C. Police were called to campus 57 times in 2001–2002, most often to remove students with substance abuse materials and/or weapons. On three occasions, the police were brought onto campus as a result of major violent confrontations (i.e., more than three combatants) that could be roughly characterized as "racially based."

D. From the informal observations of counseling staff, the cafeteria tends to be dominated by African-American and Hispanic students, though each group tends to occupy one portion of the room. Asian students rarely gather in this area; Caucasian students can be seen more frequently. It appears that the students find other gathering areas outside of the school, and that there is a generally accepted self-segregation. Of course, there are exceptions to the racial congregating. The "cowboy" group appears to mix ethnic groups, but often with hostility to other cliques. The typical "smokers' group" exists, welcoming all comers.

E. A similar division is apparent among teachers. There are three teachers' lounge areas in WHS. The north staff room, near the gym, is primarily the meeting place of coaches. Of the school's nine African-American faculty members, the four who also coach frequently can be found in the north lounge. Seven of the twenty-five Hispanic teachers also coach and therefore frequent this lounge. The remaining "north loungers" are largely male Caucasians.

The south lounge is the "academic" center of the school, largely populated by Caucasian teachers. The mix of males and females is fairly even here, though the men tend to dominate discussions. A number of the school's eleven Asian teachers use the south lounge.

The eastside lounge is predominantly a meeting place for the newer teachers, overwhelmingly Hispanic. These teachers, unlike their counterparts, tend to have three or fewer years' experience, whereas the overall average for the school is 12.7 years. This lounge is the one "adult" location where signs posted are as likely to be in Spanish as in English.

| PROBLEM DOCUMENT 7.4 | *Statistical Reports on WHS* |

Fact Sheet #475-003

Watertown High School Achievement/Retention Data

Students taking the SAT, 1999: 110   Average score: 1040 (1600 possible)

Students taking the SAT, 2000: 101   Average score: 1090 (1600 possible)

Students taking the SAT, 2001: 93   Average score: 980 (1600 possible)

Students taking the SAT, 2002: 99   Average score: 1000 (1600 possible)

Performance on CAT (California Achievement Test) in comparision with state average:

	Math	Reading	Language Arts
State	48.7	49.0	48.2
WHS	47.5	47.3	46.0

Retention rate* by ethnicity:

	African American	Asian	Caucasian	Hispanic
1998–99	62	89	75	53
1999–00	60	92	73	50
2000–01	57	95	71	48

*Retention rate as a percentage of students in all grades who were enrolled at the end of the third week of school and still enrolled as of the second week of May.

Faculty data:

Average years' experience:	12.7 years
Average age:	44 years
Educational attainment:	BA+43 credits (more than half hold Master's Degrees)
Average tenure at WHS:	10.2 years

PROBLEM DOCUMENT 7.5   *Protest Petition from AP Teachers at WHS*

Support Document #475-001

Representatives of the Advanced Placement program at Watertown High School (AP Calculus, AP History, AP Literature, AP Physics) presented a petition to Ms. Otter, the WHS principal. The full text is reproduced below:

Ms. Otter:

It has come to our attention that the Watertown Board of Education has hired Creative Consultants, International, to evaluate Watertown High School for consideration of implementing a cross-disciplinary teamed structure. We wish to register our unequivocal opposition to this plan! While some students may require the more custodial version of schooling implicit in this "middle school" organization, clearly a great many of Watertown's students are capable of independent thought, mature decisions, and superior academic performance. We shudder at the thought of what Harvard, Stanford, or Yale might think of our program if we in any way threatened the integrity of our academic rigor. The teachers at Watertown High School are consummate professionals who do not need any interference from other teachers—and especially not from business consultants! Moreover, we know that our parent clientele would rebel at this suggestion.

An argument is circulating through the halls of WHS that this suggestion arises from the recommendations of a national commission that has carefully investigated the structure of high schools. We challenge this perspective. It is our understanding that the report in question is speculative and theoretical, more committed to "political correctness" than to sound research practice. Is this an appropriate basis for such an important decision?

If the board persists in this questionable (and extravagantly wasteful!) investigation, we urge that the team structure be considered only for lower-track courses, where it is reasonable to assume a less academic program applies. Please do not damage our brightest children's futures!

Respectfully,

Martin Oister *Debra Clamm*

Esther Phish *Colin Seashore*

Ms. Otter has made no official reply to this memo. She did forward it to the Watertown Board of Education and posted a copy in the teachers' lounge.

Support Document #475-002

The following memorandum was presented to Ms. Otter, the school principal, signed by 26 teachers, two days after the AP memo.

<u>MEMO</u>

From: Undersigned teachers

To: Ms. Otter, Principal WHS

RE: AP memo

By your posting the AP memo, we have come to realize the stakes involved in the current CCI investigation at WHS. We do not wish to see this decision made prematurely, nor do we want the decision unduly influenced by a small segment of our staff. In addition, the perspective offered by the AP memo represents only a small portion of our students—primarily a group of elite white and Asian students.

We see a number of reasons why teaming should be tried at WHS—or at least seriously considered. Among these reasons are the following issues:

- We are tired of the rifts in our school, especially among various ethnic groups.
- We are weary of a curriculum that is allocated according to a student's background, with only the most privileged students receiving the best possibilities.
- We feel professionally stifled by the current arrangement and wish to explore opportunities for growth.
- We recognize changing work patterns that ought to affect what happens in schools.

Obviously the use of cooperative learning techniques has permeated education; why is it that educators continue to resist such cooperation? Think of the models we could be for our students.

We represent primarily new teachers, and as such we face some disturbing trends. Already we can see careers of professional isolation stretching out before us, broken only by casual, nonwork interchanges. This is not what we want for our careers, our school, or our students. For our kids, for our professional growth, for the community, please consider teaming at WHS.

Signed,

(The names of 26 teachers are indicated. Primary authorship has been attributed to Maria Tortuga).

PROBLEM DOCUMENT 7.7   *Summary of Recommendations*

	Fact Sheet #475-004

Summary of Recommendations from *Breaking Ranks*
(provided by CCI Research Division)

Breaking Ranks presents nine themes, with a variety of recommendations subsumed within each theme. The themes are listed below:

1. High schools are learning communities, and each school must commit itself to meeting high standards.
2. High school is a transition experience to help move students to another stage of life.
3. High school should provide students with a gateway to multiple opportunities.
4. High schools must prepare students to be lifelong learners.
5. High schools should help students understand and experience good citizenship and democracy.
6. High schools are more than academic—they must provide ways for students to grow as social beings.
7. High schools should help students succeed in a technology-based society.
8. High schools must help students to be able to live in a world of interdependent and diverse people.
9. High schools must actively advocate on behalf of individuals.

····**PROPOSE A SOLUTION** ⟶

SOLUTION SUMMARY

Before proceeding to the reflection section of this chapter, write a brief summary of your team's solution here:

Our team defined the "real" problem here as _____

_____

_____

_____

_____

_____

_____

_____

The key features of our solution were _____

_____

_____

_____

_____

_____

_____

My personal view of the problem and solution is _____

_____

_____

_____

_____

_____

_____

TIME FOR REFLECTION

Whether one tackles the issue of organizing teachers into teams from the perspective of outside consultants or teachers who are exploring this organization for their own working worlds, a number of topics surface for reflection. In this section, we consider a number of school reform issues. What does reform look like from the perspective of outside reformers? What is the role of an organizational structure for the learners, the curriculum, and the lives of teachers? Would teacher teams work at the high school level? Does it make sense to talk about an interdisciplinary curriculum?

Reform from the Outside

In one of the "models of instruction" presented by Joyce and Weils (1996), we learn of ways to make the strange familiar and the familiar strange. *Synectics* is one such model, a model that uses metaphoric thinking as a means to have thinkers move away from a familiar problem in order to come back to it with new insight. Developed for business, synectics has been a powerful tool in schools as well. It is not alone as an idea transferred from the business world to education. Arcaro (1995), for example, presents a consultant's perspective on how to bring Total Quality Management (TQM) to education, an idea echoed in Glasser (1990; 1993).

The virtue of such ways of teaching and thinking is that they do promote new insight. In the same way, there are times when it is valuable to gain the insight and perspective that belong to an outsider. In his examination of the role of school "culture" and change, Seymour B. Sarason (1982) addresses the difficulties of understanding a school completely from the inside. In fact, he invites readers to imagine how a school might look to a "being from outer space who finds himself and his invisible space platform directly above an elementary school" (p 63). What sorts of regularities would such a being notice? Fantasy aside, the point is clear: by positioning ourselves outside of schools, we experience the opportunity to see them afresh.

To address this problem, you were asked to assume the role of a non-educator, a business consultant interested in organizational patterns. This role allowed two possible benefits. First, by viewing schools from the outside, you might have gained insights into how schools are organized. Second, it allows you to think about the ways other outsiders do impact education.

When the first President Bush called for a summit on education, chaired by soon-to-be president Bill Clinton, he followed a fairly common practice: inviting people outside of the schools to offer help and advice to education. Later, IBM CEO Louis Gerstner headed up the council to reform schools. Is there an assumption that people who know how to manage a bottom line in industry have the capacity to make schools better? Numerous major metropolitan areas (Los Angeles and Seattle among them) have turned over the reform and control of the schools to non-educators. And it won't take you many parent–teacher conferences to realize that average citizens also have plenty of ideas about how to make schools better.

The key point is that teachers' work, for most of us, is public work. All sorts of individuals and groups will have ideas about what schools can do better. Some will do so for political reasons, some for economic, some out of pure altruism.

What future teachers need to realize is that reform from the outside is an ever-present force in our professional lives. It does little good to pretend it doesn't exist or to despair about it. Rather, a useful perspective is to learn how best to use such forces in the service of educating young people.

In this problem, a company of consultants had its chance to suggest changes in a school. The committed professional would hear them out, try to guide them to positive conclusions, and do whatever he or she could to learn from them—even if that professional felt that these outsiders had no business being in the schools. That's why teachers are lifelong learners.

Teacher Teaming at the High School Level

Among secondary schools, teaming has taken hold at the middle school level. Of course, there is a huge difference between accepting teams as an organizational surface feature and embracing teams as the organizing center of teachers' work. There is a good deal of evidence that teaming has been tacked on to a host of middle schools without the proper training, support for implementation, or followup (Erb, 2001). Still, teaming has opened up conversations and opportunities for professional development that were unavailable in the classic junior high model.

The implementation of teaming at the high school level has been even less successful. Traditions related to departmental structures and to the subject-based identities of teachers are powerful, well entrenched, and resistant to questioning. As Sarason (1982) has argued, the culture of the school is a force that can stifle change readily.

There are some examples of schools that have reorganized away from strict departmental groups. In his account of a high school in northern California, Neal Glasgow (1997) describes schools-within-the-school, where teachers work together across disciplinary boundaries to deliver a different kind of education. Like other schools associated with the Coalition of Essential Schools, this high school has conceptualized student learning as something that does not fit neatly into disciplinary boxes. So, Glasgow writes, "The collaborative effort of the teaching staff is focused on connecting the traditional disciplines around thematic problem-based units to create opportunities to combine teaching needs, goals, and objectives" (p. 25). In other words, teachers team flexibly to create learning experiences that cross boundaries. There would be little point to their teaming if, in fact, the teachers simply delivered the traditional, textbook-based curriculum.

To move toward a team structure in the high school goes well beyond a change on paper for the way teachers are grouped. Such a change involves a new view of the teachers' role in relation to the curriculum–student interaction. This goes to the heart of how teachers view themselves and their work. Instead of seeing themselves as dispensers of expertise in narrowly-defined areas, teachers move to the position of facilitating learning, of becoming learners themselves. Changes of this nature are painful, difficult to reconcile to, and often contrary to the cultures that schools have developed. Erb (2001) argues that as the elements of bureaucracy persist in schools, teams are not effective. "As long as teachers see themselves as individually responsible for teaching a prespecified area of the curriculum, they will self-limit their ability to function on a team. As long as administrators persist in the belief that they are ultimately responsible for what goes on in their schools so that they must make schoolwide decisions and hand them down for teachers to follow, teacher autonomy will be stymied" (p. 185).

In conjunction with the change in self-perception, teachers who move to a teamed structure need help in understanding how such teams work. Daniels, Bizar, and Zemmelman (2001) write that teaming is "unlikely to work if teachers are thrown together willy-nilly in teams and ordered to 'cooperate.' . . . Clearly, careful planning and staff development are needed for team approaches to work" (p. 80). The importance of training employees to succeed in teamed structures is well documented among organizational researchers (Fisher & Fisher, 1998; Hackman & Oldham, 1980; Wellins, Byham, & Dixon, 1994). Perhaps, if schools offer the support and training that is common in the corporate world, teams of secondary teachers can experience the kinds of dramatic improvements that businesses have witnessed.

Interdisciplinary Curriculum

One of the recommendations from *Breaking Ranks* (1996) was related to the way the curriculum is presented to students in the high school. The report calls on the high school to "integrate its curriculum to the extent possible" and to "promote cocurricular activities as integral to an education" (p. 11). The prospect of an interdisciplinary approach to curriculum excites some, frightens others, but is greeted by most secondary teachers with a yawn. Tradition maintains a mighty foothold in this arena.

But it is not beyond question that high schools might consider an interdisciplinary approach to the curriculum. A reasonable posture for inquiry might be to ask what would be gained and what might be lost by such an approach. In his article about lessons from the famous Eight-Year Study, Vars (1999) points out that there have been cases made for an "integrative" curriculum since the 1930s. He sees the call for an interdisciplinary curriculum as "mild" in *Breaking Ranks,* but a key lesson that we can apply today from the 1930s experiment in secondary schools where such curriculum designs were a major contributor to building a new vision of high school. What would be gained? Vars sees possibilities for innovation, and the use of principles from the Eight-Year Study may lead to more student-centered and democratic practices in schools. In their guide to building the "exemplary" high school, George, McEwin, and Jenkins (2000) devote an entire chapter to the reorganization of curriculum at the high school level, and they include a section on interdisciplinary organizations (including model schools). What are the potential gains? The authors argue that changes to the curriculum reflect changing times, with "higher expectations for student learning, expanded academic offerings, and efforts to teach higher-order thinking and problem-solving skills to all students" (p. 62).

It is not always essential to organize courses around the traditional disciplines. Middle schools have experimented with an integrated model advocated by Beane (1990), where curriculum is organized around the intersection of student-generated questions about themselves and questions about society. Finkel (2000) argues for organizing courses around problems and inquiry. In this model, Finkel claims, motivation becomes less of an issue. The focus shifts from arbitrary subject collections to problems that interest students and teachers alike. *"If the students are interested in the inquiry, then they will want to learn whatever is necessary to pursue that inquiry"* (p. 55, original emphasis). Is this wishful thinking? Or is it possible that the very organization of the secondary curriculum has induced some of the boredom that teachers are challenged to address as instructors?

It seems that although the idea of an interdisciplinary curriculum has not spread widely throughout the schools, it is not unthinkable. What, then, are the potential losses of such an organization of the curriculum? It is ironic that one of the chief arguments against an "integrated" curriculum at any level is the "integrity" of the subject. Notice the similarities between the two words. Both come from a Latin root meaning "whole." And, due to the nature of the ways we organize knowledge, different people see different "wholes" ("holes"?). For some, what holds a "discipline" together is a unity of a way of knowing—perhaps common methods, language, questions, and so on. This is the "whole" that should be presented to students. Others challenge the unity of a given discipline (Soltis, 1978) and argue that any sense of "wholeness" is imposed on the discipline by social conventions. That is, not the nature of the subject, but the unity of the practitioners creates the sense of "wholeness."

For teachers at the secondary level, this question deserves some attention. Is history (or math or English or any of the others) a unified area that must be taught in some pure isolation? Is it best taught in such isolation? Or is the subject a part of a less unified field that can profit from connections to other areas? Will students learn less if their math class is taught in conjunction with some other class or will they learn more? In their exploration into the potential advantages of "integrated curriculum," Daniels, Bizar, and Zemelman (2001) interviewed teachers, who listed the following benefits from teaching with colleagues in an interdisciplinary manner: building community and working relationships; improving climate through teachers knowing students better; motivating learners through authentic issues and authentic student questions; focusing on depth versus breadth; connecting disciplines; helping students with problem solving and research skills; and allowing more thorough and authentic assessment. The same teachers also indicated there were concerns about such curriculum, including what to do about the higher-level math and science courses and the loss of time to test preparation programs.

One further area of reflection has to do with the possibility of different levels of integration. In England, after the raising of the age at which children could leave school, a number of "integrated" programs were put in place to help keep potentially alienated students connected (Kain, 1993). In contrast, the American experiment with "Humanities" programs in the early 1970s (and later) saw such programs as suitable for the higher achieving students. Both examples, however, viewed integrated curriculum as appropriate for only a special population of students, removing the practice from the bulk of students. Does such an approach create stigma or status that will keep interdisciplinary curriculum an issue on the fringes?

The letter from the Advanced Placement teachers played with the idea of "rigor." Specifically, these teachers questioned how Stanford, Harvard, or Yale might view the consequences of teacher teams. What do you think of this appeal to an academic standard implied by these "sacred" names in higher education? Does organizing knowledge and schooling in some way other than the traditional means necessarily imply a lack of rigor?

Impact of Structures

We don't often consider how the organizational structures we create might impact the experience of our learners. For too long, American schools were organized around factory-model values of efficiency, size, and interchangeability. The assumption of normality prevented our seeing such oddities as funneling masses of children through roughly identical experiences. In his examination of elementary schools, Jackson (1968/1990) noticed the most compelling elements of school from a child's perspective: feeling crowded, feeling the imbalance of power, and feeling continually judged. John Goodlad's (1984) study reported a similar situation among secondary schools, with children becoming more and more passive (and bored) the longer they were in schools. The role of the organizational structure in creating this unfortunate school reality has rarely been examined.

Consider how the organization of your work as a teacher will contribute to your psychological and emotional state as you continue to work in schools throughout a career. Consider the contrast between a work environment where you actively engage your colleagues in an exchange of ideas with a work environment where the only opportunity for such exchanges is the break room. Then consider the impact of this work environment on the students you deal with. In her examination of the "contradictions of control," Linda McNeil (1986) points out how secondary teachers pass along to their students the sort of treatment they receive from the workplace.

Of course, there are many healthy and productive workplaces. This problem merely invites us to reflect on the connections between the way schools are organized for teachers and the resulting environments. As teachers, you can be active contributors in the conversations about what schools should be like. Teachers have more options than merely to complain about the social environment of an institution; they have the chance to help form it.

DISCUSSION QUESTIONS

1. What were the difficulties of taking on a role as an outsider to a school? What insights did you gather from this perspective?

2. Did you experience any positive or negative models of teacher collaboration in high school or university? What did you learn from those?

3. If it is true that the working conditions for teachers affect the environment for students, what is the responsibility of each teacher to help build a positive work environment? How does a teacher—particularly a beginning teacher—help to create such an environment?

4. In your work with colleagues in teacher preparation or graduate education, what lessons have you learned that will help you relate more effectively to your teaching colleagues?

5. What do you see as appropriate limits to place on business involvement in education or the use of business metaphors for schools? How can teachers maintain a degree of critical perspective on business without alienating potential allies?

6. Does teaming make sense without changes in the organization of the curriculum? What alternative curricular structures look promising to you?

7. Considering the PBL process, what did you learn about your interests and strengths as an inquirer through this experience?

FURTHER READING

Daniels, H., Bizar, M., & Zemelman, S. (2001). *Rethinking high school: Best practice in teaching, learning, and leadership.* Portsmouth, NH: Heinemann.
   The authors look at how high schools might be different from a systematic approach. Addressing eleven issues that they say every high school must deal with eventually, they show how a school might look if it lived up to current standards. The chapter on scheduling (Chapter 8) is especially helpful for new teachers to see beyond whatever their own experience of a daily schedule might have been like. The authors also provide insight about teacher teaming and curriculum integration in their chapters on teaching and on the curriculum.

Erb, T. O. (2001). Transforming organizational structures for young adolescents and adult learning. In T. S. Dickinson (Ed.), *Reinventing the middle school* (pp. 176–200). New York: RoutledgeFalmer.
   While Erb's chapter is written with teachers at the middle school in mind, it has excellent ideas for all secondary teachers to consider. Erb compares the demands of teaching where the duties are focused on interchangeable job descriptions—a bureaucracy—with the demands of teaching focused on problem-solving for particular students—an "adhocracy." He explores how teams of teachers can transform a school, with benefits for teachers in terms of job satisfaction and benefits for students in terms of a more supportive, less stressful environment, and potentially higher achievement. But he cautions against making surface changes: "if the practices that were created to make bureaucratic schools work (e.g., tracking, bell schedules, separate classrooms, specialized programs) are still being implemented by educators who view interdisciplinary teams as just another programmatic add-on, then teaming will fail and the educators will fail to create an adaptive, problem-solving, innovative organizational structure" (p. 188).

Finkel, D. L. (2000). *Teaching with your mouth shut.* Portsmouth, NH: Heinemann.
   Donald Finkel's book is provocative from the title page on, and even though it is directed at college instructors, it has much to say to high school teachers. Imagine what a disruption it would be to most secondary teachers to have to shut their mouths in order to instruct! In particular, Chapter 4 ("Let Us Inquire Together") has bearing on the issue of disrupting the way high schools do business. Through inquiry, teachers move their students into problems that cross disciplinary boundaries. At such opportunities, it is appropriate and valuable for teachers to work as teams, though Finkel points out that not all schools allow such organization.
   Later (Chapter 8, "Teaching with a Colleague"), Finkel looks at the particular virtues of team teaching as opposed to merely organizing into teams, which he calls "collegial teaching" to mark it as something different. Among the potential benefits of true team teaching, he points out the impact of such team teaching on democratic beliefs. He writes, "By coming together in front of students, each of the two teachers turns over to students, whether he intends to or not, that form of power most important to freedom: the power to make up your own mind" (p. 146).

Gartz, L. (Producer/writer). (1999). *Rethinking high school: Best practice in action* [Videorecording]. Portsmouth, NH: Heinemann.
   This videotape is a companion to the book *Best Practice: New Standards for Teaching and Learning in America's Schools,* written by Steven Zemelman, Harvey Daniels, and Arthur Hyde (Heineman, 1998). The brief videotape describes Best Practice High School in Chicago, a school that was created to address three big ideas that pull together the thirteen

principles of *Best Practice.* The key components of the school build a version of learning that is authentic, challenging, and collaborative. Teachers are to model the principles as well. Thus, the video tells of teachers working as teams to create integrated units for their students. In addition, teachers at the school come together to govern themselves, with peers taking turns conducting the meetings, with agendas generated by the faculty. It is a portrait of a different kind of high school—an alternative to tradition.

George, P. S., McEwin, C. K., Jenkins, J. M. (2000). *The exemplary high school.* New York: Harcourt College.
    The authors have organized a textbook for future high school teachers around the recommendations from *Breaking Ranks.* They set the historical context for American high schools and help us understand why there is a call and need for reform. Then, they build their discussion around the specific recommendations in *Breaking Ranks,* beginning each chapter with connections to the document. You may find two chapters of particular interest in light of this PBL experience. Chapter 2 looks at the high school curriculum (including interdisciplinary organization); Chapter 7 looks at the organization of teachers and learners, including academic teams of teachers and students.

Kain, D. L. (1998). *Camel-makers: Building effective teacher teams together.* Columbus, OH: National Middle School Association.
    This brief book looks at how teachers can work together in teams from a unique perspective. The fictional Dr. Drapolemac uses the notes from the original committee that developed the camel ("A camel looks like a horse that was developed by a committee") to highlight effective teaming practices. Like many other works on teaming, the focus here is on middle-level teachers. However, the principles of adult collaboration are important for teams at all levels. Besides, it's a fun read.

Sizer, T. H. (1992). *Horace's school: Redesigning the American high school.* Boston: Houghton Mifflin.
    In his fictionalized account of reforming a high school, Sizer provides two issues worth reflecting on in relation to this problem. First, the book presents a realistic—if optimistic—view of how a school might undergo reform. He gives us a glimpse of debates and discussions that a typical group of reform-minded educators might hold when approaching the problem of making an acceptable school even better. Part of the discussion focuses on basic issues of teaching (curriculum, instruction, assessment), and part of the discussion focuses on the structural issue of the organization of the school itself. Second, in examining a possibility for reform, Sizer suggests a reorganization of teachers into "houses," or teams of teachers who take responsibility for students.

WEB SITES

Breaking Ranks in the Ocean State
    http://breakingranks.org
    A network in Rhode Island committed to Breaking Ranks reforms.

Educational Impact
    www.eionline.net
    In the spirit of consultants to a school, this staff development company (from a Gates grant) is worth looking at. In fact, they have ideas for implementing *Breaking Ranks* in the schools. Here is the specific link to looking at *Breaking Ranks:* www.eionline.net/programs/breaking_ranks.html

Educational Research Service
    www.ers.org/SSP/sspsu98g.htm
    A brief paper with this headline: High School Incorporates Teaming, Career Pathways.

REFERENCES

Arcaro, J. S. (1995). *Teams in education: Creating an integrated approach.* Delray Beach, FL: St Lucie.

Ball, S. J., & Lacey, C. (1980). Subject disciplines as the opportunity for group actions: A measured critique of subject sub-cultures. In P. Woods (Ed.), *Teacher strategies: Explorations in the sociology of the school* (pp. 149–177). London: Croom Helm.

Beane, J. A. (1990). *A middle school curriculum: From rhetoric to reality.* Columbus, OH: National Middle School Association.

Carnegie Council on Adolescent Development. (1989). *Turning points: Preparing American youth for the 21st century.* New York: Carnegie Corporation.

Daniels, H., Bizar, M., & Zemelman, S. (2001). *Rethinking high school: Best practice in teaching, learning, and leadership.* Portsmouth, NH: Heinemann.

Dickinson, T. S. (Ed.). (2001). *Reinventing the middle school.* New York: RoutledgeFalmer.

Erb, T. O. (1997). Thirty years of attempting to fathom teaming: Battling potholes and hairpin curves along the way. In T. S. Dickinson & T. O. Erb (Eds.), *We gain more than we give: Teaming in middle schools* (pp. 19–59). Columbus, OH: National Middle School Association.

Erb, T. O. (2001). Transforming organizational structures for young adolescents and adult learning. In T. S. Dickinson (Ed.), *Reinventing the middle school* (pp. 176–200). New York: RoutledgeFalmer.

Finkel, D. L. (2000). *Teaching with your mouth shut.* Portsmouth, NH: Heineman.

Fisher, K., & Fisher, M. D. (1998). *The distributed mind: Achieving high performance through the collective intelligence of knowledge work teams.* New York: AMACOM.

Gartz, L. (Producer/writer). (1999). *Rethinking high school: Best practice in action* [Videorecording]. Portsmouth, NH: Heinemann.

George, P. S., McEwin, C. K., & Jenkins, J. M. (2000). *The exemplary high school.* New York: Harcourt College.

Glasgow, N. A. (1997). *New curriculum for new times: A guide to student-centered, problem-based learning.* Thousand Oaks, CA: Corwin.

Glasser, W. (1990). *The quality school: Managing students without coercion.* New York: Harper & Row.

Glasser, W. (1993). *The quality school teacher: A companion volume to The Quality School.* New York: Harper Collins.

Goodlad, J. I. (1984). *A place called school: Prospects for the future.* New York: McGraw-Hill.

Hackman, J. R., & Oldham, G. R. (1980). *Work redesign.* Reading, MA: Addison-Wesley.

Jackson, P. W. (1968/1990). *Life in classrooms.* New York: Teachers College Press.

Joyce, B., & Weil, M. (1996). *Models of teaching* (5th ed.). Boston: Allyn & Bacon.

Kain, D. L. (1993). Cabbages and kings: Research directions in integrated/interdisciplinary curriculum. *Journal of Educational Thought, 27*(3), 312–331.

McNeil, L. M. (1986). *Contradictions of control: School structure and school knowledge.* London: Routledge & Kegan Paul.

National Association of Secondary School Principals. (1996). *Breaking ranks: Changing an American institution: A report of the National Association of Secondary School Principals in partnership with the Carnegie Foundation for the Advancement of Teaching on the high school of the 21st century.* Reston, VA: Author.

Sarason, S. B. (1982). *The culture of school and the problem of change* (2nd ed.). Boston: Allyn & Bacon.

Sizer, T. R. (1992). *Horace's school: Redesigning the American high school.* Boston: Houghton Mifflin.

Soltis, J., F. (1978). *An introduction to the analysis of educational concepts* (2nd ed.). Reading, MA: Addison Wesley.

Vars, G. F. (1999). Another look back at tomorrow's high school, part one: Implications for high school curriculum from the Eight-Year Study. *Voices from the Field, 2*(1), 27–34.

Wellins, R. S., Byham, W. C., & Dixon, G. R. (1994). *Inside teams: How 20 world-class organizations are winning through teamwork.* San Francisco: Jossey-Bass.

MATH MAKES TRACKS

INTRODUCTION AND PROBLEM BACKGROUND

A fairly common distinction between the levels of teachers can be characterized by the response to this question: What do you teach? Stereotypically, the secondary teacher will answer math or English or chemistry; the elementary teacher will answer "kids." And it is generally somewhere in the middle school years that the distinction begins to be made with some regularity. Increasingly, the middle school is the level where the teacher's identity becomes tied closely to subject specialization. At the same time, strong notions about what the subject area requires of its adherents emerge. In short, it is not just that one teaches math, but that one teaches math *the way it should be taught.*

Just how a thing should be taught seems to be a combination of some understanding of psychology, some practical considerations (such as available texts), some influence from individuals, and some powerful traditions. We often associate a certain logical sequence or natural categorization with subjects. For example, consider the organization of a history class into a chronological progression through various eras. Does the nature of the discipline of history dictate that only a chronological organization is effective? What about a thematic approach? An inquiry-based approach? Such questions are difficult even to raise. In the same way, such givens as the reading groups in primary schools sit beyond our careful questioning (though it is possible that such questioning would lead us to recreate the same groups for good reasons). The tradition of placing children into a math class or sequence based on their abilities seems to be the most logical response to differences among the learners, though such a decision deserves examination.

Rarely do we question such givens in education. With the long-standing tradition, surely there is good cause for the way things are. Surely the "integrity" of a subject like math requires that we bring students along in a systematic and logical manner, and the best way to do so is to group students according to proven ability. Beyond that, what other organization makes sense for busy, overworked teachers who don't really have the opportunity to interact with each child for very long?

This PBL experience invites you to look into that assumption. While the vehicle here is math, it is important for you (as a learner) to consider several other implications. Consider, for example, how the organization of math classes by ability levels affects the mix of students in other classes. That is, do the effects of the way we organize a single subject area reach into other areas of the school? Consider also how the logic of organizing a math class applies to other subjects. After all, are there not music students who are well ahead of their peers? Are there not gifted science students? talented writers? budding historians? actors? Is the logic of sequence unique to mathematics? Finally, consider what it is that gives a teacher the conceptual basis for such decisions. In terms of the organization of schooling, what do you share with practitioners at your level and subject? What makes you tick?

PROBLEM CONTEXT AND SOLUTION PARAMETERS

Context

Burton Middle School, one of two 7/8 middle schools in this community of about 60,000 people, has proposed a major change in the curriculum. Due to reductions in student population, the school is restructuring its staffing, which spills over to the curriculum. Whereas the school previously offered an honors math section and a "basic" math section in addition to the main course, teachers are proposing a program that mixes all levels of math students together. The teachers are to gear their instruction to meet the individual needs of the students in this mixed context.

The change in math instruction is part of a larger effort to mix all the "gifted" students in with their peers. The school has seen the development of a curricular system that separates children according to abilities. And some critics have pointed out that this separation is merely a smokescreen for the true separations in the school: separating ethnic groups and social classes. The proposal to make all classes heterogeneous, in addition to solving the staffing problem, will reduce the segregation of student groups.

The teachers proposed a solution to the staffing/tracking problem, and they presented their ideas to a school site council, which indicated its support of the plan. However, when the ideas were presented to a larger audience (all "interested" parents were invited, but the audience consisted exclusively of "honors" parents), it became clear that there was widespread discontent with the plan. The teachers argued that a good school will meet the needs of all children, and that math could be taught in heterogeneous classes. Furthermore, they argued that the benefits of mixing the classes were well established, and consistent with the National Council of Teachers of Mathematics (NCTM) standards. However, parents were generally not convinced. Indeed, a number of parents made it clear at the initial meeting that they would be looking for other schools for their children. Another group of parents formally protested this plan (memo enclosed).

Problem and Solution Parameters

Your team has been appointed by the Burton school superintendent to investigate this problem. You are to make a recommendation in writing to the school board regarding the changes in the middle school curriculum. The team has educators, parents, and an administrator represented. You will present a team memo to the school board that addresses the following issues:

1. Statement of a curriculum perspective (some explanation about your team's view of the purpose of curriculum)
2. Recommendation regarding the program for honors students in math
3. Curricular and/or teaching recommendations you see as appropriate to the situation

On the day your memo is expected, the various teams will hold a discussion of the principles raised and solutions suggested.

········WORK THE PROBLEM ➞

PROBLEM DOCUMENTS

In order to assist you in your exploration of this problem, a number of documents have been included. These documents include the following:

8.1 Principal Wellington's memo to the curriculum committee, asking them to recommend a solution to problems created by staff reduction

8.2 Document created by teachers for the parent meeting at which the changes to the curriculum were announced

8.3 Memo from a concerned parent group to Superintendent Farley, complaining of the proposed changes at BMS

8.4 Letter of support from a parent, Margarita Delgado

8.5 Letter of protest from a parent, Dr. J. D. Stromberg

8.6 An open letter from members of the three high school math departments

8.7 An alternate plan, proposed by a collection of teachers from the feeder elementary schools

---

PROBLEM DOCUMENT 8.1   *Memo from Principal Wellington*

Burton Middle School

MEMO

To: BMS Curriculum Committee
From: Mr. Wellington
Date: 2/15/03
RE: Curriculum changes

As you know, I'm not one to do a lot of memo writing. I just want to remind each of you of our conversations. We have some changes for next year, as you know. We need to figure out how we're going to deal with a couple of problems, mostly caused by reduced teacher numbers.

BMS **current** staffing:

Grade 7:
23 FTE (3.5 math, 3 English, 3 reading, 3 social studies, 3 science, 1 technology, .5 library, 1.5 special ed., 2.5 P.E., 1 art, 1 music)

Grade 8:
25 FTE (4 math, 3 English, 3 reading, 3 social studies, 3 science, 1 technology, .5 library, 1.5 special ed., 2.5 P.E., .5 art, 1.5 Spanish, 1.5 music)

BMS reductions for next year:

> Grade 7:
> 1.5 FTE (.5 math, 1 reading)
>
> Grade 8:
> 1 FTE (.5 math, .5 reading)

For next year, we want to operate completely in teams. There will be no more "singleton" classes in the core areas (math, science, English, reading, social studies) that have students coming from a variety of teams. You must figure out a way to deal with this problem.

PROBLEM DOCUMENT 8.2 *Document Created by Teachers for the Parent Meeting*

BMS Moves Forward

Times change. Techniques change. What we understand about learning changes. And it is time that BMS made some changes in order to provide our students with the best possible educational opportunities.

In a move forward, Burton Middle School is making a number of changes for next year that will serve *all* our students better. The centerpiece of this change is in the math curriculum, which has traditionally been the sticking point for most reform at this level. To help our parents and students understand the changes, we have provided you with two resources in one. First, we provide a summary of the changes that we are proposing. Second, we list a series of questions and answers we anticipate to be important for the members of our community. We wish to stress that the teachers of BMS are fully supportive of this plan and what it can mean for *all* students.

Summary of Changes

In the past, the math curriculum at BMS has been organized into three separate programs for the regular student. (Our special education program offers individualized support to students in that category.) Most students have entered the main math program, which consists primarily of advanced arithmetic and some pre-algebra work at the seventh grade level, with focused pre-algebra at the eighth grade. Roughly 10 percent of our students have been in a more basic arithmetic plan, with "basics" in the seventh grade and "applications" in the eighth grade. Roughly 10 percent of our students have worked in an advanced program, with a rigorous pre-algebra course in seventh grade and high school algebra in eighth grade.

Next year, there will be only math classes, with no separation into the previous groups. All students will receive instruction together. However, through a process called "curriculum differentiation," we will address children's needs individually in each math class. This means that every class will have a broad range of abilities and interests (as is the case in almost every other subject now), and the teachers must differentiate the *activities* so that each child can progress.

Can it be done? The answer is an emphatic yes! Programs throughout the nation are able to provide adequate instruction for children in mixed groups. And many of the negatives associated with fixed math groups can be eliminated through this plan. But we know you have more questions. Read on!

Questions and Answers

Q: What does this mean for my child in pursuing high-level math in the high school?

A: We have analyzed the programs for all three high schools BMS children typically attend. For West High and Burton High School, there is no problem pursuing the full gamut of math courses. The use of "block scheduling" at those schools means that students can take far more math courses than are normally available. The freshman student who does not yet have a designated "algebra" credit can easily work through the highest math possible. For Rio de Colorado High, students face a little more challenge, but they can still easily reach the highest math with only one summer school course.

Q: Will my child learn as much math?

A: More. We have a tradition of hurrying through complex concepts in order to "cover" a textbook. The differentiation model means that students will explore concepts at their own pace long enough to develop deep understanding.

Q: What will class look like?

A: The traditional math class consists of a fixed routine: grade yesterday's homework, introduce a new skill, practice together for a while, begin homework. The differentiated model puts math in applied contexts. Students will face complicated problems, work on these alone and in groups, and meet with the teacher to examine their processes. At the end of each unit, students summarize their own learning.

Q: Is it fair to grade good math students against students who have math anxiety?

A: It's not fair to grade students against students in any case. We believe students should be graded "against" what those students' abilities suggest. As we come to know the students and their strengths and weaknesses, we believe the fairest possible grades will result.

Q: What about the state math test?

A: All students should improve on this. If there is good, solid instruction, then the students will learn.

Q: How does this change fit the school's mission?

A: Well. The mission of BMS is to build learners whose success makes them believe in themselves. The restructured math program will be the most positive step toward fulfilling the mission that we have taken to date.

Q: What about Sylvan Heights Middle School? Will they follow suit?

A: That's hard to say. We expect our example to push a lot of middle schools—well beyond the city limits—to improve math instruction. But we control only BMS.

Q: What about the students who were scheduled to start algebra next year?

A: Differentiation will work for them, too. We won't have any algebra sections.

Q: Does this mean an end to gifted education at BMS?

A: No. We know that we have an obligation to our "gifted" students, and we won't fail to meet that obligation. We simply believe that we can do so better under this system. Opportunities for expressing one's giftedness continue throughout the school—in extracurricular activities, differentiated activities, after school clubs, music, and so on. Each child, whether gifted or delayed, will find a full range of options available. But the best thing is that the children won't have as many doors closed on them as the current system allows.

We believe that what we are doing will be the best thing that has happened at this building since we changed from a junior high school to a middle school. This change lets us put action behind the words of being a developmentally appropriate school that puts the success of its children first!

PROBLEM DOCUMENT 8.3	*Memo from a Concerned Parent Group*

MEMO

Date: 3/10/03

To: Dr. Farley, superintendent

From: Burton Middle School Concerned Parents

RE: Curriculum changes at BMS

We, the undersigned parents, attended a meeting at Burton Middle School this week. While we were impressed with the care and thoughtfulness of the teachers, we were horrified at a number of things. We are requesting that you put an immediate stop to the proposed curricular changes at BMS. In particular, we wish to point out the following issues:

1) No serious consultation with parents occurred in making the decision to incorporate all math students into mixed-ability classes. The teachers indicated that parents could give input to the site council, but it is readily apparent that this site council does not represent our views. For one thing, most of these concerned parents do not currently have children enrolled in BMS--our kids are scheduled to enroll next year, and we were therefore unable to participate. Even if we had been members of the BMS community, we seriously doubt that our input would have been heard by the council.

2) What evidence is there that this change in curriculum will serve our children? The whole reason behind gifted programs and advanced courses is that some kids are bored with school and the pace of instruction. Special classes provide that extra bit of motivation that allows our kids to stay connected. What assurance do we have that our kids will get any extra attention? This will probably become another instance of teaching to the middle in overcrowded classrooms, so neither end of the extremes is dealt with fairly.

3) Where is the administration on this? We heard from a group of teachers, particularly Ms. Southwerk, but where were the administrators? We don't understand why something this important does not come from the superintendent or at least the school principal. Where were the experts from State College? We feel as though this plan came from well-intentioned and overworked teachers, but without the necessary grounding in current research.

4) The whole process seems rushed, shaky, and indefensible. Why the need to act so quickly? We are asking for one thing only: that you delay the implementation of this misguided policy until we have a chance--as a community--to fully investigate what the consequences of such a policy might be.

PROBLEM DOCUMENT 8.4   *Letter of Support from a Parent*

3/9/03

Dear Mr. Wellington:

I know I speak for many parents in our community when I applaud the recent changes described in the BMS curriculum. For far too long this system has created the most insidious form of institutional racism: tracking!

As you are well aware, the honors courses at BMS and throughout Burton are hardly representative of the student population. While our schools are roughly 60 percent majority and 40 percent minority, the "honors" programs across the city are about 90 percent students of the dominant culture. Something's wrong! And it's even worse at BMS. The upper track math courses have a makeup of 95 percent Caucasian students, with only 3 percent Native American and 2 percent Hispanic. With a school made up of nearly 20 percent Hispanic children, is it possible that we can only get a 2 percent representation in the gifted programs? And I understand this is perfectly typical of such programs all across the country.

I have heard that the methodology for teaching math--and other subjects--has advanced to the degree that tracking is really no longer serving its original purpose. This is good news for all of us, and I only hope that the teachers at BMS take advantage of this opportunity to infuse their courses with relevant, top-notch learning experiences. But I congratulate you and the school on this important first step!

Sincerely,

Margarita S. Delgado

Margarita S. Delgado

Letter of Protest from a Parent

J. D. Stromberg, M.D., 101 Lakeside Circle

3/15/03

Mr. Wellington,

I won't waste your time on niceties. I'm pulling my daughter out of your school. While I have found the school to be generally effective (there are always exceptions), this move seems to take away the opportunity for excellence.

Now, in the service of some misguided political correctness—an attempt to include everybody—we will see a lowering of standards all around. No longer will children with natural abilities and inclinations be allowed to pursue excellence. We now have a ceiling set, and we will make darn sure no one moves any farther than the crowd.

It's a sad day for Burton when our schools hop on some PC bandwagon to the detriment of the few talented and motivated children. Fortunately, I'll be able to find other options for my daughter. Unfortunately, there are people who won't have that luxury. I think the whole community will suffer.

J. D. Stromberg

*Open Letter to BMS Teachers
from High School Teachers*

As members of the mathematics departments at the three high schools in Burton, we are calling on our colleagues at BMS to reconsider their position relative to the elimination of honors math at the middle school. We have several reasons for our position, which we outline below.

- Careful groundwork must be laid in order for a math program to have the integrity and depth that life in the 21st century calls for. Students need *more,* not *less,* math than ever before. Unless we push students to achieve at the middle level, they will not have opportunities to get that math.
- A leading group of mathematicians and scientists out of Berkeley has called for a moratorium on unfounded math practices that do not permit students to achieve at their highest level.
- From a practical perspective, students arriving at the high school from BMS will be seriously disadvantaged in comparison with students from other schools in the city or from transfer sites. The simple fact is that BMS students will have nowhere to go. They will be forced to the lowest track of math at our high schools, and their aspirations will be frustrated.
- The decision to make such radical changes in the math curriculum is unwise, given the isolated conditions of the decision making. Surely this is a slap in the face of the expertise of high school instructors, who, it should be noted, have far more advanced mathematical training than the middle school teachers, many of whom teach math without even a college major in the subject!

A more thoughtful, deliberate process for your change would be to bring together key players in the math curriculum throughout the city. Let us open the discussion from a perspective that will honor the goals we have as a system.

(Signed by the chairs of the math departments of the three public high schools in Burton, and twenty-two other high school math teachers.)

*Open Letter to BMS Teachers
from Elementary School Teachers*

As your professional colleagues, we, the undersigned teachers from Burton, have heard of your intention to alter the math curriculum. We don't pretend to have any special mathematical expertise to help you in your decision, but our knowledge of children and their needs leads us to offer an alternate plan for solving the real problems at BMS.

We are all aware of the fact that enrollments are dipping throughout the city. This seems the perfect time for us to reconsider the role of the middle school in our entire system. Clearly there are first-rate teachers at both of the city's middle schools—there is no challenge to their qualifications. Yet, consistent with what has emerged across the country, the middle school may not be the best way for us to meet the needs of the children at this age. The greater specialization in math is not, perhaps, so much a response to the real needs of our learners as it is a concession to the conditions of schooling: large, anonymous schools to warehouse too many children.

Our proposal is to eliminate the middle schools completely. The students could continue to learn in the more friendly setting of a neighborhood school, where each child can be known by caring adults. By spending eight or more years in such an environment, the child has a true and powerful opportunity to be known well. The math program, or any other program, can be built around intimate knowledge of each child rather than building such a program around faceless conditions that apply in large schools in *which every child is either just arriving or about to leave.*

We ask that our ideas be given serious consideration in your attempt to solve a very real problem in our community.

(Letter signed by fifty-eight elementary teachers from all fourteen elementary schools in the city.)

SOLUTION SUMMARY

Before proceeding to the reflection section of this chapter, write a brief summary of your team's solution here:

Our team defined the "real" problem here as _____

_____

_____

_____

_____

_____

_____

_____

_____

The key features of our solution were _____

_____

_____

_____

_____

_____

_____

My personal view of the problem and solution is _____

_____

_____

_____

_____

_____

_____

TIME FOR REFLECTION

As you reflect on your experience with this PBL activity, you should draw up a list of the issues that need further exploration. This section will guide you to think about a number of such issues, though you may discover that topics you found important are not anticipated here. We will consider some of the needs of gifted students and their parents. This leads to an examination of the grouping of students more generally. Thinking about how to organize a course in mathematics may raise questions about the assumptions of subject areas—math and others. The reflections also invite you to think about the differences among models of educating children at this level. Finally, the problem suggests a number of questions about how teachers should relate to the leadership in their schools.

Gifted Students

Much of the controversy in this particular PBL experience arises from the school structures that surround the idea of the "gifted" student. What do teachers need to know about gifted students? Does any such client really exist?

A somewhat underrated part of special education, gifted education builds on the theory that each child should receive an education that is a best fit for that child. Students with disabilities receive the sort of assistance that allows them to compensate for those disabilities; students who are gifted receive assistance and opportunities that allow them to stay engaged in the learning process. Surprisingly, gifted students have unusually high levels of attrition from schools, perhaps due to the boredom they encounter.

Traditionally, giftedness has been defined in terms of exceptional verbal and quantitative abilities. That is, people who performed well on standardized tests were the ones who were identified as gifted. In recent decades, giftedness has been thought of more broadly than just a narrow range of abilities. A student might be gifted in ways that don't show up on standardized tests—gifted as a creative thinker or as a problem solver or as an artist. So, a first point to raise in reflecting on the "gifted" students represented in this PBL experience is that the students in the advanced math classes may have some "giftedness," but they will certainly not be the entire population of gifted students at a school. If the staff or the parents have somehow managed to reduce *giftedness* to the children who make up the advanced math class, the definition of giftedness is in serious need of revision at that school. (It may interest you to know that such notions as "gifted" or even "intelligence" are what we call *constructs*, human inventions that are heavily dependent on context and culture. For example, intelligence in Australian aboriginal society is often associated with the spatial ability to find one's way in the wilderness. That ability does not generally enter the American view of intelligence.)

On the other hand, there is almost no question that some of the children in an advanced math class are "gifted," and that fact deserves consideration. To neglect such children's needs would be indefensible. How, then, can teachers help gifted children without setting up special sections or classes that separate these children from their peers? The answer, addressed in part below, may have to do with the notion that the best teaching for gifted children is the best teaching for all children. Provide all children with opportunities to face interesting, relevant challenges in their work; provide all children with chances to deal with big ideas and to solve important problems. Gifted children as well as low-achieving children can benefit from rich curriculum (Haycock, 2001). And, of course, remember that giftedness appears in a variety of forms.

"Gifted" Parents and Parent Relations in General

Learning to work with parents is an important part of the job of a teacher. And this is true beyond the elementary level. In fact, one of the most crucial ages to focus on effective parent relations is at the middle school level, when children typically begin to assert more independence and realign themselves with peers more than family members (Stevenson, 1992). If for no other reason than public relations, teachers at the middle level do well to consider how they can succeed with parents. Just imagine how the world looks to a parent of a seventh-grader: "I gave you teachers my delightful child, and you gave me back a moody, unpredictable, difficult adolescent." Of course, we all know that it's not the teachers' fault, but in the turbid times families face at adolescence, it's nice to have allies among the teachers.

Ironically, many times the parents that provide the most challenges to teachers who wish to change the system are the parents of "gifted" children (Wheelock, 1992). In their work with middle schools engaged in reform, Oakes, Vasudeva, and Jones (1996) found that parents from lower income groups were most likely to trust teachers with change, while parents from upper income groups (and most often in the "gifted" category) resisted change. The "advantaged" students were doing fine, so there was no reason to change the system.

This suggests that dealing with the parents of gifted children is a delicate matter. Traditional schools have worked well for them and their children, and altering the system now may seem unnecessary and unfair. In the problem documents for this PBL experience, you may have noticed that the parents of gifted students felt excluded from the decision-making process. Do you think there might have been a better way to include them? Would some other mechanism for sharing information provide some comfort? Or does it seem that the very nature of the change will provoke opposition? Like virtually all parents, the parents of gifted students want what is best for their children. If a school is to be successful with all children, alienating any group of parents is foolish—but alienating the group most likely to support your school is exceptionally foolish.

As a member of the professional community in your school, beware of any tendency among educators to view parents as obstacles to change. Keep the notion before your colleagues that the parents want what is best, and your task is both to make sure you seek what is best and to communicate this effectively. Relating to the parents who take an interest in the larger life of your school is another of the crucial, but generally unexplored, skills a teacher must develop.

Wheelock (1992) provides several suggestions for working effectively with parents. The key element, however, appears to be communication. Parents should be offered opportunities early in the process of change to participate and express concerns and questions (which teachers should address). Parents should be informed continually as the process goes forward. Parents are far less likely to oppose a change that is committed to providing benefits for all children than they are to oppose changes they perceive to be withdrawing benefits from their own children.

Heterogeneous versus Homogenous Classes

What seems on the surface to be an organizational issue very quickly transforms into an instructional issue. That is, the demands on a teacher to employ a wide variety of teaching techniques increase dramatically when the learners have diverse abilities. Unfortunately, research isn't very encouraging about varied teaching techniques. Goodlad's (1984) massive study of schools revealed that the range of teaching options tends to get smaller as the children get older, with increasingly passive models of teaching used by teachers—and increasingly bored students. Oakes, Vasudeva, and Jones (1996) hoped to find tremendous variety in the reformed middle schools they examined. Instead, they write, "the most salient finding from our interviews and observations is that traditional, teacher-directed instruction remains firmly in place in the vast majority of middle grades classes. Upon close inspection, we found that innovative-looking curriculum and learning activities often turned out to be conventional teacher-led, coverage-driven lessons" (p. 18).

What has that to do with the makeup of classes? A great deal. The uniform teacher-dominated lesson, whether in math or language arts or social studies or any other subject, doesn't work well when the students represent a wide range of abilities. Thus, to contemplate changing the composition of the classes demands contemplating changes in instruction. Clearly it makes no sense to simply install a sequence of teacher-dominated lessons that has students alternate between passive listening, practice, and waiting their turn while kids of a different ability level receive similar instruction. Relying on the lecture, which Kauchak and Eggen (1998) call the "least effective but most popular mode of instruction" (p. 288), will not lead to much success.

But the prior question is perhaps the one that most products of a traditional educational system would ask: Why change at all? What's wrong with the homogeneous classes? Much of the investigation you have conducted with this problem will help you to formulate a response to that issue. However, for the sake of reflection, here are some questions to guide your thinking about the implications of organizing students in similar or different groups:

- What does this mean for instructional practices?
- What does this mean for the interactions among students?

- What does this mean for the opportunities students have for further study?
- How does such a decision influence high standards of achievement?
- How will community members respond to such changes?
- Who might benefit and who might lose from such reorganization?
- What new demands for teachers are created by making such changes?

In her book on tracking, Wheelock (1992) makes a powerful point. The key to changing from homogeneous to heterogeneous classrooms is "a shift from an emphasis on teaching to an emphasis on learning" (p. 191). She also reminds us of the dominance of homogeneous grouping in math, with 94 percent of students in homogeneously grouped math classes by ninth grade.

Challenging the Assumptions of a Subject Area

This PBL experience focused on the issue of mathematics instruction, but it really raises a broader question. Is there a place to challenge the assumptions of a subject area? For years, math has been sequenced in a certain manner, even when prestigious groups such as the National Council of Teachers of Mathematics have recommended changes. We find, in math, that although society has changed dramatically and our understanding of pedagogy has changed, math instruction has not. It remains "numbingly predictable" (National Commission on Mathematics and Science Teaching for the 21st Century, 2000, p. 20).

But math is not alone here. Each of the areas taught in public schools carries with it assumptions about what good teaching looks like or what the order of learning events must be. For example, must one master the sentence before writing a paragraph? Is the five-paragraph essay the building block of expository writing? Should we follow the science textbook right through to the questions at the end of the chapter? Is the right way to teach the history of a given country to proceed through key events (usually military) in chronological order? Each question pushes at the basic assumptions of the subject area.

Clearly, at the beginning of a career, teachers are probably more concerned with getting down the names of Civil War figures than with questioning how the Civil War fits reasonably in an innovative re-ordering of the topics of history. So why bother with such questions now? The fact is that the habits you develop and the structures you endorse early in your career (all influenced by the mentors you find) have a powerful, long-lasting mark on how you teach. While it is true that beginning teachers worry mostly about "survival" issues and need time to develop practitioner's expertise (Reynolds, 1992), unless you begin the practice of reflecting on the assumptions of your area, it will be very difficult to learn this practice later. For those of you with teaching experience, you will recognize two ways that these early habits limit a teacher later on. First, the organization of a subject starts to feel like "common sense," beyond question. Second, having built a template for creating lessons and units, most teachers challenge the value of disrupting this later on for a new organizational scheme.

Middle Schools, Mini-High Schools, or Extended Elementary Schools?

A group of elementary teachers and a group of high school teachers both offered suggestions for how best to organize Burton Middle School. Not surprisingly, the high school teachers urged a structure on the middle school that would make it look much like a mini-high school. And the elementary teachers urged a structure that would bring the middle school students back into the elementary fold. Both groups argue, as do many others, that the middle school is simply not an effective institution. Ruth Mitchell of the Education Trust went so far as to call the middle school a "disaster" (Norton, 2000). Thomas Dickinson (2001) points out that the middle school has fallen far short of its high goals (though he advocates its "reinvention" rather than its elimination).

The issue raised is a concern that the structure does not attend to the needs of children as well as it might. Part of your consideration for this PBL experience should have placed you in a position to consider whether middle schools are, in fact, effective. While such schools arise from a mandate to be developmentally appropriate (National Middle School Association, 1995), their effectiveness in this goal is less evident. There is good evidence that thoughtful implementation of the *Turning Points* (Carnegie Council on Adolescent Development, 1989) reforms will lead to effective middle schools (Felner et al., 1997). Among other things, these documents advocate the end of tracking students according to academic ability, and they further call for interdisciplinary team teaching so that students can become part of smaller teams where teachers can create instruction that fits their levels.

Still, the alternative of extending the elementary structure deserves thoughtful consideration. What trade-offs would be made in such a structure? For example, would there be greater sensitivity to learners, as the elementary teachers claim? Would there be a loss of disciplinary knowledge? And what of the arguments that make a case for the middle school as the most appropriate structure for the developmental needs of young adolescents? Are children in this stage different enough from their younger counterparts to warrant a separate school?

All this suggests that the way schools are put together into a system has some basis in what best serves children and young people. Reflecting on the question of how to organize the math classes invites us to contemplate why schools are structured as they are. Is there some value to the interdisciplinary team structure so widely advocated for middle schools?

Perhaps a side issue here is school size. Many districts combine multiple elementary schools into a feeder system whereby one middle school serves them all, resulting in a large, "efficient," and impersonal structure. Would a smaller middle school avoid the problems generated at BMS without altering the curriculum?

Relating to Administrative Leadership

The principal of a school is sometimes seen as the instructional leader, the lead teacher. In this role, the principal serves to model sound teaching practices for the staff, to set a direction for the interactions among learners and teachers in the school. That may or may not be the case. You may find yourself in a school with an instructional leader, a facilities manager, a clerk, a bureaucrat, or some other model. It is crucial for teachers to learn how best to relate to the administration, whatever perspective on leadership that person exhibits.

A first step in gaining this understanding is to realize that leadership is not restricted to the positions sanctioned by an organizational chart. Leadership has been widely studied in educational and business settings, making it what Bennis and Nanus (1985) call the "most studied and least understood topic of any in the social sciences" (p. 20). These authors indicate there are over 450 definitions of leaders! They draw on interviews of ninety business leaders to conclude that everyone has some capacity for leadership, and it's a matter of learning how best to exercise it. As a teacher, you will be called on many times to exercise leadership, and not just with students in your class. To relate successfully to your administrative leaders, begin by recognizing you have both the capacity and obligation to exercise leadership, too.

Still, there generally is an occupant in the principal's office, and that occupant has much to say about the quality of life you lead and the quality of the school you are part of. Desperate for that first job, teachers rarely research thoroughly the person they will be working for. To organize your reflections on the leadership you encounter as a teacher, consider the following possibilities.

Let's assume you've found yourself in a school with a leader like Mr. Wellington. How do you assess him? He apparently has seen that something must be done, but he hasn't taken it upon himself to do anything. He appears to be comfortable letting his teachers take the initiative—and whatever heat may result from that. What does a conscientious teacher do? On the one hand, you can become an active, informed participant in the conversations about the curriculum. Recognize that initially your experience level will be less than most of your colleagues, and often with teachers, "experience counts, theory doesn't" (Hargreaves, 1984). This may mean that your participation in the dialogue should be thoughtful, but quiet. In general, the new teacher can bring much to improve a school, but primarily through the process of asking questions and building rapport, an important leadership dimension (Wellins, Byham, & Wilson, 1991). Even good ideas may not be well received from the newest staff member, unless that member establishes some credibility both as a teacher and as a person who can interact effectively with other adults.

Another possibility, however, is that the principal is at the opposite end of the spectrum from Mr. Wellington. Principals are often sure of themselves, confident in their decisions, and not at all hesitant to push their staff in a particular direction. It would not be unrealistic for a principal to communicate to the teachers that certain changes would be in effect the next year, and if the teachers don't like it, they are welcome to move on. Of course, there are limits to what even principals *may* do, even if they feel they *can* do anything. How does a teacher work effectively with this sort of administrator? As in all human interactions, sensitivity to the particular context will help you succeed. Consider these general questions as you reflect on how you might respond to such a leader:

- Is it likely you would change this person's mind with direct opposition?
- Which is more important to such a leader—the *appearance* of knowledge and authority or the *substantive support* for knowledge and authority?
- What other leadership do you see in the school, and how can you connect to this leadership without jeopardizing your position?

As in most areas or occupations, it is quite possible that someone will occupy a position of authority over you without being the sort of leader who will inspire you to do good work. If you find yourself in this situation, you have some choices to consider. Leaving is an option. When your ethical position is endangered, leaving may be the only legitimate option. Generally, there are some other choices. Exercise leadership yourself, look to mentors and colleagues for leadership, become a learner. What is least likely to support you for a successful life as a teacher is to develop and dwell on the cynicism that far too many teachers have opted for in the face of mediocre or poor leadership in the schools.

DISCUSSION QUESTIONS

1. What assumptions do you have about the way your subject matter should be taught? Are there alternative ways of seeing various subjects? What gives credibility to a particular view of the organization of a subject?

2. What can you learn from the BMS approach to curriculum change? Were the teachers placed in a position that demonstrated trust in their professionalism, or were they exploited? Were parents properly involved in the decisions?

3. What do you see as some of the unintended consequences of creating advanced or gifted classes of students? Do these consequences reach to teachers, also?

4. What sort of leadership do you expect in a school? How can teachers be effective leaders, even when the "authority" rests in the principal's office?

5. What reasons are you aware of for the organization of schools (elementary, middle, high school) in your area? Do factors such as efficiency or available space dictate arrangements despite what we know about good practices? Are schools allowed to get too large?

6. Considering the PBL process, what did you learn about your ability to look at issues from a new and unfamiliar perspective? How does perspective-taking help you gain insight?

FURTHER READING

Harrison, J. (1993). Strategies for the heterogeneous math class. *Middle School Journal, 24*(4), 10–16.
Harrison recounts how a Florida middle school team restructured their math groupings so that all children could experience the subject together, with an emphasis on reducing barriers between races and socioeconomic groups. Her account provides a living example of what one school was able to do in the name of reform and math.

Kladder, R., Peitz, J., & Faulkner, J. (1998). On the right track: Connected Mathematics Project seeks to eliminate the disparities of academic tracking. *Middle Ground, 1*(4), 32–34.
A very brief introduction to a sample math curriculum that attempts to draw all students—whatever their abilities—together in order to focus on the conceptual understanding that lies beneath the math procedures children typically learn.

Ma, L. (1999). *Knowing and teaching elementary mathematics: Teachers' understanding of fundamental mathematics in China and the United States.* Mahwah, NJ: Lawrence Erlbaum Associates.
This descriptive account of teaching mathematics may be too specialized for most readers, but it is interesting to note Ma's observations on how the subject knowledge is built among teachers. Despite having an average of four or more years less education than their American counterparts, Chinese teachers manage to develop and impart a greater understanding of mathematics. The key difference appears to be that Chinese teachers continue to see themselves as learners, and they work with their colleagues to develop their understanding over time.

National Middle School Association. (1995). *This we believe: Developmentally responsive middle level schools.* Columbus, OH: Author.
This position paper from NMSA helps establish what is generally meant by the notion of a "middle school." The document establishes some of the characteristics of young adolescents, a list of characteristics of "developmentally responsive" schools, and specific recommendations about curriculum, instruction, assessment, organizational structures, support programs, and guidance services. Among other things, the document expresses opposition to tracking.
    The NMSA web site (www.nmsa.org) also provides some useful information for thinking about this particular situation. At this site you can find a link to resources, including fax sheets that provide concise information on issues such as organizing schools and heterogeneous classrooms.

U.S. Department of Education, National Center for Education Statistics, Third International Mathematics and Science Study, Videotape Classroom Study, 1994–95. Available: http://nces.ed.gov/pubs99/timssvid/index.html
This portion of the TIMSS work highlighted dif- The Third International Mathematics and Science Study provides a wealth of information about how mathematics might be taught. This portion of the TIMSS work highlighted differences among the methods of instruction in U.S., Japanese, and German classrooms during an eighth-grade lesson. The contrast between U.S. and Japanese math lessons is interesting, and not just for math teachers (since it highlights a general approach to pedagogy). The U.S. lessons followed this pattern: teachers explain a skill, teachers demonstrate, then students practice. The Japanese lessons followed this pattern: teachers pose a complex problem, students struggle with the problem, some students present ideas or solutions, the teacher summarizes the conclusions of the class, and then students practice similar problems. (See http://nces.ed.gov/pubs99/timssvid/chap7.htm#86 for a comparison chart.) The result was a different emphasis, with the U.S. lessons focusing on skills and the Japanese lessons focusing on concepts.
    The TIMSS data figure heavily in another important document, *Before It's Too Late: A Report to the Nation from The National Commission on Mathematics and Science Teaching for the 21st Century.* In this report, the commission contrasts the virtually unchanged instructional practices of math classes over the past fifty years with "high quality teaching." Among

such ideas as inquiry, high standards, and using information, the commission calls for teaching that "allows for, recognizes, and builds on differences in the learning styles and abilities of students" (2000, p. 22).

Wheelock, A. (1992). *Crossing the tracks: How "untracking" can save America's schools*. New York: The New Press.

This book provides an extended argument for eliminating tracking, with numerous examples from schools and comments from the teachers and principals in those schools. Two chapters in Part II of the book are particularly relevant to the work on this PBL experience. Chapter 5 addresses instruction and assessment in heterogeneous classes. Chapter 6 looks at math classes in particular. Wheelock acknowledges that math classes are the least likely to be untracked, pointing out that by ninth grade, 94 percent of students are in homogeneous math classes. However, Wheelock stresses the benefits to all children of simply providing better instruction and assessment in math, with more interaction among peers and better focus on the thinking behind problem solving.

WEB SITE

The Middle Web

www.middleweb.com

This web site gathers together links and resources that will assist you in thinking about the complexities of teaching at the middle level. Of particular interest to this PBL experience is the section of list serve conversations (on such topics as math and literacy or teaching math). You can access this at www.middleweb.com/MWLISTCONT/MSLstringsINDEX. html

REFERENCES

Bennis, W., & Nanus, B. (1985). *Leaders: The strategies for taking charge*. New York: Harper & Row.

Carnegie Council on Adolescent Development. (1989). *Turning points: Preparing American youth for the 21st century*. New York: Carnegie Corporation.

Dickinson, T. S. (Ed.). (2001). *Reinventing the middle school*. New York: RoutledgeFalmer.

Felner, R. D., Jackson, A. W., Kasak, D., Mulhall, P., Brand, S., & Flowers, N. (1997). The impact of school reform for the middle years: Longitudinal study of a network engaged in Turning Points-based comprehensive school transformation. *Phi Delta Kappan, 78*(7), 528–532, 541–550.

Goodlad, J. I. (1984). *A place called school: Prospects for the future*. New York: McGraw-Hill.

Hargreaves, A. (1984). Experience counts, theory doesn't: How teachers talk about their work. *Sociology of Education, 57*(4), 244–254.

Harrison, J. S. (1993). Strategies for the heterogeneous math class. *Middle School Journal, 24*(4), 10–16.

Haycock, K. (2001). Closing the achievement gap. *Educational Leadership, 58*(6), 6–11.

Kauchak, D. P., & Eggen, P. D. (1998). *Learning & teaching: Research-based methods* (3rd ed.). Boston: Allyn & Bacon.

Ma, L. (1999). *Knowing and teaching elementary mathematics: Teachers' understanding of fundamental mathematics in China and the United States*. Mahwah, NJ: Lawrence Erlbaum Associates.

National Commission on Mathematics and Science Teaching for the 21st Century. (2000). *Before it's too late*. Washington, DC: U.S. Department of Education.

National Middle School Association. (1995). *This we believe: Developmentally responsive middle level schools*. Columbus, OH: Author.

Norton, J. (2000). Important developments in middle-grades reform. *Phi Delta Kappan, 81*(10), K2–K4.

Oakes, J., Vasudeva, A., & Jones, M. (1996). Becoming educative: Reforming curriculum and teaching in the middle grades. *Research in Middle Level Education Quarterly, 20*(1), 11–40.

Reynolds, A. (1992). What is competent beginning teaching? A review of the literature. *Review of Educational Research, 62*(1), 1–35.

Stevenson, C. (1992). *Teaching ten to fourteen year olds.* New York: Longman.

Wellins, R. S., Byham, W. C., & Wilson, J. M. (1991). *Empowered teams: Creating self-directed work groups that improve quality, productivity, and participation.* San Francisco: Jossey-Bass.

Wheelock, A. (1992). *Crossing the tracks: How "untracking" can save America's schools.* New York: The New Press.

CHAPTER NINE

RAISE THOSE SCORES!

INTRODUCTION AND PROBLEM BACKGROUND

The famous fighting words of the 1983 report, *A Nation at Risk,* set a tone for raising the stakes in educational testing: "If an unfriendly foreign power had attempted to impose on America the mediocre educational performance that exists today, we might well have viewed it as an act of war" (in Berliner & Biddle, 1997, p. 140). Whether that mediocrity was real or imagined, such an accusation prompted all sorts of responses, and the ensuing years have seen increasing emphasis on testing as a means to monitor the progress of American education. Some of this testing is part of a long-term, national attempt to monitor schooling, as is the case with the National Assessment of Educational Progress (NAEP), which predates *A Nation at Risk.* Some of this testing is designed to establish comparisons among various educational systems at an international level. The Third International Mathematics and Science Study (TIMSS) attempts to do this. But perhaps the most immediate, powerful form of testing is that imposed by the states on their own schools to see how well students are meeting mandated standards. When results from such a test have a strong impact on the test-takers or the educators, an impact that is automatically triggered by the test results, this testing is considered "high-stakes" (Madaus, 1999).

There are, of course, a number of possible responses to the pressure implicit in high-stakes testing. The professional educators at a school could continue doing their jobs as they see fit, a business-as-usual approach that says "we know what is best for our students, and the test results are not our chief concern." At the other extreme, professional educators might redesign their curricula and how they teach students so that what they teach corresponds as closely as possible to the high-stakes test. The unspoken position here would say "we agree that the test is important and worthwhile, so we will guarantee that our students achieve in its terms." Perhaps a more cynical unspoken position takes the "reality" view: "the test may not be worthwhile, but our reality is that we are judged by its results, so we will change."

An increasingly popular approach to dealing with the tests stops short of altering the entire curriculum, but focuses on improving test results through test-preparation activities. Sometimes these activities are as simple as giving students practice with the format of standardized tests. In fact, many supplemental materials from textbook publishers feature tests or quizzes formatted to resemble standardized tests. Some schools create special courses or after-school programs designed to provide coaching and practice on tests. And some schools hire outsiders either to work directly with students, or more frequently, to train teachers on how to improve test performance. Linda McNeil (2000) describes one such program that "makes war" on the tests. Consultants arrive at the school dressed in camouflage clothing, provide participants with camouflaged notebooks of ideas, and carry on this theme of doing battle. McNeil also points out that such activities may raise test scores without improving actual learning.

This chapter invites you to look more deeply into the matter of test scores and the impact of such scores on the lives of teachers and students. Though the pressure resulting from standardized tests seems to come in waves, there is little to indicate that the pressure will recede any time soon. Teachers in today's classrooms must understand enough about the issue of high-stakes testing to make sound choices as instructors and to be informed participants in the crucial decisions being made for our students at the system level.

PROBLEM CONTEXT AND SOLUTION PARAMETERS

Context

Totem High School is one of two high schools in this Northwest community. At one time, THS was the only high school, with a relatively homogeneous population. As the population grew in this commuter community, another high school was opened on the outskirts of town, and this new school drew off many of the students from more affluent homes. The older neighborhoods fed THS with a strong working class population, people less likely to drive BMWs into the city each day. The student count at THS has grown steadily over the years, but some community members have seen the school slide from "an above-average high school of 600 to a mediocre high school of 2,400." Whenever the standardized test scores of the two high schools are compared, THS comes out well below the newer Ray High School. There are comments about the low score on the totem pole.

The superintendent of schools in the community was recently hired as a forward thinker, someone who could anticipate what's in store for schools and help to place the city schools "on the map for this state and beyond." Superintendent Hamburg has, as a result, been far more proactive than her predecessors; in fact, some teachers see the superintendent more as a disruptor than a pace-setter. This is particularly true in the elementary schools, where Superintendent Hamburg began her campaign to change the system. However, the superintendent has recently made some pronouncements indicating that the secure secondary schools are not to be allowed complete autonomy, as they had in the past. The informal network of rumors is indicating that secondary principals will soon be brought into alignment with the superintendent's agenda.

Problem

One area in which Superintendent Hamburg hopes to beat out surrounding school districts is in performance on standardized achievement tests. As a fairly recent immigrant from the state of Texas, Dr. Hamburg knows what a powerful force standardized tests can be, either to build or crush the credibility of the school. And as a forward thinker, Dr. Hamburg can see that the state will be building its own graduation tests similar to the Texas Assessment of Academic Skills (TAAS). For now, student scores on the Stanford Achievement Test (SAT-9) serve a similar purpose. School results on the SAT-9 are published in newspapers and on the state's Department of Education web site. At the very least, real estate agents and potential business relocators are well aware of how schools rank in terms of their test scores. To move the community beyond its "bedroom" status and make it into a real player, Dr. Hamburg knows she must make the schools more attractive to businesses.

And the big problem, according to Dr. Hamburg, is that the city's schools don't rank very high. The city averages by grade level were near the state average, certainly not disastrous. However, for a city that wants to sell itself as a model of education for the state and beyond, the scores are simply too low. Worse yet, there are only two high schools in the community, and your school, Totem High School, always has lower scores. The facetious nicknames for RHS and THS among the real estate community are Right High School and Trailing beHind School.

Superintendent Hamburg worked with an advisory council to discuss the test issue and she has now come to a decision. As indicated in her memo (which is included here), she is dedicating all professional development funds and a portion of the textbook budget for the next two years to purchasing the services of the STAR™ test preparation program. From her own experience and from her reading of the professional literature, Dr. Hamburg concluded that this program was just what was needed to take the city to the next step. Your principal was cautiously supportive initially, but after returning from a STAR information session, she has become a strong advocate, too.

You are a relatively new teacher at THS, which makes you a bit reluctant to get too involved in what some of your colleagues are calling a "political issue." On the other hand, you are too idealistic to simply accept a directive without at least looking into its justification and potential effects. When you heard that some of your THS colleagues were exploring the issue and had already reserved a speaking time at the school board meeting where the superintendent expected to receive final approval for her plan, you decided to join the investigation.

Solution Parameters

Your team has been allotted ten minutes of the board's agenda time, with up to five minutes for questions and answers following your report. You're not at all sure what should be done at this point. Clearly, the team could endorse Superintendent Hamburg's ideas, offer an alternative plan, or urge a complete rejection. But that is why you have an investigation to conduct first.

••••••• **WORK THE PROBLEM** ⟶

PROBLEM DOCUMENTS

To assist you in understanding various aspects of this situation, the following documents have been provided to you:

9.1 Memo from the Superintendent of Schools

9.2 Letter of support from the Business-Partnership for Effective Schools (B-PES)

9.3 Advertising brochure from the STAR (Standardized Test Achievement Renaissance) test-preparation program

9.4 District test data from the past three years

PROBLEM DOCUMENT 9.1	*Memo from the Superintendent of Schools*

Forest City Schools—
Where Education Still Pioneers!
Bobbi Lee Hamburg, Ed.D., Superintendent

Memorandum

To Forest City Board Members

Cc School Administrators and Faculty

From Superintendent Hamburg

Date 2/10/03

RE Test Performance

As you recall, I received a very clear charge from the Board on my hiring—to put our city schools on the education map. It is no secret that the vitality of any community is intimately tied to the vitality of its schools. We know that attracting businesses to this community cannot be accomplished without the prior step of building a model school environment. More importantly, we owe it to the fine students of this community to provide them with the best opportunities for education available anywhere in the Northwest.

I believe it is evident from the Annual Report to the Board that I filed in the fall that much progress has been made in this endeavor. Changes in the structure and personnel policies at our high schools have begun to move this community to a position of athletic preeminence in the state. Students from our schools have been recognized across the state for literary and artistic works, and our extra-curricular drama program was honored as the best in state last year.

However, the core of our work as educators remains largely unaffected. I am referring to the academic centerpiece of education—the achievement of our students. As many of you are aware, our state is rapidly joining nearly every other state in mandating a standards-based assessment of student learning as a requirement for graduation. Not only will this affect individual students' life decisions, but it will also affect—most dramatically—the credibility and status of our school system. Best indicators tell us such a test will be in place within two years, perhaps sooner, and our schools simply must prepare for this now.

The standard measure for the state at this time is the Stanford Achievement Test (SAT-9). As you can see by the data I have provided, our schools have been, at best, mediocre in performance on these tests. While we are not a "low-performing district," as the state defines this, we are clearly not a model district yet. However, I have every confidence that the fine educators and tremendous students in this community can move us quickly to a position of prominence on this test—and later on the state exam. All that is needed is for us to devote deliberate, sustained attention to the performance of our students on this exam.

I am, therefore, offering a proposal for the Board's consideration. This proposal is similar to the work I did in Texas, work which the Board acknowledged in its hiring me. The essence of my proposal is that we channel existing resources that have been targeted for professional development of teachers into a focused program of professional development dedicated to enhancing the performance and opportunities of our students. I also recommend that a portion of the money be reserved for incentive bonuses for principals and teachers in outstanding schools.

In past years, professional development monies have been allotted on a formula of FTEs and controlled at the building level. This has resulted in sporadic, fragmented, and inefficient professional development. For example, one member of a high school department might use up the entire department's budget to attend a national convention in the subject area. I do not doubt that this is rejuvenating for that faculty member, but it hardly serves to provide the entire department with professional growth. At one elementary school, the entire professional development budget was turned over to creating a community-intervention program, while another elementary school utilized its budget by allowing teachers to purchase whatever books they wanted with the money. Clearly there is no defined goal or even theme for the expenditure of these monies.

I propose that our district purchase the services of the STAR program. In order to do this, for the next two years, all professional development money must be earmarked to fund this venture. In addition, we should delay the purchase of materials designated for upgrading elementary art programs and eliminate library discretionary funds. This STAR program *guarantees* improvement in student performance on standardized tests. That is, if we find our scores do not improve, the entire expenditure will be refunded to us. If our scores improve, we are moving forward in our goal to become an exemplary district. Either way, we profit.

Having worked with a similar program in Texas, I am completely convinced that this is the best possible use of our resources. When I was a principal, my students' scores jumped by 10 percent in the first year of our contract with the test-preparation firm. Moreover, I believe we provided students with transferable skills to take into other testing situations. Our teachers became better teachers through the principles they learned in their training. Soon after the test-preparation program began, we were recognized as a U.S. Department of Education A+ school!

Perhaps the best element of purchasing the services of STAR is that our teachers can continue their great work, but with the systematic support of experts in the testing field, freeing our teachers to bring the best possible education to our students.

All the logistics of the program are handled by the STAR case managers. In short, we buy opportunities, focus, growth, and success with this investment. I would stake my career on the value of this move.

Letter of Support from the Business-Partnership for Effective Schools (B-PES)

Business-Partnership for Effective Schools (B-PES)

Arthur V. Johnson, Chair

To the Board of Education:

On behalf of the Business-Partnership for Effective Schools (B-PES), I am pleased to write in support of Dr. Hamburg's proposal to purchase STAR services for the city schools. The considerable business acumen represented in the membership of our organization has been put to work in investigating the claims of the various test-preparation companies serving our area, and we are pleased to report that we see STAR as the clear value leader. Not only does STAR provide a comprehensive program, with support materials and the ever-crucial human support element, but STAR also provides a money-back guarantee for its product. As responsible business persons and taxpayers, we see the features of STAR as the sort of investment this school system cannot afford *not* to make!

Indeed, the members of B-PES feel so strongly about this matter that we have organized a matching grant program to assist the schools in this venture. Through contributions of members, we propose to match school district expenses in acquiring STAR at a one-to-ten rate. That is, we will increase your budget for purchasing STAR features by 10 percent as our way of emphatically endorsing this educationally-sound decision.

Why should B-PES concern itself in this matter? Essentially, we have two broad reasons for our involvement. First, we recognize that the children who stand to benefit through this enhancement are our children, the children of our workers, and the children of our clients. We are part of this community, and this is our way of giving back. Second, we also acknowledge that we have a vested interest in the success of our schools. We cannot recruit good workers if the school system has a mediocre reputation; we cannot see a broadening of the business opportunities in this community if the conditions of the schools discourage the potential relocation of complementary business firms. As business people, we are attuned to the "bottom line," which is the most convincing component of any organization's ability to sell itself. For schools, that bottom line is student success. To improve opportunities for our students' success, we are willing to put up a meaningful investment.

It is truly our hope that this moment of community-wide collaboration will engender future partnerships between the business and education communities.

Sincerely,

Arthur V. Johnson

Arthur V. Johnson, Chair

ST☆R

**Standardized Test
Achievement
Renaissance**

Making
your students
Stars in their
own futures!

What's at stake?

By now, education professionals around the country have seen what kind of impact test results are having on the business of learning. State legislatures are clamoring for accountability. Members of the professional and business communities are on the doorsteps of the schoolhouse, not to bring help, but to demand results. Newspapers throughout the nation are plastered with the failures—and rare success stories—of public schools. Principals and administrators are justifiably anxious, and teachers are pressed to add to their already overloaded lives. Nothing short of the survival of schools is at stake here. If test scores do not please the pressure groups, schools will find themselves out of business.

The phrase "high-stakes testing" has more bite to it now than ever before. And help is needed.

What do we offer?

STAR™ is the most comprehensive assistance for high-stakes testing available today. At STAR™, our goal is to provide training and materials to reduce the impact of high-stakes testing. We provide the means for schools to address the test so that learning will not be lost. Here are some of the key features of the STAR™ program:

- On-site in-service workshops for all affected teachers
- Hands-on, activity-based techniques with exemplary facilitators
- Practice drills and activities built from the national standards
- Adaptation of focus to your particular high-stakes environment
- Follow-up sessions on a negotiated schedule at your schools
- Cutting-edge materials to take directly into the classroom for instruction
- Computerized practice tests that are readily scored onsite and reports that offer content and test-taking strategy feedback
- Special guides for family support (family sessions available at extra cost)
- Money-back guarantee!

What have we found?

The results are impressive. Our average gain-score improvement has been .48 standard deviations in the language-use tests, .47 standard deviations in the mathematics tests, and a whopping .62 standard deviations in the reading sections of the tests. These results are reported as standard deviations because of the variety of tests used in different districts. There are also dramatic improvements in tests of other specific content domains, demonstrating the adaptability of the STAR™ program.

Here's what a few of our satisfied customers have reported:

> *"I'm a convert! I have always disdained prep programs as a waste of time and money. But our teachers report that they can teach even more now that they have confidence in the testing results. We're stars!"* Annemarie Westcoat, Superintendent of Schools, Remington, VA

> *"When they promise, they deliver. Our scores went up from the 43rd [percentile] to the 53rd in just one year. I got a bonus!"* Dave Pallinger, Principal, Arnodt Elementary School, Grand Rapids, MI

> *"My principal practically had to drag me into the first session of the STAR workshop. I thought I knew it all, with twenty years of experience under my belt. But from the first minutes, I saw that I would be getting new ideas not just for getting the kids ready for the Arizona state test, but also for making my own class a better environment for learning. I'd have to say that STAR™ is worth it, even if test scores don't matter that much in your school."* Jane Thomas, math teacher, Regent Middle School, Phoenix, AZ

How do we become a STAR™ school?

Our professional staff will work with a school or school district on an individual basis to tailor a program to your needs. Costs are established based on the particular needs of your school and testing situation. Our staff members are experts not only in the test-score enhancement process, but also in creative financing possibilities. Ask a representative about potential grants and cost-sharing opportunities in your region.

Making your students Stars in their own futures!

ST☆R
Box 44723, Orlando, Florida
1-800-KIDSTAR
www.startestprep.com

District Test Data from the Past Three Years

Grade	Content area	1999–2000			2000–2001			2001–2002		
		THS	RHS	SA	THS	RHS	SA	THS	RHS	SA
09	Reading	43	49	49	42	50	49	41	51	49
	Language	44	46	48	44	50	49	41	47	50
	Math	44	51	53	48	52	53	45	54	53
10	Reading	45	49	50	42	51	50	41	50	49
	Language	44	49	49	42	43	51	42	51	49
	Math	47	50	50	46	53	52	46	51	53
11	Reading	48	48	49	45	51	49	41	51	51
	Language	43	47	50	43	50	49	42	52	52
	Math	49	51	51	47	51	50	46	54	53

THS = Totem High School
RHS = Ray High School
SA = State Average

•••• PROPOSE A SOLUTION ➤

SOLUTION SUMMARY

Before proceeding to the reflection section of this chapter, write a brief summary of your team's solution here:

Our team defined the "real" problem here as _____

_____

_____

_____

_____

_____

_____

_____

The key features of our solution were _____

_____

_____

_____

_____

_____

_____

_____

My personal view of the problem and solution is _____

_____

_____

_____

_____

_____

_____

_____

TIME FOR REFLECTION

This PBL experience raises a number of issues for you to consider. Of paramount importance is the role of the professional educator as an informed participant in debates about testing and accountability. The reflection is organized first around issues of standardized testing: its role in schools and school reform, the pressures this testing places on students and teachers, and how we prepare students for the tests. In addition, we will consider the impact of accountability on schools in general. Finally, this section focuses your attention on the professional development of teachers.

The Place of Standardized Testing

With tremendous pressure placed on most schools to perform well on one standardized test or another, it is a commonplace of schooling today to find educators—especially administrators—judging any potential innovation in terms of how it will affect the test scores. Thus, standardized test results become, perhaps unintentionally, the standard by which progress is measured. Consider Tanner's (2000) portrayal of the role of standardized testing: "Nonetheless, the prevailing attitude of the school superintendent and principal is that curriculum is determined at the state level and is manifested by means of statewide achievement tests in the mandated individual core subjects. The clearest path to educational efficiency resides in 'teaching to the test,' and the demonstrated measure of educational excellence resides in the test scores, pure and simple. The job of the teacher is to 'deliver' the curriculum" (p. 193). Tanner's skepticism is entirely missing in similar comments from testing advocates, such as (then Texas governor) Bush's education advisor, Margaret LaMontagne, who said "If you teach to the test, and the test has just what you want the kid to know, it's kind of a 'So what?' deal here in Texas" (Henry, 2000).

The extremes are there: Testing as the de facto ruler of the curriculum and testing as no big deal. At a position quite the opposite of Dr. Hamburg's, some teachers see standardized testing of any form as a dirty word in education. That is, they see such testing as irrelevant in its best forms and insidious in its worst. Such testing is not a measure of progress, they would argue. It is a meaningless measure.

If we step away from the politics around standardized testing, we can see that one place the tests may be useful is in providing information. We can do much with information if we know how to use it well. Some have argued that information from standardized tests can help us target deficiencies among average students to help them move forward (Whitehead & Santee, 1987). Key, however, is finding valuable uses of this information and resisting misuses that don't consider the social and legal implications of test use (Airasian, 1987). Informed teachers can help their constituents understand what it means to use test data appropriately (Heubert & Hauser, 1999).

Is Test-Prep "Teaching to the Test"?

Theodore Sizer (1992) writes that "Teaching to the test is eminently sensible if the test is worthy, and a travesty if the test is corrupt or mindless" (p. 113). He uses the word "test" more broadly than the sense of "test" in this problem. However, his words provide us with an important perspective. The idea of "teaching to the test" is widely scorned among educators at the same time that this idea is widely implemented. Does using a test-preparation program necessarily mean we are teaching to the test? And where do we draw the line for ethical behavior here? That is, if we can improve student scores through some sort of test preparation, whether we improve student learning or not, do we owe it to the students to provide them with that assistance? Or do we owe it to the students to protect them from such a perversion of the learning process?

The view expressed by Sizer (1992), of course, assumes that the "test" is something far more significant than an externally-imposed standardized test. Madaus (1999) argues that the very presence of standardized testing that has high stakes associated with it will lead to teachers teaching to the test. Airasian (1987) lays out the proposition that "Given the important consequences that ensue from policy-oriented testing, not to teach to a test may be a greater disservice to pupils than to teach to it" (p. 408).

Thus, we have two extremes: we are obligated to teach to the test and we are obligated *not* to teach to the test. The question we must consider is whether we can accept either extreme or work out some middle ground. In his editorial on standardized testing, Gordon Vars (2000) writes that it would be nice if we could turn over the test preparation to someone else and, as teachers, focus on student learning. This is, however, an impossible dream. "The skills and information assessed by even the more poorly conceived test have no value unless they are *applied* in real life. . . . Instruction in the mandated competencies, however trivial they may be, must not be separated from the major goal of educating whole human beings" (p. 1).

The climate of testing doesn't allow much room for educators to simply ignore this question. As a professional, you need to reflect on what position you take. Do you see justification in teaching to the test? How would you address a parent who thought you were neglecting or over-emphasizing test-taking skills?

The Real Pressures on Teachers

To what extent do teachers feel pressure to have their students achieve high standardized test scores? Apparently the pressure is real and significant. Survey recent news stories on education, and you will find ample evidence both of the pressure for accountability and of teachers' reactions. In the fall of 2000, voters in Oregon turned down a proposition which had proposed tying teacher pay to the performance of students on standardized tests, and this proposition was not unique to Oregon. Writing against this idea, principal Jan Ophus (2000) of North Bend High School argued, "Surely even the angriest voter understands that in education the result of a teacher's skill, effort, dedication, and even love is not always graphable on a chart of student assessment. There are simply too many powerful social and economic factors that get in the way. . . . The hurting, troubled, hungry children who pass into our schools each morning are often better off when they leave at the day's end if only because they've learned they're known and cared for by the adults who work in those schools. Not giving a raise or a cost-of-living increase to a teacher of such children because his students didn't gain a point at the end of the year on a state multiple-choice reading and math assessment is wrong" (p. 7).

Whether the test scores are tied to monetary rewards or simply a part of the work climate in schools, teachers cannot easily ignore such pressures—especially if the pressure is personalized in the form of a bonus-seeking administrator. Innovations in curriculum and instruction are quickly judged by their potential to influence standardized test scores, and even ideas that may promise greater aesthetic development, greater interpersonal success, greater wholeness as a human being, are set aside if they do not lead to improved multiple-choice performances. Teachers have been known to abandon exciting, engaging units for their children in favor of drill for the tests; in some elementary schools, recess has been eliminated for primary students in order to provide extra time for practice. As Oakes and her colleagues found in their research on reform in middle schools, standardized testing programs "had a chilling effect on experimentation" (Oakes, Vasudeva, & Jones, 1996, p. 29).

Thus, beyond the merits of being accountable or focusing on student achievement, the testing movement must seriously consider the impact of this pressure on the lives of teachers. And, of course, there is no such being as "the testing movement." Instead, there are politicians and educational leaders and disgruntled community members and committed advocates and even teachers. There are people. These people, loosely drawn together to create a national force called the testing movement, affect the careers and lives of educators and the children they serve. It is crucial that teachers be both aware of the pressure (to deal with it productively) and prepared to be participants in the debates about standardized testing.

Students and Standardized Testing

In virtually every call for accountability through standardized testing, the language of protecting or assisting students comes into play. Perhaps there is a basic distrust of the educational system or of teachers beneath the calls for accountability, but at an overt level, everyone seems to agree that such testing is really put into place for the sake of the children. Is this so? As a participant in the educational venture, you do well to consider this question.

In his article about the role of the state in establishing a vision for education, French (1998) points out that in a society stratified by race and economic status, the lack of standards will doom minority students to an inferior education. Standards, in this context, become a means of guaranteeing that all children have the opportunity to be educated. However, as French points out, when educators discussed implementing standards without a broader vision of the democratic basis for schools, the result was an insensitive, rigid implementation that worsened inequities. His examination of the Massachusetts example found that the original vision for complex, multi-faceted standards was reduced to results on a single multiple-choice test. Instructional practices that had proven to be successful with diverse learners were abandoned in favor of "coverage" to get ready for the tests. McNeil's (2000) investigations in Texas found something similar, with a greater emphasis on how such teaching actually damaged the educational opportunities of minority youth.

You should recognize in the examples given above that there can be contradictions between *standards* and *standardized tests*. It is important, therefore, to be clear about the differences. Standards focus on what students should know and be able to do. These standards can be carefully selected to produce the kinds of graduates we can be proud of. However, in most views of what it means to be well educated, not all standards are reducible to what can measured by standardized tests.

Another issue related to student performance is the actual testing situation and the discomfort it may generate. We know that students find the testing situation generally unpleasant, and increasingly so as they progress through the years (Wheelock, Bebell, & Haney, 2000). We know that some students suffer from serious anxiety about testing, particularly when time limits influence their performance (Woolfolk, 1998). But the same things might be said about making a visit to a physician. Virtually no one enjoys going to the doctor to find out what's wrong; some people have such serious anxiety about the doctor's office that they avoid it altogether, even though they may suffer serious consequences. An argument could be made that the discomfort of the testing situation is a necessary evil in the attempt to diagnose and correct what is "wrong" with any given student.

Of course, we must ask if that is truly how we use the information garnered from standardized testing. Imagine if the information gathered from a visit to a doctor was pooled so that whole neighborhoods received health ratings—even to the extent that we could say that a certain neighborhood was the healthiest in town, while another was the most sick. The information the doctors gathered was not effectively used to help any given patient, but only to label the community. Eventually, business and real estate representatives might start coaching citizens on how to handle the doctor's appointment or even whose information should not be included in the neighborhood report.

As ludicrous as this analogy seems, it is worth some consideration. We have to ask who is benefiting from the information gathered from standardized tests. Are individual students helped or harmed? This sort of question is asking about what some have called "consequential validity" (Gipps, 1994), the idea that we need to consider seriously how the uses of assessment information will affect students' lives. Standardized testing raises some serious questions in this regard. Data from Massachusetts indicate that the implementation of high-stakes testing related to graduation in that state has caused an increase in the dropout rate, especially among African American and Latino students (FairTest, 2000), a finding corroborated in Texas (McNeil, 2000). In fact, nine of the ten states with the highest dropout rates have high-stakes testing; none of the ten states with the lowest dropout rates have such testing (FairTest, 2000). Schools have eliminated arts programs, class meetings, recess periods, electives, and even whole programs in order to focus on the areas covered by standardized tests (Kohn, 2001), and one must raise the question of consequences: Are students better off because of these cuts? Kohn (2001) takes the position that a rise in test scores may actually indicate teachers are doing a worse job of educating children, since they are probably focusing on more superficial matters, or sometimes leaving out important subjects (such as science and social studies) that are not covered by the tests.

The necessary reflection, then, focuses on what such testing does to the children with whom we work. Responsible educators must be guided by this sort of thinking. Given the predictable relationship between test scores and socio-economic status (Kohn, 2001), we must be hesitant to exult in high scores and just as hesitant to condemn low scores.

The Impact on Schools

Perhaps the most important issue we need to reflect on is the kinds of schools we will create for the young people we meet each day. Ideally, the schools we create will be places of high engagement, curiosity, and learning. Such schools are likely to produce graduates who will do well on standardized assessments, though that may be a side effect. Drilling students to prepare for tests may improve the scores; the question is whether or not that will make schools places of engaged learning. Seymour B. Sarason (1998) argues that schools ought to be places of productive learning. He phrases well his hope for graduates, a hope that is worth reflecting on. In considering what a person should leave school with, he writes, "*I would want all children to have at least the same level and quality of curiosity and motivation to learn and explore that they had when they began schooling*" (p. 69). Not a bad target, even in the secondary school!

Business Allies?

As the Forest City schools began to investigate test score improvement, they found ready allies in the business community of their city. This experience raises some interesting issues. What is the proper relationship between the schools and the businesses?

In the early 1990s, the province of British Columbia articulated a new mission for its schools. This mission included enabling learners to develop knowledge, skills, and attitudes that would help them contribute to a healthy society and "a prosperous and sustainable economy" (British Columbia, 1990, p. i). Certainly such a statement generates controversy, and just as certainly, it bears the mark of business influence on education. While educators are likely to nod at statements about critical thinking, statements that link the schools to business more often raise eyebrows.

In this problem, the business representatives actually volunteered funding to assist the schools. At one level, this is not surprising. Schools do influence the desirability of a community—and businesses seek to enhance this desirability. However, the high profile role of the business group's support of testing here should not disguise the fact that in many communities, businesses also support music programs, service learning, after-school enrichment, and so on.

So are these business allies welcome? Perhaps the most important consideration is the difference between support and control. Schools need allies. In most places, schools need financial support; schools also need opportunities for students to connect with the larger community; schools need the human capital of their neighbors. When the schools have a clear sense of what they stand for, the ways that outsiders can be supportive become clear. However, when there is confusion about the direction of schools, community members and business persons may step in to set that direction. In the Forest City example, the business allies may have seen an opportunity in the new leadership of Dr. Hamburg to influence the direction of the schools, rather than merely to support the efforts of the schools. Is this appropriate? Is it a manifestation of democracy or a manipulation of influence?

Professional Development

One of the superintendent's recommendations was to channel all professional development money into the STAR program. Just what would be lost in such a diversion of funds? Is professional development important to teachers? Is it professional? Do teachers develop through this avenue?

When I began teaching, I was given some provocative advice: "It's okay to teach for twenty years; it's just not okay to teach one year twenty times." I wish I could credit my advisor, but I don't recall who said it. The statement made the point to me early in my career that continuing to develop as a professional was essential for teachers.

As a beginner, I was startled to find that there were actually days set aside for teachers to engage in professional development. Like most of my colleagues, I entered the work of those professional development days with mixed emotions: grateful for the break from the routine of the classroom, but ill-prepared to learn in the professional development setting. I had plenty of work to do, and I would have been much more pleased just to be given time to spend grading papers, preparing units, and doing the thousand chores of teaching. I was not receptive to the in-service workshop.

This problem invites you to think about turning over all professional development time and money in a school system to test preparation activities. One question worth contemplating is what would be the opportunity cost of such a bargain? That is, whether or not the workshops were good, what would a teacher give up in professional growth by giving up all other development efforts?

To answer that question, one must reflect on what it means to be a growing professional. Surely a teacher can carry on such growth independently, through readings and taking the odd graduate course. The trade-off would involve the kind of workshop activities most schools engage in, what Quartz (1996) calls marginal expert-driven learning opportunities that don't have much impact on teachers anyway. Quartz argues that most professional development in schools is stabilizing, reinforcing what's going on rather than inviting new ideas. If this is so, and the evidence appears to support it, then perhaps there is no great loss in turning over the paid development time to test preparation activities.

Perhaps. But perhaps not. The idea of a community of professionals joining together to consider their practice and the effects of their practice on their "clients" may be the essence of professionalism. If we take away the conversations about teaching, the structured whole-group conversations that make up professional development in the schools, do we lose important connections? Do we eliminate the chance for ideas to spark?

As a teacher stepping into the classroom and the school community, you must give careful thought to how you will continue to grow as a professional. Taking charge of your professional development, or at least entering into the opportunities you have with enthusiasm, may make the difference between teaching for twenty years and teaching one year twenty times.

DISCUSSION QUESTIONS

1. If there is a balance to achieve between preparing for standardized tests and just educating your students, how does the professional educator strike such a balance?

2. What ways can individual teachers help to win the public relations battle associated with test scores and schools? How can a school get out its story of student learning in terms other than such scores?

3. One portion of the superintendent's plan for implementing a test-prep program was to create incentives for performance. She suggested the possibilities of bonuses for principals and teachers. What do you see as the potential positive and negative effects of such a reward system?

4. What legitimate role can outside consultants, such as the STAR program, perform in helping schools accomplish their goals? How does a school maintain a shared sense of purpose and commitment with such outside forces?

5. Some students and parents around the country have organized protest boycotts of standardized testing. If such a boycott were promoted in your school, what would you see as the ethical response of a professional educator?

6. In your contacts with model teachers, what have you discovered about their perspectives on professional development? How can this become a priority for the busy beginning teacher? How can a teacher who has neglected this make it a part of the everyday world of teaching?

7. Considering the PBL process, what did you learn about your tolerance for a different model of learning?

FURTHER READING

Berliner, D. C., & Biddle, B. J. (1997). *The manufactured crisis: Myths, fraud, and the attack on America's public schools.* White Plains, NY: Longman.
    This book examines a series of myths about American education. Chapter 2, "Myths about Achievement and Aptitude," provides helpful lenses on how to interpret information from standardized tests. In contrast to what the media report about performance on such tests, Berliner and Biddle explain how proper interpretation of test data does not support the

notion of a crisis in education. Their work is an important reminder that tests can provide useful information, but we must understand how to use such information.

Heubert, J. P., & Hauser, R. M. (Eds.). (1999). *High stakes: Testing for tracking, promotion, and graduation.* Washington, DC: National Academy.

Heubert and Hauser represent the Committee on Appropriate Test Use from the National Research Council in putting together this book. The work addresses a variety of issues in high-stakes testing, including promotion and retention, tracking, granting diplomas, disabilities, and more. The second chapter, on policies and politics, is especially useful for developing an understanding of what it means to use test data appropriately.

Madaus, G. F. (1999). The influence of testing on the curriculum. In M. J. Early & K. J. Rehage (Eds.), *Issues in curriculum: A selection of chapters from past NSSE yearbooks: Ninety-eighth yearbook of the National Society for the Study of Education, Part II,* (pp. 71–111). Chicago, IL: University of Chicago.

This important essay is reprinted from an earlier (1988) NSSE Yearbook, and it's a timely reprint. Madaus lays out a clear depiction of the issues that follow from what he calls "measurement-driven instruction" (p. 75). He identifies seven principles that describe what can happen when tests gain excessive power in the system, and the principles are disturbing from an educator's point of view. In particular, he argues that as the stakes get higher for tests, the curriculum and instruction narrow, and the control over learning moves farther away from teachers and students.

Popham, W. J. (1987). The merits of measurement-driven instruction. *Phi Delta Kappan, 68,* 679–682.

W. James Popham writes a defense of "measurement-driven instruction," arguing that in this practice "we have a potent and cost-effective intervention that can substantially boost the quality of schooling in our nation. It's time to use it" (p. 682). He acknowledges that, like anything else that is poorly done, MDI can have negative consequences. However, he sees its positive consequences as more convincing. Popham addresses the concerns of critics who argue (as Madaus does) that such testing will narrow the curriculum or stifle creativity. Instead, Popham sees such testing as "a powerful curricular magnet" (p. 680) that can pull the schooling experience away from the boring, irrelevant, unmotivating reality most students face. Popham has raised other perspectives in more recent works (for example, see *Educational Leadership,* Volume 56 Number 6, March 1999, "Why Standardized Tests Don't Measure Educational Quality"), but this essay provides a strong case for a positive use of "measurement" to influence instruction.

Wheelock, A. (1998). *Safe to be smart: Building a culture for standards-based reform in the middle grades.* Columbus, OH: National Middle School Association.

Anne Wheelock takes a positive approach to the standards movement, trying to redeem what otherwise might be a disastrous trend. She makes a clear case that standards and standardized tests are not the same thing. She even points out, as Kohn (2001) does, that practices associated with raising the test scores do not necessarily improve learning, that such practices may actually harm learning. In the end, Wheelock offers three key ideas rooted in the notion of a supportive school culture for making standards work to the students' advantage in schools: focus on student work and rich pedagogy, focus on relationships that nurture motivation, focus on teachers' role in a community of professionals.

WEB SITES

Center for Education Reform
www.edreform.com/pubs/testing.htm
Provides a positive reason for using standardized tests.

Consortium for Equity in Standards and Testing
  www.csteep.bc.edu/ctest
  The mission of this organization is to focus on how standards and tests can be used more fairly.

FairTest
  www.FairTest.org
  This web site is dedicated to challenging the way in which standardized tests may disadvantage certain students. It is an ongoing, up-to-date reference for information on what is going on at the national level in connection with standardized testing. Despite the name, this site maintains a highly critical perspective on testing.

Alfie Kohn
  www.alfiekohn.org
  He has plenty to say about standards and standardized testing.

REFERENCES

Airasian, P. W. (1987). State-mandated testing and educational reform: Context and consequences. *American Journal of Education, 95*(3), 393–412.

Berliner, D. C., & Biddle, B. J. (1997). *The manufactured crisis: Myths, fraud, and the attack on America's public schools.* White Plains, NY: Longman.

British Columbia. (1990). *Year 2000: A framework for learning.* Victoria: Ministry of Education.

FairTest. (2000, September). MCAS: Making the Massachusetts dropout crisis worse. *MCAS Alert.* Retrieved from www.fairtest.org/care/MCAS%20Alert%20Sept.html

French, D. (1998). The state's role in shaping a progressive vision of public education. *Phi Delta Kappan, 80*(3), 184–194.

Gipps, C. V. (1994). *Beyond testing: Towards a theory of educational assessment.* London: Falmer.

Henry, T. (2000, November 1). 'Teaching to the test' becomes the learning standard. *USA TODAY,* p. 8D.

Heubert, J. P., & Hauser, R. M. (Eds.). (1999). *High stakes: Testing for tracking, promotion, and graduation.* Washington, DC: National Academy.

Kohn, A. (2001). Fighting the tests: A practical guide to rescuing our schools. *Phi Delta Kappan, 82*(5), 348–357.

Madaus, G. F. (1999). The influence of testing on the curriculum. In M. J. Early & K. J. Rehage (Eds.), *Issues in curriculum: A selection of chapters from past NSSE yearbooks: Ninety-eighth yearbook of the National Society for the Study of Education, Part II* (pp. 71–111). Chicago, IL: University of Chicago.

McNeil, L. M. (2000). Creating new inequalities: Contradictions of reform. *Phi Delta Kappan, 81*(10), 728–734.

Oakes, J., Vasudeva, A., & Jones, M. (1996). Becoming educative: Reforming curriculum and teaching in the middle grades. *Research in Middle Level Education Quarterly, 20*(1), 11–40.

Ophus, J. (2000). Measure 95 should be defeated. *Oregon School Board Association, 27,* 6–7.

Popham, W. J. (1987). The merits of measurement-driven instruction. *Phi Delta Kappan, 68,* 679–682.

Quartz, K. H. (1996). Becoming better: The struggle to create a new culture of school reform. *Research in Middle Level Education Quarterly, 20*(1), 103–130.

Sarason, S. B. (1998). *Political leadership and educational failure.* San Francisco: Jossey-Bass.

Sizer, T. R. (1992). *Horace's school: Redesigning the American high school.* Boston: Houghton Mifflin.

Tanner, D. (2000). Manufacturing problems and selling solutions: How to succeed in the education business without really educating. *Phi Delta Kappan, 82*(3), 188–202.

Vars, G. F. (2000). An impossible dream? *The Core Teacher, 50*(4), 1.

Wheelock, A. (1998). *Safe to be smart: Building a culture for standards-based reform in the middle grades.* Columbus, OH: National Middle School Association.

Wheelock, A., Bebell, D. J., & Haney, W. (2000). What can student drawings tell us about high-stakes testing in Massachusetts? *Teachers College Record.* Retrieved November 2, 2000 from www.tcrecord.org

Whitehead, B., & Santee, P. (1987). Using standardized test results as an instructional guide. *The Clearing House, 61*(2), 57–59.

Woolfolk, A. E. (1998). *Educational psychology* (7th ed.). Boston: Allyn & Bacon.

CHAPTER TEN

SERVICE LEARNING BEATS DOING HOMEWORK

INTRODUCTION AND PROBLEM BACKGROUND

Students in secondary schools make several complaints almost universally. The food's bad; there's nothing to do outside of school; the older generation doesn't understand us; this place is like a prison. But perhaps the most common complaint is worded as half question, half proclamation: "Why do we have to do this? This stuff doesn't have anything to do with the real world."

While there is no single solution to the kinds of complaints students continue to make, two perspectives on secondary education claim to address the last issue, the relevance of learning to life. On the one hand, supporters of service learning argue that students can find relevance in carefully organized learning experiences, with reflection, in the context of caring for others. On the other hand, school-to-work advocates maintain that students can learn better if they are able to embed their learning in real-world work contexts. Critics of both positions raise objections on the basis of time lost to instruction and a narrow and limiting career perspective students acquire. In fact, Vo (1997) reports that school-to-work programs have been condemned from both extremes: as tools of corporations and as Marxist plots. Critics of service learning have denounced the idea of mandatory volunteerism.

The similarities of service learning and school-to-work programs suggest at least a coordination of efforts, as has occurred in the programs of Ellington Township High School, the focus of this chapter. Both service learning and school-to-work claim to connect students to their communities, to engage students in applying knowledge and skills, and to enhance student attitudes and values related to citizenship and the workplace (Brown, 1998). The common benefits of the two programs make them natural allies (Dunlap, 2001).

Here's what some advocates (Yoder, Retish, & Wade, 1996) of service learning claim:

> Students are able to make a meaningful link between daily activities, work skills, and the curriculum through problem-solving and action. Students learn to take pride in themselves and their social contributions while engaging in activities that establish positive connections among the school, students, and community. (p. 17)

The National School-to-Work Learning and Information Center (1996) makes this claim for school-to-work on its web site:

> Years ago, non-academic, vocational classes were only for those students who did not plan to go on to college. However, today's high-skill job market demands that all high school graduates have both advanced academic knowledge and workplace skills and training. The school-to-work, or school-to-careers, movement aims to improve the way students are prepared for college, careers and citizenship.
>
> The goal is to improve learning through more interesting and relevant experiences that integrate school-based and work-based learning and foster real-world applications of principles and concepts.

As is so often the case in education, the clear claims of any advocacy group get muddled in the complexities of a society trying to come to agreement on the purpose of schooling. Such complexities come to the surface in examining the troubles at Ellington Township High School.

PROBLEM CONTEXT AND SOLUTION PARAMETERS

Context

Ellington Township High School had begun working with partner learning experiences (PLEs) well before the 1994 School-to-Work Opportunities Act made such programs widely available to secondary students. In fact, ETHS began working with PLEs even before the National and Community Service Act of 1990. This innovative high school had sent its students out to do service-learning projects at the local hospital, animal shelters, the library, to numerous businesses, and to a host of government agencies (such as the Forest Service). One reason for the success of Partner Learning Experiences at ETHS was the recognition that the extensive demands of such a program would require a full-time director, and the school had acquired a noncertified employee to do just that.

As an early innovator in School-to-Work, ETHS became a source of pride. Visitors from around the state and even beyond the state boundaries came to see just how to make such a program thrive. Many teachers at ETHS learned ways to incorporate PLEs into their curricula so that the experience of partnering was becoming more business-as-usual than an exception. Of course, certain teachers had managed to resist and oppose the idea of PLEs, and there was the usual array of critics who argued that this sort of learning was not rigorous and that such experiences were contrary to the spirit of an academic institution. Still, the system was in strong working order.

Problem

In the most recent school board election, a coalition of voters joined behind a candidate who represented a position critical of ETHS for a variety of reasons, but especially for the school's PLE program. This candidate, a local physician, campaigned with the slogan, "Getting our kids back in school." Her supporters agreed that too much time was lost to instruction because of the extensive school-to-work activities. Dr. Moreau's promise to her supporters was that she would get in and shake up the fluff in the system.

Most teachers did not expect Dr. Moreau to win the election, but she did. Now there is a current of fear about the program as evidenced by the letter from the PLE director, soliciting active lobbying for his program. Teacher leaders suspected that Dr. Moreau would make a move to eliminate PLEs and the director's position early in her time on the governing board. They were correct. Dr. Moreau, in a surprisingly indirect move, has asked that the PLE program be up for discussion at the next meeting. She provided a discussion document for all board members to read prior to the meeting and distributed copies to the public and ETHS faculty members.

As a faculty member at ETHS, you have been drawn into this issue. The informal network of hallway and lounge discussions has elevated the PLE controversy to a place where it represents not just a threat to one program, but a symbol of outsiders trying to push the school back to the basics. A number of faculty members are portraying this controversy in dramatic terms that strike you as more emotional than rational. You have, therefore, joined as a volunteer to a task force coordinated by the principal of ETHS to examine the role of service learning and school-to-work programs in U.S. high schools. You want to develop a dispassionate, carefully reasoned position even in this climate of emotions running wild.

Solution Parameters

Your task force will present a report to the school board on the results of your investigation. The Board has agreed to give your task force up to fifteen minutes to address this issue, followed by an opportunity for Board members to question your committee. Each member of the task force will provide a two-page summary of his or her position on this issue—allowing all task force members to build on their agreements but to maintain independent opinions.

········WORK THE PROBLEM ──▶

PROBLEM DOCUMENTS

The following documents have been provided to assist you in your investigation of this problem situation:

10.1 Program description of the Partner Learning Experience at ETHS

10.2 Discussion document on the effects of PLEs at ETHS, written and presented by Dr. Saundra Moreau

10.3 Student testimonial on PLEs included with Dr. Moreau's open letter (the school board received dozens of letters, but Dr. Moreau highlighted only one)

10.4 Letter soliciting support from PLE director, Alberto Juarez

10.5 Job description, Director of Partner Learning Experiences

10.6 Student petition to retain PLEs at the high school

10.7 Letter of support for PLEs from the director of a local Humane Society

10.8 Test score summaries from the previous five years for ETHS

10.9 Principal Pearlmutter's charge to the task force

The Partner Learning Experience (PLE)

at Ellington Township High School

The ancient Chinese proverb claimed simply and profoundly, "I see, and I remember a moment; I hear, and I remember a day; I do, and I remember a lifetime." The Partner Learning Experiences of Ellington Township High School are rooted in the belief that true learning only occurs when students are given the opportunity to *do something* with their learning. The cornerstone of learning, we believe, is in the application of learning.

The Impact of PLEs

PLEs have a long history at ETHS. Some of the accomplishments of the PLEs can be seen in the following examples.

At the school itself:

- Since the founding of PLEs, there has been a steady decline in the dropout rate at ETHS.
- Student satisfaction at the high school, as measured by self-reported survey data, has increased.
- Teacher support for the program has steadily increased throughout the PLE experience.

At the community level, here are some of the accomplishments of the PLE program:

- PLE students completely reorganized the Humane Society animal shelter, and have had a major hand in running the shelter for four years.
- PLE students joined with Habitat for Humanity, both to raise funds and to plan and build houses. PLE students have been major contributors to acquiring housing for more than ten families!
- PLE students initiated and supported the development of a "traveling library" from the Township Library System.
- PLE students have tutored over 500 elementary students.

Clearly, these accomplishments are profound, yet they are only a historical footnote to an ongoing, living program. PLEs continue to offer students and teachers opportunities to make learning come alive.

Current PLE Opportunities

Our current offerings include the following categories:

COMMUNITY HEALTH: PLEs involving such venues as the Humane Society, Mercy Hospital, Golden Days Nursing Home, the Salvation Army homeless shelter and soup kitchen, the Forest Service trail maintenance crews, and the Eastside Recreation Center.

EDUCATION: PLEs involving such venues as tutoring at several elementary schools, the Catholic Social Services Afterschool Tutoring Program, Township Library Systems, and the Museum of the Past (docent program).

BUSINESS: PLEs involving such venues as assistance to the Township Council Intergovernmental Board, CLICK Software Firm, Peaks Outdoor Manufacturing, the Mainstreet Coalition, and others.

Commonalities of the PLEs

Whatever PLE a student participates in will include several commonalties.

First, there is a **training** period before any PLE. This training is provided through collaborative efforts of the PLE director, experienced ETHS students whose current PLE is a training assignment, and Partners from the community. No ETHS student goes into the community without adequate training.

Second, there is an ongoing **mentoring** for each PLE. Mentoring is done primarily by the Partners, with suggestions from the PLE director.

Third, there is a required **reflection** for each PLE. ETHS students are required to submit a log to the PLE office weekly, and group sessions to discuss what is being learned are held with each PLE participant at least once a semester.

Finally, there is an **accountability** system. Reflections, evaluations from site mentors/supervisors, and summaries of the experience are generated for every student in the PLE program.

Your Involvement?

Educators at ETHS are welcome to propose new PLEs and/or "curriculum links" (a PLE term for course credit tied to PLEs) at any point. Proposals are made through the simple filling out of the **Curriculum Link** proposal form.

Community members who have ideas for PLEs should contact the director of PLEs at Ellington Township High School. After an initial discussion, community partners simply provide a list of the work or service opportunity expectations, a plan for mentoring and accountability, and a contact person.

Partner Learning Experiences at ETHS:

Where Learning Meets Life

SAUNDRA MOREAU, M.D.

Board Member

On the Effects of Partner Learning Experiences for Academic Achievement
at Ellington Township High School

As we launch into a period of reflection and renewal for the schools of Ellington Township, I am urging thoughtful deliberation about the practices and policies in all our schools. I have made a personal commitment to work for academic <u>excellence</u> in our schools, the sort of excellence that will serve our students in their lives beyond the classroom and will bring recognition to our community for its accomplishments. In light of this commitment to excellence, I am calling for an examination of the effects of Partner Learning Experiences (PLEs) at Ellington Township High School.

While the experimentation with PLEs began some ten or more years ago, the formal adoption of the program, including the hiring of a Director, took place five years ago. It is important to note that this decision was made at the school level, with the *tacit* approval of the Board in its allocation of the funds to support the Director's salary (see Ellington Township Governing Board Minutes, August, 1997). As far as I can tell, there has been no serious evaluation of the impact of this decision at any level, and no consideration of the consequences, intended and unintended. Anecdotal evidence alternately supports and challenges the program; test data would indicate that the program has had a negative rather than a positive effect on student outcome. I have included a student testimonial that supports this program, but I think you'll agree, its effect is to cause us to have even graver doubts about PLEs. I believe it is time for the Board to seriously question the costs and benefits of PLEs at ETHS.

In terms of costs, I direct the attention of the Board to two general categories, the cost in terms of financial outlay and the cost in terms of time for learning. Considering the former, the PLE program is relatively inexpensive. The average annual salary and benefits for the Program Director is at 70 percent of the median teacher salary for the district. While that does not represent a hardship for the financial obligations of the District, it should be noted that this salary does represent the equivalence of hiring another teacher, perhaps a teacher who could assist some of the students whose reading scores lag at ETHS. The operations budget for the program is more difficult to determine, since most expenses incurred by the program (e.g., photocopies, office supplies, telephone/fax bills) are not separated from the general budget of ETHS, a practice that also deserves reexamination. Clearly, the travel budget for the PLE program is exorbitant, matching the entire travel budgets of the two largest departments at the school, which translates into a spending ratio (by staff compared to teachers) of 25 to 1!

However, the more significant cost of the PLE program lies in its effect on student learning. Perhaps the most solidly established research fact in the past several decades is that student learning can be predicted by the amount of time spent on task. When students are engaged in rigorous and challenging learning activities, they learn. When students are allowed to wander off task, to become distracted by the innumerable concerns of adolescence or the lack of skillful guidance from their instructors, they don't learn. It's that simple. The amount of time our students spend learning has steadily decreased as the PLE program has gained popularity. Students spend time traveling from the school to community work sites; students spend time in training to do menial tasks for local businesses; students spend time completing questionable documentation of their hours (logs and reflections); and students are not in class, engaged in the curriculum for any of that time. That cost, I submit, is enormous. As leaders of education in our community, I do not see how we can sustain this.

In fairness, we must also look to the benefits. Supporters of the PLEs from the community claim that the students gain valuable work experience. Perhaps this is true, and were we a vocational education institution, this might be persuasive. I see little value in providing work experience to students if that work experience serves to limit their potential for greater occupational opportunities later in life. It must also be pointed out that these community supporters have found a source of free labor for half a decade now at ETHS. Supporters of the PLEs within the school argue that student satisfaction has increased, and that this is in evidence in the reduced dropout rate at the school. While it is true that the dropout rate has steadily declined (from 19 percent to 9 percent) over this period, it is not clear that this reduction can be attributed to any one program. What other factors might explain this? Even if we assume the dropout reduction is connected to PLEs, we are obligated to explore the reason for this. Surely, having turned a serious place of learning into a site for developing job skills in a relaxed atmosphere can explain why fewer students drop out. Yes, learning is hard work, and yes, many adolescents prefer not to work hard. If we transform the school into a social club, of course they will be more likely to stay.

There is yet one more concern that I feel obligated to underscore. A glance at the sorts of activities our students engage in reveals not only an unfair benefit accruing to certain members of the business community (free labor), but also a Constitutionally questionable merging of church and state. Our students go out from a public school to work in various religious organizations in the community. While I have nothing against organizations such as Habitat for Humanity on a personal level, I vehemently oppose the merger of public education with religious charity.

The spirit in which I offer my remarks is one of commitment to making our schools the best possible environments for real learning. It is in that spirit that I hope we can discuss the state of affairs at ETHS.

| PROBLEM DOCUMENT 10.3 | *Student Testimonial on PLEs Included with Dr. Moreau's Open Letter* |

Dear Dr. Moreau,

I am one of the students' who works with the PLE's at Ellington. I herd you were considering getting rid of the program, and I wanted to tell you not to.

Just over a year ago or so, I was so close to dropping out of school. I thought it was real boring and a total waist of time. Their is hardly anything that is more boring than school, except maybe doing homework.

Then I talked to Mr. Juares about the PLEs. He got me a PLE at the animal shelter where I spend part of everyday taking care of the abandoned pets. For me, you can't imagine how important it is to do this kind of work. I make a difference to these animals, and they're as important as anyone else. But more important, I found a reason to stick with school because I'm going to run my own shelter later on. It was the PLE that helped me see I could do something important and I had a reason for school. My grades have gone up, and I think I care a lot more now.

Besides, service learning really beats doing the boring homework of high school.

Sincerely,
Marcie West

Dear Colleagues at Ellington High,

No doubt you have heard that our recent school board election has prompted a flurry of criticism of the PLE program here at Ellington Township. While no official word has been offered, there are rumors throughout the hallways that the program is on the chopping block. My head is the first to go.

I am appealing to you to express your support of the PLE program in whatever way you can. I am ready to stand by the record of this program. I firmly believe that we have accomplished great things at ETHS, I think we have made the school a better place and you will agree. Our students have stronger social skills and academics. We no longer are seen by this community as a place to guard against (remember the horror stories of adding guards during the noon hour?), but as a source of good works.

It is well known that the dropout rate has gone down because of the PLE program. We simply reach more kids than we could before, and this is no negative comment about the work you teachers have done. It's tough teaching high school students, and whatever we can do to make that easier is worth doing.

Before the School Board makes a terrible mistake, do your part to help our students. Gather the evidence of how PLEs have helped you do your job. Talk to parents and urge them to let their voices be heard. We can make a difference, but only if we join together as one for the students.

Sincerely,

Alberto

Alberto Juarez, PLE Director, ETHS

Partner Learning Experiences at ETHS:

Where Learning Meets Life

Director of Partner Learning Experiences
Ellington Township High School

The Director of the Partner Learning Experience program at ETHS will be a noncertified staff member, subject to staff conditions of service, as opposed to faculty. This means the Director will be hired on a year-by-year basis, with no possibility of tenure. As with all staff contracts, the continuation of employment is subject to satisfactory completion of the duties outlined in the job description.

Primary Duties	• Coordinate Partner Learning Experiences connections between community agencies and ETHS (through personal contacts)
	• Document PLE hours, activities, and accomplishments
	• Supervise or arrange supervision for all PLE students
	• Provide liability counsel to Partners and parents
	• Write curriculum appropriate to the PLE
	• Train students prior to their commencement of PLEs
	• Evaluate the PLE program yearly and report to the Principal
Secondary Duties	• Seek external support (grants) for the PLE program
	• Network with Partners and other service/work programs in other school districts
	• Enhance the program through innovations
	• Provide guidance to Partners on mentoring and supervising activities
	• Advocate for the program in the school and community

The Director of the Partner Learning Experience Program will report directly to the principal of ETHS for purposes of supervision and evaluation.

Student Petition to Retain PLEs at the High School

Petition

As students at Ellington Township High School, we appeal to the Board of Education to support the Partner Learning Experience program at our school. We have heard that the PLE program is under consideration for elimination. We oppose this. We have all participated in PLEs, and we list the following benefits of the PLE program.

1. We have found no experiences at ETHS that let us apply our learning as well as the PLE program.
2. We have learned a great deal about what it means to be a member of this community.
3. Numerous students have said that they would not have stayed in school if the PLEs had not made school seem somehow more worthwhile.
4. Mr. Juarez is one of the only teachers in this school who will listen to students in a way that respects us for who we are.
5. Grades in other classes are better because of the success we achieve in the PLE program.
6. We understand more about the world of work because of the PLEs.

We urge the school board and the leaders of Ellington Township High School to consider the wishes and needs of those most directly affected by this decision, the students.

(Signed by 273 students.)

Letter of Support for PLEs from the Director of a Local Humane Society

Ellington Township Humane Society
Alexandra Kinsky, Director

Mr. Alberto Juarez, Director
Partner Learning Experiences Program
Ellington Township High School

Dear Mr. Juarez,

I am pleased to be able to express my unconditional support of the PLE program at your school and of the students who are the heart and soul of that program. As Director of the Humane Society for the past ten years, I am well acquainted with the power of the PLE program. Indeed, our efforts to care for the animal community of this region would be severely hampered were it not for the sincere and consistent efforts of the students at your school.

Let me give you an idea of what kinds of contributions the PLE students have made to the Humane Society. Each day, PLE students assist with the care and feeding of the animals. Displaced dogs and cats find positive human interaction because of the PLE students. Community clients who come to the Society are assisted in making mutually beneficial choices by the PLE students, who come to know the animals better than anyone else at the site. PLE students assist with inventory, delivery, cleaning, and public relations. In fact, the entire public relations campaign, which has successfully put our name and location in the minds of thousands of community members, was initiated, organized, and conducted by PLE students working out of an ETHS marketing and business class.

Some five years ago, PLE students analyzed the processes and procedures of the Humane Society, including the monitoring system for euthanization of animals. Under my guidance, but substantially on their own, these PLE students reorganized our operation, increasing both its efficiency and its "compassion index," a term coined by the students themselves. At least one of the students who worked on this reorganization has since contacted me to inform me that she is working in an administrative position at an animal shelter in Colorado!

I think it is apparent that the PLE program has impacted both our organization and the students who have participated in it. Without question this is the sort of program that deserves our continued support and participation.

Sincerely,

Alexandra Kinsky

Alexandra Kinsky, Director

Summary Data on Stanford 9 Percentile Rank Scores for ETHS

Grade, Subject		1999			2000			2001			2002			2003		
		%	S	ST	%	S	ST	%	S	ST	%	S	ST	%	S	ST
9	R	82	53	49	84	50	48	85	48	48	90	45	49	95	41	49
	L	84	55	48	87	52	47	90	48	48	92	51	48	97	48	49
	M	83	47	49	85	50	50	89	47	49	95	47	48	97	46	50
10	R	79	56	50	83	56	49	83	53	50	87	49	49	90	47	51
	L	82	57	49	80	58	51	87	52	40	90	48	49	95	46	50
	M	81	51	49	84	52	49	90	47	51	93	49	51	97	47	49
11	R	84	54	53	79	58	50	90	49	53	94	50	52	92	47	47
	L	77	60	52	85	54	50	90	51	49	93	49	53	95	51	52
	M	80	58	49	87	51	49	93	49	51	95	51	52	96	48	50

R = Reading
M = Mathematics
S = Mean percentile rank score at ETHS
ST = Mean percentile rank score in the state

L = Language
% = percent of students at ETHS tested

Principal Pearlmutter's Charge to the Task Force

ELLINGTON TOWNSHIP HIGH SCHOOL

Memorandum

To: Interested Faculty Members

From: Aaron Pearlmutter, Principal

RE: Task force on PLE issues

As most of you have heard by now, the Ellington Township Governing Board will be discussing our school's use of Partner Learning Experiences at the upcoming meeting (one week from Wednesday). From what I can tell, the Board will be holding an initial discussion, which will lead to a motion about the program. The nature of that motion and any subsequent vote are not clear at this point, but given the critical perspectives aired recently, I expect a serious challenge to the program.

I spoke with Superintendent Winston about this issue, and she is reluctant to advise us on how to proceed. She did, however, agree to arrange for a time for us to speak at this meeting. When the Board Agenda reaches item 7 (approximately one hour into the meeting), representatives from ETHS will be given fifteen minutes to address the Board and to respond to questions. Superintendent Winston indicated it would be "futile" to trot out testimony about the PLE program without reference to the "larger picture" of these issues. She adamantly opposed any presentation by the PLE director, indicating that this might do more to incite opposition than to quell it.

Upon reflection, I have decided that our best hope is to pull together a disinterested group of faculty members to look into the issues surrounding PLE-style programs. I suspect that strong advocacy will not help our case; rather, if we show that we have a good grasp on the full range of issues and implications for this issue, we may have more power. I suppose, in fact, that our inquiry into the issues could, conceivably, cause us to change our direction.

I am requesting that you inform me by this afternoon if you are willing to serve on this investigative task force. We will meet tomorrow immediately after school to discuss how to proceed. I will be providing one day of release time for each participant, which I anticipate we will use to meet at the end of this week after we have established our initial plan of action.

I realize this comes at a busy time (what time isn't?), but I feel it is important that we take charge of this issue and set a positive tone as the new Board begins its work.

····PROPOSE A SOLUTION ➞

SOLUTION SUMMARY

Before proceeding to the reflection section of this chapter, write a brief summary of your team's solution here:

Our team defined the "real" problem here as _____

_____

_____

_____

_____

_____

_____

_____

The key features of our solution were _____

_____

_____

_____

_____

_____

_____

_____

My personal view of the problem and solution is _____

_____

_____

_____

_____

_____

_____

_____

TIME FOR REFLECTION

You may have decided to defend the PLEs, or you may have decided the school was in need of some changes. Either way, a number of issues probably drew your attention in this problem. This reflection section opens with questions about the power of a single person in criticizing a school's program. Then, you are invited to think about components of service learning and school-to-work: what is the range of such programs, what is learning like in these models, and how do we determine goals in such programs? Finally, the reflection looks at public relations for schools and the ways people use data in arguing for or against school programs.

The Power of One

Can a single school board member, supported by a relatively small coalition of supporters, actually have the kind of impact suggested by this problem?

There appears to be some evidence that one person can have a tremendous impact on the direction of a school system. For example, Littleton High School, in Littleton, Colorado, instituted a series of reforms in early 1990s that moved students toward more interdisciplinary work, graduation by exhibition, critical thinking, and student control of the learning process (Oppenheimer, 1992). Widespread faculty involvement was coupled with community partnerships to transform the school into what reformers hoped would be a powerful place of learning. However, even before the "restructuring" of Littleton had been completed, school board elections changed the plan. What some have described as a conservative restoration occurred. The newly elected school board completely dismantled the work of restructuring, fired the superintendent, and launched the school district in a different direction. This is only one example, but it does highlight the power of a small group in setting the direction of a school system. Elections for school board membership are typically determined by a very small minority of voters. It gives reason for teachers to think about how they represent their schools and how they participate in the community discussions about school governance.

A Range of Programs

The Partner Learning Experiences program described at Ellington Township High School is a somewhat unique notion, combining service learning and school-to-career into one program, under the control of a single administrator. This is one version in a wide array of possibilities. Clark and Welmers (1994) list several options of programs, but conclude that the ideal program of service learning is built around an interdisciplinary team. Fertman (1996) describes a continuum of possible programs based on how well the programs link to the curriculum. For example, service clubs are at the low end, since these clubs have virtually no connection to the curriculum. At the high end of this list of options, Fertman places school-wide themes that involve the whole school in projects linked across the curriculum. Such a perspective reminds us that schools can incorporate the ideas of service learning in a host of creative ways.

In a similar vein, school-to-work or school-to-career programs have a wide range of options. In some cases, the experience is entirely extra-curricular, unconnected to the normal classroom work or seat-time associated with a course. In other cases, such as the academies that *Seattle Times* reporter Frank Vinluan describes (2000), the school-to-work experience becomes the organizing center of a student's entire high school experience. In such cases, students might find themselves in a tourism academy, where math skills and writing skills are contextualized in the business of tourism. *Let's Get Real* (Holt & Willard-Holt, 2000) is an example of a corporation-sponsored competition that involves students in solving the real-life problems business persons face in their companies.

One programmatic question deserves special attention. Should schools require participation in service learning for students to graduate? Roughly twenty percent of high schools have done so, based on the positive impact that service learning can have on young people and the importance of developing citizenship (Sauerwein, 1996). However, this requirement has also generated controversy. Is compulsory volunteerism justifiable in schools? Students sometimes protest this, even when these students are already participating in service activities. One high school student, who chose not to graduate rather than give in to this requirement, unsuccessfully sued her high school (Sauerwein, 1996). This question deserves our consideration.

Learning through Service and Work

A number of challenges face educators as they consider learning through service and work opportunities. Consider some of the following issues:

- How do we assess the learning students achieve in these contexts?
- What provides program continuity for students in such programs?
- How do we manage the potential problems associated with the connections between schools and the community? (For example, liability!)
- What is the "opportunity cost" of such programs? That is, to participate in either service learning or school-to-work, students must give up something else. Does the trade-off serve students?
- How can seasoned educators, well-versed in their own methods of teaching, be brought to the discussion table on this issue? And can novices withstand the resistance that the veterans throw up to changes in the school?

These questions represent the sort of thinking and discussion we must engage in if we are to guarantee that learning is the centerpiece of these programs.

Competing Goals in Service and Learning?

In their article on service learning, Kahne and Westheimer (1996) note that service learning is enormously popular and widely supported. However, they are concerned that "more attention has been focused on moving forward than on asking where we are headed" (p. 594). To understand the direction of the movement, they contrast two historical positions on the issue of learning through service projects. From one perspective, which they call the "charity" view, service projects are a civic duty that young people should learn to perform. Students learn to give back to their communities, and they see a place to apply some of their learning. The other perspective Kahne and Westheimer describe is the "change" perspective. This view of service calls on the learners to develop relationships of caring as opposed to giving; this position also asks students to engage in changing the social order, rather than ameliorating suffering. Notably, the "change" perspective looks to make transformations in the learner rather than merely providing opportunities to practice skills. These two contrasting positions suggest serious differences in the way service learning plays out in a school. These positions also serve to remind the beginning professional to dig beneath the slogans of advocacy in order to better understand what educational practices lead to.

Think about this fairly typical example. Students in a middle school are told that they will not get their December dance unless they gather 6,000 cans of food for the local food bank. One wonders what message about service is embedded in this. Does the child learn that there is a personal payoff for providing service? Does the child come to believe that such giving—which nearly always means pestering parents for contributions—relieves him or her of the obligation of a more personal involvement? Does this child come to see accumulating a box of canned goods as the end of civic responsibility? The responsible educator must reflect on such issues and questions.

Some writers even challenge the otherwise glowing reports of what students get out of service learning experiences. Sauerwein (1996) reports negative psychological consequences students sometimes experience, including fear and depression. Willison (1994) worries that such activities as working to serve food to the homeless will merely reinforce negative stereotypes unless there is adequate thoughtfulness about preparation for, participation in, and follow-up to service learning activities.

The matter comes back, once again, to the serious posing of questions about what it is we hope to accomplish through the experiences we offer our students. Advocates of school-to-work programs tell us that it is not training for a career, but building a context for good learning (National School-to-Work Learning & Information Center, 1996), learning that is relevant whether students go straight to work or to college. Advocates of service learning likewise argue that it is the learning that is central, not providing service (Yoder et al., 1996). Somewhere beyond the slogans, serious educators must be ready to address the question of the goals such programs will serve.

Public Relations for the Public Schools

The discussion document that Dr. Moreau used to launch the examination of PLEs at ETHS illustrates an issue that many people would have found unthinkable a short time ago. Do schools need to concern themselves about public relations? In the long story of American education, schools have generally been regarded as not needing to promote themselves. That is, though there has always been a persistent voice worrying about the younger generation, schools have generally enjoyed the support of their communities.

That may not be entirely true. Public education has been assaulted at regular intervals, especially when sparked by dramatic events that call for someone else to get the blame. When Sputnik launched the Russians into the lead in a race for space, it was the fault of the schools. When U.S. market dominance was in question in the 1970s, it was the public schools that took the blame. Cold war problems? "It's the schools, stupid." In fact, there's a rich tradition, as Daniel Tanner (2000) points out, of politicians' bashing schools in order to claim to be great supporters of education.

But there is something that seems different in recent years, and the public image of schooling has taken a beating. Certainly inflamed language, such as the defeat in war metaphor used in *A Nation At Risk* (1983) is the sort of rhetoric that is bound to put schools on the defensive. But the presence of charter schools, advocacy for vouchers for private schools, and even the home schooling movement move educational institutions out of the position of monopoly they once seemed to hold. Add to this the sensationalized reports of school violence, and it's easy to see why schools now must be serious about their public relations.

For the particular case of service learning and school-to-work, it is clear that there will be both strong advocates and critics. The question, then, is what obligations does the teacher face in representing the school publicly? Most educators are likely to feel that their job is to teach young people, and that the responsibility for representing the school rests with the administrators or someone else. However, this may not be the best attitude to take if our real focus is to help the students and assure the survival of important programs in the schools.

Data?

You may have noticed the way Dr. Moreau used data in her letter to the board. In one letter, she used the decline in test scores at ETHS as an indictment of service learning, while dismissing the reduced dropout rate. She indicated that the dropout rate is complicated, and can be attributed to a number of factors. One wonders, what about test scores? Are these not complicated, too?

Also, consider the student testimonial Dr. Moreau included with her letter. The note from Marcie West was one of dozens of support letters. Why did Dr. Moreau select this letter to include? Do the errors in Marcie's letter have more rhetorical power than the sentiment she expresses? What do you learn about the use of data from this example?

The caution that is well worth contemplating is that data can be used in ways that are misleading and inaccurate. When professional educators hear someone claim that there is a correlation between falling scores and this or that innovation, it serves you well to examine that correlation very carefully.

DISCUSSION QUESTIONS

1. Consider how to position yourself in a community where there is such obvious jockeying for support. Dr. Moreau and Mr. Juarez, without directly sparring, are clearly in conflict. The former has great power, the latter only symbolic power. What risks does the teacher face in taking sides in such an issue?

2. The PLE program appeared to be widely supported. How do teachers apply critical perspectives to such programs and still maintain their own credibility?

3. In your reflections on service learning, what do you see as the key benefits and the major drawbacks?

4. What is the relationship of school-to-work with the business community? What effect does this focus have on more "academic" aspects of the high school? Do you see school-to-work as more appropriate for certain students than others?

5. How can either service learning or school-to-work experiences be organized to maximize student benefits? What is the role of reflection for the students?

6. As is true with all problems teachers face (and all PBL experiences), data can be used in a variety of ways. What is the ethical obligation of teachers concerning the use of data?

7. Considering the PBL process, what did you learn about your ability to work with messy details in an unstructured situation?

FURTHER READING

Bolt, L., & Swartz, N. (1997). Contextual curriculum: Getting more meaning from education. In E. I. Farmer & C. B. Key (Eds.), *School-to-work systems: The role of community colleges in preparing students and facilitating transitions (New directions for community colleges)*, pp. 81–88. San Francisco: Jossey-Bass.
A brief article that helps establish the *learning* basis for service learning. The authors provide features of contextual learning that make it more effective than traditional approaches, and they offer suggestions deriving the content/process for contextual learning, for organizing the curriculum, and for assessment.

Linking Learning with Life Series, produced by the National Dropout Prevention Center, College of Health, Education, and Human Development, Clemson University, 209 Martin Street, Clemson, SC 29631-1555.
This series has more than 20 booklets that address aspects of service learning, from guiding athletes into service off the field to connecting generations through service learning. Also included is a booklet on school-to-work, a focus on multiple intelligences, and a reflection guide. The booklets are all short and very user-friendly. One volume especially useful to this PBL experience is listed below.

Dunlap, N. C. (2001). *School to work to life: Linking service learning and school-to-work.* Clemson, SC: National Dropout Prevention Center.
This volume provides a comparison of service learning and school-to-work, developing a blended model. Very readable, with numerous examples, ideas, and potential partners.

Steinberg, A., Cushman, K., & Riordan, R. (1999). *Schooling for the real world: The essential guide to rigorous and relevant learning.* San Francisco: Jossey-Bass.

This brief book helps bring together two important contemporary movements in education, and especially in high school education. On the one hand, the book examines the claims of school-to-career programs, particularly the claim that such programs lead to better engagement and academic performance. The other force for reform is the Coalition of Essential Schools, a movement founded on the ideas of Theodore Sizer (1984; 1992; 1996). This movement began with a commitment to ending the "mindlessness" of schools, but comes together with school-to-career programs in a joint commitment to learning in meaningful contexts. Steinberg, Cushman, and Riordan are clearly advocates of the kind of learning that is possible through connecting to the community, whether in service projects or apprenticeships. The authors list numerous examples of what high schools are doing in the community. The authors also provide various principles for sound learning and suggestions for how to go about changing a school. Overall, this book argues that school-to-career programs are not just vehicles for dealing with weak students; instead, such programs are a means for all students to learn a more rigorous and relevant curriculum.

WEB SITES

National Service-Learning Clearinghouse
www.servicelearning.org
A web site to collect resources and support for service learning.

The National Youth Leadership Council (NYLC)
www.nylc.org
The site of an organization that bills itself as a leading advocate for service-learning and national service.

REFERENCES

Bolt, L., & Swartz, N. (1997). Contextual curriculum: Getting more meaning from education. In E. I. Farmer & C. B. Key (Eds.), *School-to-work systems: The role of community colleges in preparing students and facilitating transitions (New directions for community colleges)* (pp. 81–88). San Francisco: Jossey-Bass.

Brown, B. L. (1998). *Service learning: More than community service* (ERIC Digest No. 198 ED421640). Columbus, OH: ERIC Clearinghouse on Adult Career and Vocational Education.

Clark, S. N., & Wlemers, M. J. (1994). Service learning: A natural link to interdisciplinary studies. *Schools in the Middle, 4*(1), 11–15.

Dunlap, N. C. (2001). *School to work to life: Linking service learning and school-to-work.* Clemson, SC: National Dropout Prevention Center.

Fertman, C. I. (1996). Linking learning and service: Lessons from service learning programs in Pennsylvania. *ERS Spectrum, 14*(2), 9–16.

Holt, D. G., & Willard-Holt, C. (2000). Let's get real: Students solving authentic corporate problems. *Phi Delt Kappan, 82*(3), 243–246.

Kahne, J., & Westheimer, J. (1996). In the service of what? The politics of service learning. *Phi Delta Kappan, 77*(9), 593–599.

National Commission on Excellence in Education. (1983). *A nation at risk: The imperatives for educational reform.* Washington, DC: U.S. Department of Education.

National School-to-Work Learning & Information Center. (1996, March). *Dispelling myths about school-to-work.* Retrieved from http://icdl.uncg.edu/ft/081799-01.html

Oppenheimer, J. (1992). *Restructuring the high school: A case study* [Videorecording]. Alexandria, VA: Association for Supervision and Curriculum Development.

Sauerwein, K. (1996). A compelling case for volunteers. *The American School Board Journal, 83*(3), 29–31.

Sizer, T. R. (1984). *Horace's compromise: The dilemma of the American high school.* Boston: Houghton Mifflin.

Sizer, T. R. (1992). *Horace's school: Redesigning the American high school.* Boston: Houghton Mifflin.

Sizer, T. R. (1996). *Horace's hope: What works for the American high school.* Boston: Houghton Mifflin.

Steinberg, A., Cushman, K., & Riordan, R. (1999). *Schooling for the real world: The essential guide to rigorous and relevant learning.* San Francisco: Jossey-Bass.

Tanner, D. (2000). Manufacturing problems and selling solutions: How to succeed in the education business without really educating. *Phi Delta Kappan, 82*(3), 188–202.

Vinluan, F. (2000). Career academies: Expanding the world of work. *The Seattle Times.* Retrieved from http://texis.seattletimes.nwsource.com/cgi-bin/texis/schoolguide/vortex/article?ArticleID=8

Vo, C. (1997). "Not for my child." School-to-work faces a growing backlash from nervous parents. *Techniques: Making Education & Career Connections, 71*(9), 20–23.

Willison, S. (1994). When students volunteer to feed the hungry: Some considerations for educators. *The Social Studies, 85*(2), 88–90.

Yoder, D. I., Retish, E., & Wade, R. (1996). Service learning: Meeting student and community needs. *Teaching Exceptional Children, 28*(4), 14–18.

CHAPTER ELEVEN

CONSTRUCTIVIST LEARNING ON TRIAL

INTRODUCTION AND PROBLEM BACKGROUND

Ask any veteran teacher about some new approach to teaching or learning, and it's likely she or he will tell you that it's been around before. You're likely to hear that every few years some consultant or theorist manages to sell a "new" approach that's already been tried somewhere. Your veteran source may see it as a humorous trapping of the profession or a tragic example of manipulation. You could make a safe bet that the veteran will have an opinion.

And yet ideas come along that seem to shake the field significantly. One such shaking can be traced to the idea of "constructivist" teaching. That is, this idea might lead to such a shaking of the school world if it were tried. Brooks and Brooks (1999) describe two contrasting classrooms to help illustrate what constructivism might look like. In a seventh-grade classroom, the teacher works students for the "correct" responses to a poem—what the poet really means, what the poem is supposed to evoke. As students realize they are generally wrong in their understandings, they shut down, end their participation. In contrast, a ninth-grade teacher turns the students loose to develop their own experiments on how muscle movement is affected by temperature. This teacher challenges the students' thinking and forces them to structure their investigations, to seek relevance in relationships. This teacher is practicing constructivism.

Presented in a number of guises (Perkins, 1999), what most constructivist perspectives seem to hold in common is a de-centering of the teacher and a move toward students' making sense of their learning. Oh, and the seasoned teacher will remind us that the ideas were present in Dewey's, Kilpatrick's, and others' work early in this century.

Just how dramatic this move might be can be imagined when you look at works like John Goodlad's study, *A Place Called School* (1984). Based on thousands of hours of observations, Goodlad concluded that the pattern of education is one where students are passive recipients of information and that this pattern gets stronger as students progress through the grades. Teachers talk; students listen. Goodlad points out that students make few decisions, that they mostly sit passively as members of the whole class, and that their interest wanes as they progress through years of schooling. They encounter little novelty in their years of schooling. Moving from a vital interest in kindergarten, students can become jaded cynics before they leave middle school. Goodlad concludes that it is pointless to help teachers get better at what they are already doing way too much of. And this pattern of passivity is everywhere and powerful, a pattern that Dewey noted in his 1918 text, *The School and Society* (cited in Phillips, 2000).

So when professional groups such as the National Council of Teachers of Mathematics or the American Association for the Advancement of Science call for a different kind of teaching, they are fighting against a weighty tradition. Is it a futile battle? Can the traditions change? *Should* the traditions change? Is there room for compromise? These are some of the questions you should think about as you address the problem in this chapter.

PROBLEM CONTEXT AND SOLUTION PARAMETERS

Context

Alton High School has a history of being one of the "troubled" schools in the Northeastern urban community it serves. Local news media find plenty of opportunities to highlight the school's performance, but the stories never focus on the academic achievement of the AHS students. News items from Alton typically bring a shaking of the head and a "here we go again" from readers. "Can you believe those kids? What could make teenagers act like that? That place is a mess!"

In his third year at Alton High School, principal James, "Jamie," Busch has worked hard to combat the perceptions of the school as a holding pen for future criminals. He has also worked hard to help instill in the faculty a belief that they can somehow make a difference in the lives of these young people. Part of his task has been to weed out teachers he says have "sunk to the bottom and landed at Alton." Another part of his job has been to encourage the active participation of teachers in building a positive school climate, where teachers feel a sense of professional worth. To this end, he created the Council of Chairs.

The Council of Chairs is made up of the department heads from the following areas: Mathematics, Science, History and Social Studies, English, Foreign Languages, Arts, Health, P.E., and Vocations. Over two summers, Mr. Busch has arranged for all the members of the council to attend workshops at a major university to enhance teaching skills. The focus of the workshops has been on constructivist teaching methods, and with a year of practice and two summers of instruction, the council has decided to go public with its ambitious new agenda.

Problem

Teachers received a letter near the end of their summer vacation. This letter, signed by all the members of the Council of Chairs but not the principal, called on the faculty at AHS to make the school a "lighthouse" of learning instead of a "sideshow" of combating delinquencies. Some faculty members received the letter as a hostile assault on their professionalism, and somehow the letter ended up in the hands of a local editorialist. Much controversy followed, with the principal at first appearing to support the council and later appearing to call for restraint and thoughtful deliberation.

As a member of this high school faculty, you are concerned that this division may cause more harm than good. You have questions about the plan. Clearly, in your view, the tradition at AHS has not moved anyone toward excellence or high standards. The few students who have achieved well are the sort of students, you believe, who would achieve anywhere. The school, you suspect, is plagued with drudgery and boredom—both from the students' perspective and the teachers'. On the other hand, to have a small group of "leaders" announce to the faculty that there must be a change of methods smacks of elitism to you.

Your puzzlement about this issue prompted you to volunteer for the task force the principal has asked to form. This group has been given a wide-ranging task: recommend to the Council of Chairs what to do about teaching at AHS. Your group has also been asked to represent one side of the debate or the other, even if you consider a compromise position to be the best.

Solution Parameters

Mr. Busch wants to build his decision on the basis of good information. To accomplish this, he has appointed a number of task forces. Yours is one of these task forces. You will be instructed to make a case for or against the shift to constructivist practices. Mr. Busch has indicated that the council will consider the "advocacy" positions in an attempt to come to a fair and productive decision.

The format you will face is as follows: The Council of Chairs will hear from a variety of groups, each wholly committed to one position. Each group will be given fifteen minutes to present its case to the council. Following this, the council will ask questions, which Mr. Busch has characterized as "challenges" to the ideas of the task force. Following the presentation of the various positions, the council will hold an open discussion with all members of the faculty before voting on an action.

Because you may have to suppress your true beliefs in this matter, you will also be asked to write an individual report on the council discussion. In this report, which should be about two pages in length, you will indicate what you see as the best solution for AHS and your reasons for this opinion.

········WORK THE PROBLEM ➞

PROBLEM DOCUMENTS

To assist you in understanding various aspects of this situation, the following documents have been provided to you:

11.1 Joint statement from the AHS Council of Chairs calling for all classes to build on a foundation of responsive teaching; this is the letter that teachers received prior to the beginning of the school year

11.2 The principal's initial ruling on "responsive teaching" at AHS

11.3 Editorial from a community weekly paper concerning the plan to change pedagogy at AHS

11.4 The principal's revised ruling on "responsive teaching" and the need for a task force

11.5 Summary evaluation data from the previous academic year

11.6 A version of the "constructive controversy" technique, adapted by the principal from ideas outlined by Johnson and Johnson (1994)

PROBLEM DOCUMENT 11.1   *Joint Statement from the AHS Council of Chairs*

ALTON HIGH SCHOOL
Where Learning Happens

August 15, 2003

Dear <<teacher first name>>,

As members of the Council of Chairs, we are pleased to welcome you back to AHS for another year. We believe this will be the best year ever for AHS for several reasons. First, you are probably aware that our recent changes have diffused criticism of the school in the local press. Fewer and fewer of our students are appearing in criminal reports or lists of victims in the newspapers. Second, there has been a concerted effort this past spring by the council and Mr. Busch to hire only the most competent and committed teachers to replace our retiring colleagues. We are pleased to report that for the first time in two decades, we will be starting this academic year with all teaching positions filled. Kudos to Mr. Busch's energetic recruiting.

Our third reason for optimism is the most powerful of all. As you may know, the council has spent the last two summers in careful study of effective teaching methods. We have worked many hours to understand and implement principles of effective teaching in our own classes, and we have worked diligently with consultants from the State University to be certain our knowledge base is at the cutting edge of what works for students. The results have been dramatic. Now we believe it is time for us to go one step further. Aware that changing our practices is a great challenge for most of us teachers, we deliberately choose to disrupt the patterns of pedagogy at AHS. For too long, we have been a school devoted to holding our own as we combat juvenile delinquency. Serious learning has taken place in small pockets in our school, but for the most part, teachers have had to fight for control rather than lead into learning. We are calling for ALL classrooms to change this academic year. We are calling for ALL classrooms to implement effective instruction. Specifically, each classroom should evidence the following characteristics of good learning environments:

- Students actively build meanings rather than passively receive information.
- Students actively discuss and cooperate with their peers in building meaning.
- Students regularly experience learning in authentic contexts and in areas that are relevant to their own lives.
- Students continually see their own growth as lifelong learners.

In our participation with Mr. Busch to perform supportive faculty evaluations, the council will look for manifestations of these principles in every classroom, every lesson. We are calling for the end to lectures, worksheets, true-false tests, and mindless video watching. By moving our students to active participation, we expect to transform AHS into a lighthouse of learning for our community. It is time for responsive teaching at AHS.

We realize that some will believe our decision to be too abrupt. In fact, we are convinced that the only hope to make a real change is to do it now and to do it completely. Half-hearted efforts to reform schools have a failure rate that rivals that of the alchemists! To support this change, the council members are available individually to teachers every day through appointments. In addition, we will be holding weekly after-school support sessions (alternating Tuesday and Wednesdays, from 3:00 to 4:00).

We are truly grateful for your dedication to our students, and we look forward to working together this year.

(Signed by all the members of the Council of Chairs.)

PROBLEM DOCUMENT 11.2 *The Principal's Initial Ruling on "Responsive Teaching" at AHS Alton High School*

ALTON HIGH SCHOOL

Where Learning Happens

August 20, 2003

Dear Faculty Members,

I was thrilled to see the proactive, exciting recommendations of the Council of Chairs. I believe we should all count ourselves fortunate to be working with such a dedicated group of professionals. What I admire most of all is that the council took two summers and an academic year to pilot their ideas, to hone their skills, to test the waters, even before bringing in the rest of the faculty. These colleagues of ours are not arm-chair quarterbacks who sit back and tell us what to do; these colleagues are pioneers who are leading us into greater opportunities by helping us understand what it means to be responsive teachers for high school students.

I wish to express my support of the council's call, and I will back this up by providing extra release time for teachers who feel they need further instruction in how to teach with student involvement. Up to two days' time will be available for any teacher who needs the time to reorganize curriculum or to meet with consultants, visit classrooms, or otherwise carry on the learning necessary to succeed. In addition, our opening-of-school work day will be devoted to "constructivist" techniques for the high-school instructor. We have arranged for a local expert, Dr. Melton, to conduct our workshop.

There are, of course, other issues for us to address this year. Nothing, however, is as important as the transformation of this place into a house of learning, responsive to the needs and interests of our students.

Jamie Busch

Jamie Busch

Editorial from a Community Weekly Paper

No Light in the Lighthouse

STAFF EDITORIAL

A recent letter from the leaders at Alton High School demonstrates just how silly jumping on the band-wagon can be. Deluded by the educational establish-ment and intoxicated by educational jargon, the "Council of Chairs" at AHS recently called for an end to teachers' teaching at their school. You heard that right—an end to *teaching!* Instead, these pundits would have us believe that all a school has to do is make a warm place for the kiddies to hang out, and they will "construct" their own understandings. Balderdash. We all know what the inmates of AHS construct when they're left on their own: drug deals and muggings and vandalism and theft and worse.

Who do these "educational leaders" think they are kidding? According to their letter, they would have the teachers abandon any formal instruction. In its place, students would be given opportunities to dis-cover meaning in relevant experiences. Sounds great if you're the kind of kid who wants a place to hang out with nothing to interrupt your day! One veteran math teacher at the school, who asked that his name be left out for obvious reasons, had this to say. "I was hired to teach math because I know math. If my hands are tied so that I cannot explain and teach the math except in those moments when students find some relevance, I simply can't teach. I came here to be a teacher, not the keeper of a lighthouse." Word is that the teachers' union is about as upset on this one as this math teacher and one fuming newspaper writer.

Come on, Alton! Dump the psychoeducational babble and teach these kids something. Just because most of the students come from poorer neighbor-hoods doesn't mean they don't deserve an education. Maybe that's what this *community* sees as relevant. And it's our school.

ALTON HIGH SCHOOL

Where Learning Happens

August 25, 2003

Dear Faculty Members,

I am sorry to greet you with this note, but it has become an urgent matter that I clarify issues surrounding the controversy at AHS even before our meeting this afternoon. As you are aware, I expressed my endorsement of the ideas of the Council of Chairs for transforming our school's instructional patterns from passive to responsive learning. I believe the mandate from the council was created with the best motives and with solid research backing. In my enthusiasm for supporting such innovation, I'm afraid I was less than sensitive to other forms of expertise and experience on our faculty. For this, I apologize.

It would be rash for us to completely overhaul the evaluation of teachers' work without giving serious consideration to the consequences of such a decision. So, while I maintain my enthusiasm for the ideas of the council, I am suggesting another approach to this problem. I am calling for a delay in the implementation of these changes, and for our own people to investigate this matter more fully. To accomplish this, I would like to adapt the technique known as a "constructive controversy." In this approach to sound decision-making, various people represent the possible positions in the decision. Because these positions are assigned, it is not a matter of representing your own view and winning a debate. Instead, it is a matter of fully advocating a position so that all of us can understand it from its best side. Then we will be in a position to decide fairly.

For those of you willing to help with this, you will be assigned to investigate and defend either completely transforming to constructivist teaching or completely ignoring this position. It is my sincere hope that in this spirit of inquiry, we can discover what is best for AHS.

Jamie Busch

Jamie Busch

*Summary Evaluation Data
from the Previous Academic Year*

STATEMENT	DEPT.	% COMPLETED	LO 1 (%)	2 (%)	3 (%)	4 (%)	HI 5 (%)
This course helped me learn a lot about the subject.	H/SS	75	30	30	14	16	10
	SCI	90	25	33	22	10	5
	MATH	80	35	33	30	1	1
	LA	95	25	40	25	5	5
	FL	100	10	20	42	13	15
	VTech	65	5	8	23	40	24
	H/PE	65	10	15	35	20	20
	ARTS	72	4	16	22	30	28
This course was important to issues in my life.	H/SS	75	30	35	30	3	2
	SCI	90	50	25	13	6	6
	MATH	80	44	43	10	3	0
	LA	95	35	32	15	8	10
	FL	100	25	45	15	15	0
	VTech	65	10	12	35	20	23
	H/PE	65	5	8	22	35	30
	ARTS	72	5	17	30	20	28
This course was worth recommending to a friend.	H/SS	75	20	24	31	20	5
	SCI	90	32	31	17	15	5
	MATH	80	40	33	20	5	2
	LA	95	20	23	20	21	16
	FL	100	15	45	22	9	9
	VTech	65	5	12	25	25	33
	H/PE	65	42	22	20	10	6
	ARTS	72	4	4	31	21	40
This course encouraged me to learn more about the subject.	H/SS	75	43	30	5	15	7
	SCI	90	12	32	30	14	10
	MATH	80	35	40	20	2	3
	LA	95	24	26	30	15	10
	FL	100	43	27	17	7	6
	VTech	65	5	15	22	30	28
	H/PE	65	25	13	12	30	20
	ARTS	72	5	7	23	30	35

A Version of the "Constructive Controversy" Technique

Constructive Controversy Procedure

Jamie Busch

Adapted from *Joining Together* (Johnson and Johnson)

The point of a constructive controversy is to build a process that can allow the *best* solutions to emerge without tying those ideas to individual people. Because people advocate for positions whether or not they agree with these positions, the best reasoning from all perspectives comes out.

In a true constructive controversy, teams work together and eventually argue for both sides of a controversial issue. Our process at AHS will be as follows:

1. Teams are assigned to take strong positions (either for the recommended changes or against them).
2. Teams research their positions.
3. In the context of a Council of Chairs meeting, a team presents its case.
4. Council members (me included) challenge these ideas in a spirit of inquiry.
5. Another team presents the opposite case.
6. Again, council members challenge these ideas.
7. Drawing team members from both extreme positions together with the council, an open discussion of the best points of each is held.
8. Each team member presents his or her personal view in writing (formed as a result of the debates and discussion).
9. The council considers the written responses and decides on a course of action.

••••PROPOSE A SOLUTION

SOLUTION SUMMARY

Before proceeding to the reflection section of this chapter, write a brief summary of your team's solution here:

Our team defined the "real" problem here as _____

_____

_____

_____

_____

_____

_____

_____

_____

The key features of our solution were _____

_____

_____

_____

_____

_____

_____

_____

My personal view of the problem and solution is _____

_____

_____

_____

_____

_____

_____

_____

TIME FOR REFLECTION

This PBL experience gave you the opportunity to explore how a theory of learning might have an impact on schools. In reflecting on the issues raised, this section examines the following topics: constructivism in the schools, how schools make decisions about innovative practices, the role and use of student evaluations, whether unity in teaching leads to a negative uniformity, and how schools change. The last section focuses on the constructive controversy as a learning/teaching technique.

What Is Constructivism?

In her essay to answer that question, Constance Kamii (1991) reminds us that constructivism is really a theory about *learning*, not teaching. She elaborates on three kinds of knowledge that we all acquire: physical (which amounts to the empirical or sense observations we make), social (which are agreed-upon issues, such as the designation of a certain season of the year as "Spring") and logico-mathematical (which consists of the web of relationships a learner constructs inside her or his head). This last form of knowledge is how we make sense of the world, how we make meaning. And this last sort of knowledge cannot be delivered to students, Kamii says, though the actions of teachers can either encourage or block the construction of such knowledge. As Eric Jensen puts it, "Ultimately, everyone has to make his or her own meaning out of things" (1998, p. 98).

In the writing about constructivism, one generally finds some common features. These features include the following: students control some of the learning focus and activities, teacher-centered strategies such as lectures are minimized, multiple ways of knowing (through arts, for example) are honored, learning activities and assessments are often rooted in authentic situations, and much learning occurs in groups. These elements are extrapolated from our understanding of cognitive psychology. In other words, these features of practice are logical outgrowths of a view of learning found in cognitive psychology.

Some writers remind us that there really is no such thing as a "constructivist technique," though various techniques can be used in a constructivist manner (Howe & Berv, 2000). A fair question for teachers to raise is this: Are the logical applications of cognitive psychology supported in the actual research conducted in schools? Do we see evidence that students learn more from teachers using constructivist ideas? Some work in this area has revealed that students using "constructivist" methods do better than "traditional" classes in terms of achievement (Lord, 1997, 1999). The videotape studies connected with the Third International Mathematics Science Study (TIMSS) revealed that high-achieving classes in Japan, for example, were using the constructivist techniques recommended by the National Council of Teachers of Mathematics (U.S. Department of Education, 1999), whereas U.S. classrooms were not.

Of course, the controversy about what counts as constructivism suggests teachers have a great deal of flexibility in using so-called constructivist techniques. An appropriate line of inquiry might be to compare your own personal beliefs about learning with what the "constructivists" claim. See where your beliefs match or depart from the constructivist approach. Then consider how your teaching practices can be consistent with what you believe to be the central principles of how people learn. But notice something powerful here: As soon as you begin to focus on the learning as opposed to your actions as a teacher, you will find tremendous growth possibilities for your students.

A final thought about this focus on learning. Seymour Sarason presented a powerful goal for our educational systems when he wrote what he would want for graduates of our schools: "I would want all children to have at least the same level and quality of curiosity and motivation to learn and explore that they had when they began schooling" (1998, p. 69). We do well to consider how our teaching keeps such curiosity alive.

Decision Making in Schools

This problem began with the proclamation of a council of leaders, which was part of a whole school-reform package instituted by the principal to help this struggling school. How realistic is such a decision-making process?

In recent years, there has been a greater and greater emphasis placed on what is sometimes called site-based decision making (SBDM) or site-based management. Some states and/or districts require this to take place. The form of SBDM varies, though generally it involves more than a council of chairs. Generally, community members and other staff members (such as a secretary or cafeteria worker) are also involved in what is sometimes called a site council. Some theorists have claimed that there is no evidence that such decision making has any effect on students (Johnston, 1995; Midgley & Wood, 1993; Weiss, 1993), especially if the focus is on *who* decides rather than *what* is decided. Other theorists argue that site-based decision making, done well, is the best avenue for reform (Lange, 1993). If such councils have authority and are careful to communicate with their constituencies, they can succeed (Guskey & Peterson, 1995–1996; Wohlstetter, 1995). However, there are always risks involved with the new roles and responsibilities in teachers making decisions that they may not be accustomed to making (David, 1995–1996).

In the context of this problem, how effective was the site-based decision making? The Council of Chairs seemed to be an integral part of the reform of Alton High School, and this is clearly consistent with the best hopes for SBDM. At the same time, it is apparent that the council alienated a number of teachers and community members by its action. Did it overstep reasonable boundaries in calling for a change in the dominant model of teaching at the school? Or, as some would argue, was it necessary for the council to call for a radical change to be made immediately rather than hope that gradual, incremental change might work? In essence, educators need to decide if they want such councils to make decisions with the potential to alter practices, policies, and environments radically, even if this is contentious, or if such councils are to be symbolic means of legitimizing others' decisions.

You may find yourself, even early in your career, in a position to participate in a school's decision-making body, such as a site council. In this capacity, perhaps more than in any other role, you are called on to see the school from the perspective of the students and to think in terms of the "big picture." Teachers grow accustomed to concerning themselves with their own classrooms, subject areas, or departments, but participating on a site council calls on teachers to think differently. What does the whole school experience look like from a student's perspective? What are the patterns of learning, and how do they all fit together into some meaningful experience for these young adults? As a participant in site-based decision making, you may be able to make real improvements to the students' experience, but only if you step outside your subject-expert role.

Related to the issue of decision making and school change, this PBL experience gave you a glimpse of a school leader's role. Mr. Busch appears to be a respected, change-oriented leader. He certainly could not be accused of being an old-school, stuck leader. At the same time, he also appears to have shifted positions or backed off of his support. What might explain this? What sorts of pressures do school leaders face that cause them to have to reverse themselves? We can only speculate, but some of the forces that might have influenced this school leader include the pressure of the newspaper editorial, concerns from the school district offices, protests made by the teachers' association, and even the reactions of respected faculty members. Mr. Busch may have found himself in the position of advocating for changes, but not considering the implications of his advocacy carefully enough. Does his backing down on the decision indicate weakness as a leader or humility?

Unity or Uniformity?

Another issue raised by this problem goes beyond the circumstances of how the decision about instruction was made. Instead, our focus shifts to the decision itself, and the implications of a whole school moving in one direction for instruction. How sound is it for a school to adopt a central theme or approach to pedagogy? For example, should a school be known as a "cooperative learning" school, where all teachers use a form of cooperative learning daily? And what about those teachers who have seen successes without using cooperative learning or arts-based education or whatever technique is advocated?

We do know that a characteristic of productive schools is that there is a unified vision for learning (Lockwood, 1996) and an understanding of the "big picture" for the school as a whole (Felner, Kasak, Mulhall, & Flowers, 1997), though some theorists, such as Michael Fullan, see vision as overrated (1996).

So, should a school adopt a single vision? As you visit schools and converse with your colleagues, you might ask whether the school itself has a central vision. If so, what is the role of this vision in the school's success? One account of a series of public high schools that experienced major turn-arounds spoke of how school personnel came together to support central visions (Gest, 2000), suggesting that this may be very important. Of course, this vision may or may not address the instructional techniques employed by teachers.

That said, it is well worth remembering that the patterns of pedagogy teachers hold on to may be nothing more than the traditions they are accustomed to. Seymour Sarason observes that "Teachers teach the way they have been taught to teach, but what they have been taught produces the polar opposite of a context for productive learning" (1998, p. 76). Thus, to get teachers to consider alternatives to the traditional patterns of teaching is potentially revolutionary.

It may be that the issue of instructional methods is only a tiny portion of the problem or solution. The high schools cited above (Gest, 2000) also looked at such factors as the school size, expectations, and parental involvement. Perhaps the unity that promises healthy reforms for schools is a unity of school culture, with a diversity of techniques. In her comments about how to move forward in school reform, Deborah Meier writes, "The next phase will do well not to ignore the lessons learned: it's easier to design a new school culture than to change an existing one. And it's the whole school culture—not this or that program—that stands in the way of learning" (1995, p. 372).

Student Evaluations?

Part of the information provided with this problem was a summary of the general performance of each department as measured by student evaluations. Your group may have found this information unnecessary for the problem, or you may have decided this information was crucial in determining whether a change ought to be made. Either way, the presence of the data reminds us that student evaluations are one important means for teachers to receive feedback about their performance. What role should such evaluations take in deciding on the effectiveness of teachers and teaching methods?

At first glance, it seems logical that such evaluations ought to have significant impact. After all, who is in a better position to understand a teacher's effectiveness than the ones who are supposed to learn? Who can determine the power of a teaching technique better than the learner can? Indeed, teachers do well to seek feedback from their students, though this feedback can come from a variety of sources beyond evaluations (e.g., student performance on tests, student projects, and informal observations).

Glasser (1993) argues that students should be involved in evaluating their own work, and he maintains that quality work always feels good, clearly implying the important role of students in assessing the feel of their work. Some cautions may be in order, though, as we consider the role of evaluations. In his account of the pedagogy of poverty, Haberman (1991) explains that students will often resist teaching strategies that call on them to think and make decisions; often students prefer the "dumbed-down" version of instruction that calls on them to complete worksheets. In fact, other researchers have pointed out that teachers and students come to implicit agreements that the teachers will not push the students too hard in exchange for student compliance and positive evaluations (McNeil, 1986; Powell, Farrar, & Cohen, 1985), and that student evaluations are often associated with grade inflation (Edwards, 2000; Haynes & Hunt, 2000). Obviously, this is not always the case. Sometimes students capably identify good or bad instruction (Stroh, 1991). The point is that information from student evaluations must be carefully examined. Numerous factors influence how students view the effectiveness of a given teaching model (such as their own comfort level, their relationship with the instructor, and their performance on assessments). As professionals committed to improving practice, teachers do well to see beyond the numbers such evaluations produce.

School Change

The problem presented here arises from an energetic principal's attempt to change a school. Teachers at all levels, particularly beginning teachers, wonder about their roles in changing schools. If the continuum for change attitudes ranges from "If it ain't broke, don't fix it!" to the Japanese notion of *kaizen* (continuous improvement), some would say it seems sensible for teachers new to a school to stay near the former end. After all, you've just arrived on campus. Do you want to greet your new colleagues with this message: "Hi. I'm glad to be here. Now let's fix this mess!"?

On the other hand, even if you had a great experience in school, isn't there a nagging sense that things could be better? Couldn't we do more to make students learn and to make this place of learning more inviting and effective? That's why, paradoxically, even though schools are very similar to what they were like generations ago, there is always pressure to make changes in the way schools are.

Developing a perspective on change may be an important feature of your sense of professionalism. One doesn't have to be negative or critical to be a change agent. In fact, it is often the negative staff members who block change with cynicism and inaction. It does help, however, to be purposeful about change. That is, your job is not to try out every new idea that passes through the popular and educational literature. In contrast, your job is to have a learning disposition (Darling-Hammond, 1998; Senge, 1990) and a commitment to making the whole school—not just your little piece of it— a great place to work and learn. Fullan and Hargreaves (1991) argue that there is "an overwhelming need for greater involvement of teachers in educational reform outside as well as inside their own classrooms, in curriculum development and in the improvement of their schools" (p. 15). The provocative title of their book, *What's Worth Fighting For? Working Together for Your School,* suggests that teachers can be active participants in school change, not victims of the way things have always been. In another book, Fullan (1991) points out the importance of making personal meaning of potential changes, again emphasizing that teachers can do something. While you would be wise not to enter a new school as a crusader, recognizing your own obligation to improve the schools is a powerful aspect of becoming a professional.

The Constructive Controversy Process

The principal in this PBL experience made something of a unique proposal. He recommended that teachers use a teaching method (the constructive controversy) to address a real problem. In a sense, this is a reversal of the way most people, including teachers, view school: real life can actually gain something from school techniques. The method in question has been used in the business world as a way to assist in making good decisions (Johnson & Johnson, 1994), but it still would probably surprise most teachers to have a teaching technique proposed to them as a means to solve a problem.

There is a sort of radical endorsement of an instructional method when the learners apply it beyond the confines of the classroom. When teachers apply the principles of effective problem solving to their interactions over real problems, it says that the principles really work. So, Mr. Busch's recommendation of the constructive controversy served to demonstrate that he believed it was more than an exercise. What did you learn from the process? Were you able to separate your personal beliefs and opinions from the task of advocating for a particular position? How does such a separation allow you to develop a new perspective on the issue? Could you use the technique in your classroom and beyond?

DISCUSSION QUESTIONS

1. What elements of "constructivist" teaching and learning did you see as appealing to you as an instructor? How would you implement these? Are there elements of constructivism that you see as negative from the perspective of a classroom teacher? What limitations do you perceive?

2. What may be some potential advantages to students of a school with a consistent and united approach to instruction? What might be the potential losses to students in that situation? Is a vision important to a school as opposed to a teacher?

3. What is the new teacher's role in the issue of school change? How do you balance the competing pressures to conform and to be a change agent?

4. Having been at the sending end of student evaluations for some time, how do you view the practice as a means of improving instruction? Are there ways that teachers can guide students to write more effective and relevant evaluations? What would you want to learn from your students? Are there other sorts of information the school should seek to use for judging the students' experience?

5. What do you see as the potential benefits and limitations of site-based decision-making? Would you want to participate on such a group? Why or why not?

6. Considering the PBL process, what did you learn about collaborating with colleagues?

FURTHER READING

Brooks, J. G., & Brooks, M. G. (1999). *In search of understanding: The case for constructivist classrooms.* (2nd ed.). Alexandria, VA: Association for Supervision and Curriculum Development. Brooks and Brooks provide a three-part structure to their "case." First, they describe why schools should change, based primarily on how children learn. Second, they lay out key principles of constructivism with chapters on each principle. Finally, they address what needs to be done to make the changes. Chapter 9 is particularly interesting because it provides a dozen suggestions about what constructivist teachers do.

Educational Leadership, 57(3), November 1999. "The Constructivist Classroom." This issue of the journal is devoted to constructivism in education. In addition to Perkins's clarification of versions of constructivism, there are articles about constructivism in general, constructivism in literature, PBL, mathematics, art, science, brain-based learning, interdisciplinary connections, and research in constructivism.

Perkins, D. (1998). What is understanding? In M. S. Wiske (Ed.), *Teaching for understanding: Linking research with practice* (pp. 39–57). San Francisco: Jossey-Bass.

Given that much of constructivism is devoted to enhancing our students' understanding, it is, perhaps, important to get some agreement on what it means to understand. If you were to ask five different science teachers, for example, what it means to understand the concept of "ecosystem," you could easily get five different answers. Here is where Perkins is helpful. His essay, in a book about a framework called Teaching for Understanding (TfU), brings some clarity to what it means to understand. The short version of understanding is that it is the ability to "to think and act flexibly with what one knows" (p. 40). He makes a powerful distinction between representational understanding, which involves building a mental model, and performance understanding, which involves activity beyond rote memorization. Performance understanding ought to be our goal, he argues, and it is "always something of a stretch" (p. 42). I think the idea of stretching ourselves and our students is inspiring.

Sprague, D., & Dede, C. (2000). If I teach this way, am I doing my job? Constructivism in the classroom. *ISTE Journal, 27*(1). Retrieved from www.iste.org/L&L/27/1/index.html

This brief article provides helpful scenarios to contrast what a constructivist classroom might look like compared to a traditional classroom. The authors also raise the issue of how an administrator might misunderstand what is going on in a constructivist classroom. Finally, the authors portray the role of technology for both students and teachers engaged in a constructivist learning experience.

Tomlinson, C. A. (1999). *The differentiated classroom: Responding to the needs of all learners.* Alexandria, VA: Association for Supervision and Curriculum Development.

For anyone considering widespread changes in the way instruction looks in a school, Tomlinson's book offers some helpful guidance. Her overall theme is that teachers should create learning environments and experiences that help students grow and succeed. With a focus on differentiating, she provides many examples of different ways of teaching, ranging from stations and centers to PBL to investigations. She gives ideas about how to make change happen in a school, and offers ways of accommodating the real pressures on teachers while making such change. One important point she makes is the value of situating change in the collaboration of teachers rather than in independent work.

Woolfolk, A. E. (1998). *Educational psychology* (7th ed.). Boston: Allyn & Bacon. See especially pp. 277–281 and 346–367.

Woolfolk provides a good overview of the range of ideas about teaching that fit in the "constructivist" perspective. She notes differences, such as the distinction between exogenous, endogenous, and dialectical constructivists, and she gives examples of the kinds of teaching strategies she considers to be constructivist. In addition, she has sections on constructivism in reading, writing, mathematics and science.

WEB SITES

The Association for Supervision and Curriculum Development (ASCD)
webserver2.ascd.org/tutorials/tutorial2.cfm?ID=27&TITLE=Constructivism
A tutorial on constructivism.

School Improvement in Maryland
www.mdk12.org/practices/good_instruction/constructivism.html
This site presents a different, more graphic exploration.

REFERENCES

Brooks, J. G., & Brooks, M. G. (1999). *In search of understanding: The case for constructivist classrooms* (2nd ed.). Alexandria, VA: Association for Supervision and Curriculum Development.

Brooks, M. G., & Brooks, J. G. (1999). The courage to be constructivist. *Educational Leadership, 57*(3), 18–24.

Darling-Hammond, L. (1998). Teacher learning that supports student learning. *Educational Leadership, 55*(5), 6–11.

David, J. L. (1995–1996). The who, what and why of site-based management. *Educational Leadership, 53*(4), 4–9.

Edwards, C. H. (2000). Grade inflation: The effects on educational quality and personal well being. *Education, 120*(3), 538–546.

Felner, R. D., Kasak, D., Mulhall, P., & Flowers, N. (1997). The project on high performance learning communities: Applying the land-grant model to school reform. *Phi Delta Kappan, 78*(7), 520–527.

Fullan, M. (1996). Professional culture and educational change. *School Psychology Review, 25*(4), 496–500.

Fullan, M. G. (1991). *The new meaning of educational change* (2nd ed.). New York: Teachers College Press.

Fullan, M. G., & Hargreaves, A. (1991). *What's worth fighting for? Working together for your school.* Andover, MA: Regional Laboratory for Educational Improvement of the Northeast and Islands.

Gest, T. (2000, October 9). Fixing your school. *U.S. News & World Report, 129,* 65–73.

Glasser, W. (1993). *The quality school teacher: A companion volume to The Quality School.* New York: Harper Collins.

Goodlad, J. I. (1984). *A place called school: Prospects for the future.* New York: McGraw-Hill.

Guskey, T. R., & Peterson, K. D. (1995–96). The road to classroom change. *Educational Leadership, 53*(4), 10–14.

Haberman, M. (1991). The pedagogy of poverty vs. good teaching. *Phi Delta Kappan, 73*(4), 290–294.

Haynes, D. C., & Hunt, H. (2000). Using teaching evaluations as a measurement of consumer satisfaction. *Consumer Interests Annual, 46,* 134–139.

Howe, K. R., & Berv, J. (2000). Constructing constructivism, epistemological and pedagogical. In D. C. Phillips (Ed.), *Constructivism in education: Opinions and second opinions on controversial issues* (Vol. 1, pp. 19–40). Ninety-ninth yearbook of the National Society for the Study of Education. Chicago, IL: University of Chicago.

Jensen, E. (1998). *Teaching with the brain in mind.* Alexandria, VA: Association for Supervision and Curriculum Development.

Johnson, D. W., & Johnson, F. P. (1994). *Joining together: Group theory and group skills* (5th ed.). Boston: Allyn & Bacon.

Johnston, S. (1995). Curriculum decision making at the school level: Is it just a case of teachers learning to act like administrators? *Journal of Curriculum and Supervision, 10*(2), 136–154.

Kamii, C. (1991). What is constructivism? In C. Kamii, M. Manning, & G. Manning (Eds.), *Early literacy: A constructivist foundation for whole language* (pp. 17–29). Washington, DC: National Education Association.

Lange, J. T. (1993). Site-based, shared decision making: A resource for restructuring. *NASSP Bulletin, 76*(549), 98–107.

Lockwood, A. T. (1996). Preliminary characteristics of productive schools. *New leaders for tomorrow's schools, Fall.* Retrieved from www.ncrel.org/cscd/pubs/lead31/31prdlst.htm

Lord, T. R. (1997). A comparison between traditional and constructivist teaching in college biology. *Innovative Higher Education, 21*(3), 197–216.

Lord, T. R. (1999). A comparison between traditional and constructivist teaching in environmental science. *Journal of Environmental Education, 30*(3), 22–27.

McNeil, L. M. (1986). *Contradictions of control: School structure and school knowledge.* London: Routledge & Kegan Paul.

Meier, D. (1995). How our schools could be. *Phi Delta Kappan, 76*(5), 369–373.

Midgley, C., & Wood, S. (1993). Beyond site-based management: Empowering teachers to reform schools. *Phi Delta Kappan, 75*(3), 245–252.

Perkins, D. (1999). The many faces of constructivism. *Educational Leadership, 57*(3), 6–11.

Phillips, D. C. (2000). An opinionated account of the constructivist landscape. In D. C. Phillips (Ed.), *Constructivism in education: Opinions and second opinions on controversial issues* (Vol. 1, pp. 1–16). Ninety-ninth yearbook of the National Society for the Study of Education. Chicago, IL: University of Chicago.

Powell, A. G., Farrar, E., & Cohen, D. (1985). *The shopping mall high school: Winners and losers in the educational marketplace.* Boston: Houghton Mifflin.

Sarason, S. B. (1998). *Political leadership and educational failure.* San Francisco: Jossey-Bass.

Senge, P. M. (1990). *The fifth discipline: The art and practice of the learning organization.* New York: Doubleday.

Sprague, D., & Dede, C. (2000). If I teach this way, am I doing my job? Constructivism in the classroom. *ISTE Journal, 27*(1).

Stroh, L. (1991). High school student evaluation of student teachers: How do they compare with professionals. *Illinois School Research and Development, 27*(2), 81–92.

Tomlinson, C. A. (1999). *The differentiated classroom: Responding to the needs of all learners.* Alexandria, VA: Association for Supervision and Curriculum Development.

U.S. Department of Education. (1999). *National Center for Education Statistics, Third International Mathematics and Science Study, Videotape Classroom Study, 1994–95.* Retrieved from http://nces.ed.gov/pubs99/timssvid/index.html

Weiss, C. H. (1993). Shared decision making about what? A comparison of schools with and without teacher participation. *Teachers College Record, 95*(1), 69–92.

Wohlstetter, P. (1995). Getting school-based management right: What works and what doesn't? *Phi Delta Kappan, 77*(1), 22–26.

Woolfolk, A. E. (1998). *Educational psychology* (7th ed.). Boston: Allyn & Bacon.

CHAPTER TWELVE

REFLECTING ON THE PLACE OF PROBLEM-BASED LEARNING

At this point you've worked through a number—perhaps a great number—of PBL experiences. You have been forced to take on new roles, to perceive the occupational world of teaching from a host of new perspectives, and to make recommendations about issues that you may not have even realized were a part of the teacher's work. If the experience has helped you to see that the teacher's work goes beyond preparing lessons, lecturing, and giving tests, then it's been a good addition to your career. Given this base of experience, the challenge now is to incorporate what you have learned into a framework that assists you in becoming successful in the multi-faceted role of a secondary teacher. In the next chapter you will have the opportunity to work through a process to help you design PBL experiences for your future students. This chapter will provide some guided reflection to help you make sense of your experience.

One caution. I realize that you may not have worked through each of the problems here. When I refer to a particular problem as an example, my intention is to draw on the reader's experience. It might be helpful for you to review the types of problems that have been featured in this text (Figure 12.1).

The selection of problems in the text was designed to expose you to the wide variety of issues you might face as a teacher. Of course, you will face more types of problems than these, and you'll face problems that are similar to these, but which will send you in completely different directions for a solution, based on the community and school where you work. Thus, reflection is designed to help you use this experience to help in the face of the certainty of new problems.

This chapter is organized around several questions. First, what can you as a learner transfer from your experience with PBL? Second, what does your experience in PBL tell you about yourself as a problem-solver and what does this mean for you as a self-directed learner? Third, what have you learned about working with your peers? What do you take away from your experience related to the specific issues that have provided the focus of the problems? And finally, how can you shift your thinking from the perspective of a student to that of a teacher?

FIGURE 12.1   Summary of Problems Presented in Part II

CHAPTER	TITLE	BRIEF SUMMARY
3 (pp. 28–45)	What Should We Do about Andy?	A child study team cannot come to agreement about what is best for a middle-school student's IEP.
4 (pp. 46–64)	Whose Discipline Problem Is This?	A principal at a combined middle school and high school demands that teachers adopt a uniform policy/procedure for classroom management.
5 (pp. 65–83)	Change This Grade!	A high-school athlete is denied the opportunity to participate in basketball due to his failing English grade; a teacher committee must rule on his grade appeal.
6 (pp. 84–100)	An Afrocentric Curriculum?	An ad hoc parent committee demands that the high school curriculum be altered to serve the neglected African-American students in the school.
7 (pp. 101–119)	To Team or Not to Team?	Consultants must help a school staff decide whether to implement the recommendations from a national commission to have team teaching in their school.
8 (pp. 120–141)	Math Makes Tracks	A middle school committee must respond to charges that the elimination of honors math sections is merely an example of political correctness interfering with best practice.
9 (pp. 142–161)	Raise Those Scores!	A superintendent calls for schools to institute a "test-prep" program in order to enhance the schools' performance on the state standardized test.
10 (pp. 162–182)	Service Learning Beats Doing Homework	A newly-elected school board member challenges a popular high school service learning program, and a task force examines what to do about this recommendation.
11 (pp. 183–201)	Constructivist Learning on Trial	Members of the high school faculty question the mandate to transform their class practices into a "constructivist" model.

THE TRANSFER ISSUE

One question that ought to be addressed by all teachers arises from what the educational psychologists term "transfer." Think of it this way. When you learn a particular skill, are you able to apply it in a situation that is similar to the learning situation? If so, then you have "transferred" the skill. For example, you learn the skill of estimating a solution through a series of math activities. Later, in solving a different kind of math problem, you draw on the estimating skill to come to a solution. That's transfer. It would be even more exciting if that estimating skill surfaced when you were dealing with an area other than math, such as purchasing materials for the creation of a theatrical set. Woolfolk (1998), citing Salomon and Perkins, calls this "low-road" transfer, which she says involves practicing a skill so often that it becomes automatic. "High-road" transfer, in contrast, is when you apply abstract knowledge to a new situation. Woolfolk's example is the application of what you learn in an anatomy class to a drawing class. When you hear someone arguing that lessons learned in World War I have a message for us in our global politics, you are seeing a conscious effort at transfer.

There is some controversy over how and whether transfer works, though that controversy is beyond the scope of our examination (it suggests a new PBL focus!). In short, most people agree that the closer the new situation is to the learned situation, the more likely transfer will occur. But not always. I recall a situation in a school where I was an English teacher. The department had just finished working on creating some learning modules for our students. One of the modules was on "creative problem solving," where we designed an experience to teach the process to our students. A key element of that process was to defer the solving of problems until the students had generated a variety of potential solutions to evaluate. We emphasized over and over again with the students that even if that first solution proves to be the best, it is crucial to generate a pool of possibilities so that creative ideas are not neglected. Even while we were taking our students through the process, a problem arose for the department related to resources. As one of the novices in the department, I was surprised and a little horrified to watch our group jump on the first solution presented without even pausing to consider what some other possibilities might be. This isn't a case of a lazy student—*we were teaching this stuff, and still we could ignore it.* That's anecdotal evidence, I know, but not atypical. It suggests to me that all of us need to consider how we can enhance transfer.

Specifically, from your experience in PBL, the question of transfer asks what you will take with you from your work. Will it be specific content knowledge, such as learning the definition of an IEP from Andy's case or learning how to communicate your grading system effectively from the grade appeal problem? Will it be cognitive practices, such as engaging in perspective-taking in order to identify the "real" problem, a practice that should have been helpful in deciding whether or not to use teams at a high school? Will it be presentation skills, useful in persuading audiences of your view? Will it be skills of collaboration, such as drawing out a quiet, but crucial, group member or resolving conflict without damaging a person's self-esteem? All these are examples of potential areas where you might transfer your learning to new situations. The likelihood of your transferring what you learn is increased if you consciously consider how you might do so. In a sense, this chapter is a model for you. I'm attempting to help you maximize the chances of transfer, just as you will one day want to maximize such chances for your own students.

And there is cause for a cautionary note here. Experience can lead you to insight, but it can also lead you to erect limitations. Far too often, a student teacher's experience with only one mentor teacher leads that future teacher to view the world in a very restricted manner. It's not uncommon for a student teacher to dismiss a wealth of information and techniques because one "real-world" experience doesn't match what he or she was told. In a similar manner, your PBL experience should not be used to impose limitations on yourself. You want to be careful that you don't assume too much from your experience with PBL in the situations you face later. For example, your team may have reached a decision to implement an Afrocentric curriculum for Layton, California, based on the evidence you discovered. That doesn't mean that every similar situation would call for the same solution. Having gone through one grade appeal through PBL should sensitize you to the various issues; it should not persuade you that every grade appeal must be resolved exactly as your team decided in this case, nor should it persuade you that anyone who uses multiple intelligences in teaching is misguided or unprofessional. A decision about school-to-work in the Ellington Township example is not the final word on school-to-work. Transferring what you have learned in these complex situations always demands that you exercise professional judgment, which should have been stimulated and encouraged through the process of addressing the problems.

HOW DO I SOLVE PROBLEMS?

A second area for contemplation is the area of problem solving. What did you learn about yourself as a problem solver through your PBL experience?

In previous work with students new to PBL, I've found some surprising things. Some students have discovered, for example, that they actually enjoy research. Given an authentic context for discovering information rather than simply acquiring facts without a meaningful reason, they have learned that this activity motivates and interests them. Research often has a bad reputation with students and—surprisingly—with teachers. Too often we hear comments such as "you can make the research say anything you want" from teachers. By divorcing their practice from a scientific basis, they become vulnerable to criticism that what they do is arbitrary and ultimately indefensible. For the future teacher to discover a value to research is a powerful lesson in one part of the problem-solving process.

Consider what you might have learned about your own problem-solving tendencies. How do you respond to the ill-structured and complex nature of PBL experiences? Does it bother you that the details are "messy," with extra facts but never enough information? Some students have a definite preference for very clear limitations on the problems and very clear expectations about the solutions. In fact, most problems you will face as a teacher will be similarly complex and messy. There might be a clear "due date" (deadline), but exactly what constitutes an ideal solution will likely be more complicated than "write 500 words explaining why your major needs technology." So, if you are a problem solver who is made uncomfortable by the mess, what should you do? Part of the response involves career guidance. The world of teaching is messy and uncertain, and if this generates discomfort for you, you may want to consider seriously whether teaching is a good fit for you. Should you put yourself in a situation that calls for traits that you don't possess? Even if you love your subject and you can communicate it well to others, the realities of teaching suggest that you need a high degree of tolerance for uncertainty. That is not to say that you cannot develop a higher level of comfort with uncertainty. I indicated in Chapter 2 that medical students who encountered PBL as a learning method often went through an extensive period of "grieving" about this change in their lives. But such a change was important for them, given the nature of medical practice they were hoping to engage in (which is far different from the conditions of a traditional educational system). These students continued to practice PBL, continued to work together to overcome their discomfort. If you found the messiness of PBL to be difficult, you may need to continue more practice with such frameworks. You may also want to discuss with your professors and mentors ways of dealing with the uncertainties of the teaching profession.

Consider, also, where your particular strengths and weaknesses were in the problem-solving process. Were you a leader for the group's attempts to identify the problem? Did you resist looking at the problem from different perspectives? Were you able to encourage divergent viewpoints in generating solutions, or were you frustrated by those who seemed to distract the group from a clear focus? Were you one who encouraged mixing of ideas and discussion of both the nature of the problem and the possibilities of solution and presentation? Were you one who wanted to get to solutions quickly and directly? Did you advocate a strict division of labor or did you see the mixing of roles as worthwhile?

These questions may seem to sit out there without any practical value, but the reality is that you need to consider them for two basic reasons. First, as a member of the community of professionals in schools, you will find yourself involved in problem solving. Patterns you see from your work in PBL are likely to intensify in your professional practice, particularly since it is unlikely anyone will ask you to reflect on your problem-solving practices with detachment. Are you pleased with yourself as a problem-solver? The reality you will encounter in your occupation is that there will be people who not only don't contribute to solving problems, but who actually block the problem-solving efforts of others. While there is no magic pill you can take to be a great problem solver, your awareness of your own tendencies, abilities, and limitations in this area can help you become better.

Second, you will probably want to teach your own students to be problem solvers. Your awareness both of the general process and your own application of that process will help you to be a more effective teacher. For example, it is unlikely you will convince your own students to consider multiple perspectives if you don't believe—and practice—this principle yourself.

SELF-DIRECTED LEARNERS?

One of the claims of research about PBL is that it encourages people to become self-directed learners (or SDLs). For example, Blumberg's (2000) review of the (limited) research literature indicates that medical students using PBL actively use libraries, utilize study strategies that enhance deep understanding, and see themselves as on a path to continuously improve their SDL skills. As professional educators, you should find the possibility of creating self-directed learners to be a promising idea.

Even if your focus right now is not on what kind of learners you turn out, it's worth your time to consider how you can make your own growth a priority throughout your career. As knowledge workers, we need to keep the ideal of continuing stimulation and growth alive. While the notion of "teacher burnout" is a complex issue in our system, at least a small part of the problem rests with teachers who do not choose to make learning a constant feature of their professional lives.

In her research on what makes effective elementary teachers of mathematics, Ma (1999) compared Chinese and American teachers. Ironically, though the Chinese teachers had far less formal education (and math courses, specifically) than their American counterparts, the Chinese teachers developed a deeper understanding of the math concepts they were teaching. Part of the explanation for this paradox, Ma concludes, rests with the fact that the Chinese teachers saw themselves as active learners, and in addition to careful study, these teachers spent time working with their colleagues to build understanding.

To put it at a personal level, do you see yourself as a self-directed learner? Does the pursuit of understanding motivate you? Is your curiosity alive? Or, in contrast, do you gather information for practical purposes only? Once the assignment is completed, has the curiosity subsided?

Problem-based learning is intended to assist you in becoming more self-directed in your learning, but it is only an environment to encourage such growth. You are the one who must make the decision to embrace lifelong learning. You alone can decide that as a professional educator, you will continue to inquire into what is best practice. Unlike members of most other professions, teachers tend not to read the professional journals in their fields. Far too many teachers end their own education with the last class in their college preparation—and even the courses they are required to take for re-certification tend to be viewed as hoops to jump through. By developing a self-image as a self-directed, lifelong learner, you can provide yourself with the limitless stimulation of a progressing career, and you can do much to enhance the credibility of the profession. There's also something infectious about a person who is passionate about learning—an important role model for the students who come to us.

WORKING TOGETHER—DOES IT WORK IN SCHOOLS?

Among the most thoroughly researched techniques in education, cooperative learning has become well established in the schools. As you may have learned in your professional education, cooperative learning is more than putting kids into groups where they do the same things they used to do individually. Cooperative learning involves changing the environment of the classroom, the goal and reward structure for the students, the structure of tasks, and even the assessment of student work. In light of problem-based learning, are such changes worth making? Does this working together work in schools?

If you've been through a relatively faithful version of PBL, you've had some significant experiences in working with groups. And if you're like most people, you've had a range of quality in your experience. It's likely that you've encountered someone who was *not* cooperative, who actively resisted the spirit of PBL and the efforts of your instructor and classmates to make the groups work. You've probably met a student who talked too much, another who knew too much, and another who had absolutely nothing to say. You may have even met someone who taught you a great deal.

Congratulations. You've met another slice of reality. In fact, in almost any walk of life, there are no perfect groups. Employers frequently complain that their new workers can be trained to do the technical aspects of their work, but that the new workers lack the ability to get along with co-workers. In too many cases, students in K–12 schools have learned what Haberman (1997) calls an ideology of nonwork, where the learners focus on excuses, developing a victim mentality, and living at a low level of expectations. Among other problems, students too often fail to see that they can play an important role in performing tasks as a group.

I have been surprised to find how often students in higher education have similar problems. Indeed, many post-secondary students make it through their educational experiences without any serious need to collaborate with peers. This was a concern among medical educators, and a key reason for the development of PBL in the professional education of physicians. Teachers, like doctors, find themselves frequently in need of collaboration in their working worlds. Even though a classroom may be a private and isolated work world (Lortie, 1975), the school world beyond the classroom door calls for all sorts of collaboration.

And as any teacher could tell you, virtually all the problems you might encounter as a member of a group in college will await you in your future job. There will be people who are late to group meetings, people who don't do their assigned tasks, people who will try to pull rank, people who will make personal attacks. You may find yourself assigned to a teaching team where your colleagues have little training in effective ways of working as a unified group (Kain, 1998). A key difference will be that there is no threat of a grade to pull your groups into focus and no professor with a clear line of authority. You will need to be an effective group member, not only in attending to your own behavior, but also in steering your groups to better performance.

So what have you learned about yourself as a member of a group? Consider both your actions and your colleagues' actions in the PBL experiences you have encountered. Perhaps you recall some of the roles of group members (Chapter 2). Did you find it helpful to establish formal roles? That is, when someone was assigned to be the group leader, did leadership emerge more effectively than when no one was assigned this task? How did you provide leadership for your groups? How did you handle conflict in your groups? Were you able to discuss this openly, or did your groups develop a means of addressing conflict that relied on denial? Were you and your peers consistent in addressing problems directly, or did you find yourself gossiping about other group members as a third party?

These questions are not merely an exercise for your time as a student. The career path of a teacher will put you in a place where effective group skills are central, and flashing a set of *A*'s from your education courses is no substitute for being a positive contributor to the collaborative environment of an institution (Little, 1982). As you reflect on your experience, consider what strengths you can build on and what areas of weaknesses you might have to address. The prompts in Figure 12.2 might help you in this reflection.

FIGURE 12.2   Prompts for Reflection on Group Behavior

1. I was most comfortable in group situations when I took the role of _____

2. I found the most difficult interactions with my peers to be when _____

3. My greatest strength as a group member appeared when I _____

4. If my group members had been fellow teachers in a school, they would probably have perceived me as _____

5. I think practicing teachers would be different from the group members I worked with in that the practicing teachers would _____

6. The area I need most to work on in order to be a more effective group member is _____

7. As an honest evaluator of my work in PBL group situations, I would summarize my performance as follows: _____

ISSUES AS VEHICLES FOR LEARNING

One difference between this book and most that you are likely to encounter in professional education is that it deals with a number of issues but brings closure to none. While you may have formed strong opinions about the issue of standardized tests, for example, your peers may have come to different conclusions—and this book doesn't arbitrate. The perspective I have tried to communicate here is that all of these issues are complex and multi-faceted and need the careful deliberation of ethically-guided and competent professionals.

What I'm hoping to have you reflect on is the idea that the particulars of the problems you have faced in this experience are of a secondary importance. Surely the particulars give you reason and context to investigate issues. However, in the long run, your decision about what to do about Andy or what school-wide management system to use or whether Darrin gets to play ball or whether every teacher should use constructivist techniques is not the crucial issue. You will face these questions in different forms throughout your career. While the strength of PBL here and elsewhere rests with the specifics that make learning seem relevant, in a sense, the least important thing of all is the specifics. What you have learned about the "issues" through your experience may not impact your practice as much as the fact that you have learned a professional way to address the issues you will face one day.

STUDENT OR TEACHER?

The transition from thinking like a student to thinking like a teacher can be uncomfortable. As a *student* facing a problem such as whether to organize a high school into interdisciplinary teams, you are likely to wonder what you need to do to get an A. You may find yourself calculating what effort you can exert without jeopardizing other course work. You may place undue emphasis on the quirks of your professor. Looking at the same problem from the perspective of a *teacher* whose every working day may be affected by the outcome is quite different. You would want to be assured not only that the organizational structure is sound for your students' sake, but also that the particulars in your building would not make your life miserable. The world looks different, quite different, from these two points.

As a student of teaching, you may come to realize that the attributes that serve you well as a student are not sufficient for success as a teacher. Your success depends, in part, on the conscious decision to adopt a teacher's perspective. You no longer look at the assessment you face in class as your pathway to a good grade; you begin to examine that assessment as the teaching tool of a colleague, which may help you to design an effective tool for your own purposes. Attending class or a group discussion is not simply a matter of earning participation points, but a matter of answering real and pressing questions for your career.

Think back over the PBL experiences you've had throughout this text. Step outside of your trench of the student earning a high mark for your transcript, and consider what the experiences have shown you about the world that teachers occupy. Each of the problems included a reflection section that was intended to prompt the sort of processing that would help you see the world from the teacher's perspective, but it may be that in the throes of solving the problems, you still were caught in the student's world. Consider your experience once again, but with a very specific lens. Here are some prompts for you to tackle alone or in cooperation with your colleagues, who are also making this dramatic shift:

The problem that revealed the most surprising part of a teacher's work was _____

_____.

The reason I was surprised was _____

_____

_____

_____.

The problem that disturbed me the most was _____.

It made me realize that teachers _____

_____

_____

_____.

I still want to question the issues raised in the _____

problem. Can it really be that teachers _____

_____

_____

_____?

The biggest change in my thinking about the work of teaching came through the

_____ problem. Prior to this, I thought that _____

_____

_____

_____.

Now I think that _____

_____

_____

_____.

These prompts are designed to help you bring together the various problems for comparison, rather than considering each in isolation. Another approach might simply be to generate a list of teacher attributes and responsibilities connected to the PBL experiences. However you approach it, your greatest profit from the PBL experiences will come as you contemplate the specifics of becoming a teacher—or becoming a better teacher. It's your career; it's your choice to develop as a professional. Take charge.

LOOKING FORWARD: WHAT'S THE PLACE OF PBL IN MY CLASSROOM?

As you close your reflection on what you have experienced through PBL, a final important question to think about is what role PBL will play in *your* classroom. Is there space for this technique in the array of tools you plan to use with your future students?

I was startled once to read this comment from one of my students, who had completed several PBL units: "I really like PBL, but I don't see how I could use this in my subject—biology." My surprise, of course, arises from the fact that sciences tend to build so much on the inquiry process embedded in PBL that the fit seems natural and effortless. Part of the problem was with this student's understanding of the nature of her subject. To complete a degree in biology without seeing the role of inquiry in the discipline is an amazing (and discouraging) feat. But I also take the student's comment as an indictment of my presentation of PBL. Somehow I had not managed to communicate to this student the value of PBL for her future students. I believe a central factor in this is that I didn't actively call on my students to connect their learning experiences with their future learners through deliberate reflection.

For that reason, the next chapter walks you through the process of building a PBL experience for your students. You will be able to use the chapter to guide the construction of a problem-based learning unit in your subject area. However, even before that step, it is valuable for you to consider what kind of classroom you want to create for your future students. The PBL classroom draws on a view of learning as student-centered, collaborative, and centered around inquiry. How does that match your developing conception of what counts for an effective learning environment?

Obviously I have a bias in this, and I believe you serve your students well to move them into greater inquiry and problem-solving. However, what you think is what counts in this matter. Have you given thought to the overall climate that you will create for your students? Have you considered the messages you will give students by the way you organize their learning for them?

And is this a matter of all or nothing—either a student-centered PBL classroom or a traditional approach? Can a teacher be eclectic in pulling together teaching techniques? Is it appropriate for you to mix various models of teaching and learning, even if some of them appear to be contradictory in spirit? (I remind you of the thinking you did on this matter when you considered "Constructivist Learning on Trial.") Can you do good lectures and guide your students through PBL experiences?

Such questions as these are important for you to think about as you build the classroom that matches your strengths, goals, and interests with the needs of your students and the communities you serve. It is appropriate as you complete or enhance your professional education to move beyond the learning of techniques and to begin to contemplate the impact on your students of the experiences you provide them.

DISCUSSION QUESTIONS

1. As a student of teaching, what are the three most important observations you have made in your work with PBL? Compare these with your colleagues' ideas. What does your experience tell you about the nature of learning and teaching?

2. What issues in the PBL experience surprised you as you think about the complexities of the teaching career? What areas of concern appear as a result of your encounter with teachers' work? How do these compare to your colleagues' areas?

3. When do you shift from your role as a learner in a teacher-preparation program or graduate school to your role as a lifelong learner? What are the implications of this for how you actually organize your learning?

4. What areas of problem solving do you see as your own strengths and weaknesses? How can you build on your experience to provide a more powerful experience for your future learners?

5. Where can you see connections between the subject or subjects you will be teaching and the PBL technique? Where can you find allies to help in the creation and implementation of inquiry teaching strategies?

6. Given the focus of most of the PBL units on "occupational" issues of teaching, which areas do you think you need further education? How might you enhance your understanding of occupational issues in the teaching career?

FURTHER READING

Levin, B. B. (Ed.). (2001). *Energizing teacher education and professional development with problem-based learning.* Alexandria, VA: Association for Supervision and Curriculum Development.
This collection addresses a number of issues that might be worthwhile as you reflect on the relationship between PBL and your future classroom. There are some sample PBL units, some principles for organization, and perhaps most useful to the new teacher, a final chapter of frequently asked questions.

Woods, Donald R. (1994). *Problem-based learning: How to gain the most from PBL.* Waterdown, ON: Author.
I recommended this book at the end of Chapter 2, but it's worth coming back to at this point. Woods does a wonderful job of focusing on the student's perspective in a PBL environment. His work was useful for preparing to learn; it is just as powerful as you reflect on what your experience has been in the PBL model.

REFERENCES

Blumberg, P. (2000). Evaluating the evidence that problem-based learners are self-directed learners: A review of the literature. In D. H. Evenson & C. E. Hmelo (Eds.), *Problem-based learning: A research perspective on learning interactions* (pp. 199–226). Mahwah, NJ: Lawrence Erlbaum Associates.

Haberman, M. (1997). Unemployment training: The ideology of nonwork learned in urban schools. *Phi Delta Kappan, 78*(7), 499–503.

Kain, D. L. (1998). *Camel-makers: Building effective teacher teams together.* Columbus, OH: National Middle School Association.

Levin, B. B. (Ed.). (2001). *Energizing teacher education and professional development with problem-based learning.* Alexandria, VA: Association for Supervision and Curriculum Development.

Little, J. W. (1982). Norms of collegiality and experimentation: Workplace conditions of school success. *American Educational Research Journal, 19*(3), 325–340.

Lortie, D. C. (1975). *Schoolteacher: A sociological study.* Chicago: University of Chicago.

Ma, L. (1999). *Knowing and teaching elementary mathematics: Teachers' understanding of fundamental mathematics in China and the United States.* Mahwah, NJ: Lawrence Erlbaum Associates.

Woods, D. R. (1994). *Problem-based learning: How to gain the most from PBL.* Waterdown, ON: Author.

Woolfolk, A. E. (1998). *Educational psychology* (7th ed.). Boston: Allyn & Bacon.

CHAPTER THIRTEEN

USING PBL IN
YOUR CLASSROOM

Now that you've experienced problem-based learning from the perspective of a learner, it is appropriate to look at the world from the other side of the desk. Indeed, all the problems found in this text have pushed you, as a learner, to see the occupational world of teaching. You have been urged to think like a teacher in a host of situations. The one role you have not been asked to assume is the one most commonly associated with teacher education: preparing lessons. This final chapter asks you to do just that. In this chapter, you will draw on your experience as a learner in PBL situations to assist you in planning PBL experiences for your students.

The process described in this chapter involves a number of steps. First, you must select a problem that is worth developing and that connects in a reasonable manner to your curriculum. Next, you develop the problem situation, including the roles your students will assume (if any) and the parameters of the solution. After this, you must create any problem documents and assemble necessary resources. Although you will have already considered the solution parameters, you must next give further attention to the ways in which students will frame their solutions, including how you will assess the learning that takes place. Throughout this process, it is important to be aware of the role of the instructor, who, having developed the basic problem and documents, steps into a tutorial posture as opposed to a provider of information. Finally, the prospective PBL teacher must consider how to put it all together into a coherent program.

A PBL Option

This chapter is written in a fairly traditional, explanation-based manner. That may be most helpful for some learners, but other learners might profit from a different approach. You can take on this last PBL task in the same manner you took on the others—solving a problem.

Here are your parameters: Select an area of your curriculum that you feel is appropriate to a PBL approach. Design a PBL unit directed at a specific group of learners in a specific place. Create a problem description, the necessary problem documents, an assessment plan (with a rubric), and an evaluation of your work. You may use any of the documents in this text as a model and refer to whatever sections of this chapter you find appropriate.

SELECTING AND CONNECTING GOOD PROBLEMS

Judging the Value of Problems

To use problem-based learning in a way that benefits students, teachers must select and develop worthwhile problems. Barrows (1996) explains the importance of organizing learning experiences around good problems: "The curricular linchpin in PBL—the thing that holds it together and keeps it on track—is the collection of problems in any given course or curriculum with each problem designed to stimulate learning in areas relevant to the curriculum" (p. 8). Before considering what such a "collection" might look like and how the collection relates to the curriculum, think about what makes an effective problem.

Selecting a problem might be an individual task if a teacher intends to develop and implement the problem alone. On the other hand, given the interdisciplinary nature of most "real life" problems, selecting a PBL experience provides a powerful opportunity for teachers to collaborate. Together, teachers can select problems that highlight the big ideas of their own subject areas, while helping students make connections among what sometimes seem like the fragmented bits of school life. In either case, teachers need to have a sense of what constitutes effective problems, and when teachers work together, a common language. The following section provides both a discussion of good problems and a rating scale to use in judging the potential of a problem idea.

The experience of educators in a variety of fields suggests a number of characteristics for effective problems. These characteristics are listed in Figure 13.1.

Delisle (1997) adds that a problem should be developmentally appropriate to the students, curriculum-based, and grounded in student experience (p.18). Torp and Sage (1998) emphasize the importance of student interest and learning characteristics in selecting good problems. The criteria outlined in Figure 13.1 are elaborated below.

Relevance. If the experiences provided to students seem to be "teacher issues," then PBL becomes nothing more than business as usual. This is not to argue that

---

FIGURE 13.1   **Characteristics of Effective Problems**

- Problem has relevance (contemporary) to students, touches their interests

- Problem is real versus contrived (students sense it could be or is an actual event)

- Problem has significance

- Problem has contextual details, but not enough to solve without going beyond the problem documents

- Problem is ill-structured (messy), opening the way for multiple solutions

- Problem has important learning targets embedded in it

Source: Adapted from Bridges and Hallinger (1995) and Glasgow (1997).

effective learning experiences must have a novelty to them; clearly, learning can occur in all sorts of situations. However, the unique demands of PBL require student engagement in order for students to take initiative and control their learning. Thus, a problem must not resemble the stereotypical application problems at the end of a chapter ("one train left Boston at 4:00 p. m., traveling west at 60 miles per hour; another train left Chicago . . . "). Instead, an effective problem gives credence to student perspectives. That is, a problem designer must learn to see the world through students' eyes and seek problems that will engage students. The best learning, according to Wiggins and McTighe (1998), is found at the intersection of what is effective practice and what is engaging to students.

Real. This criterion may be a refinement of relevance. Effective problems have an authenticity to them. That is, effective problems arise from what is actually going on or what could happen. We often cast students in roles to address problems, and these roles may be far from the students' current perspectives. However, whether students assume distant roles (acting as consultants or government researchers, for example) or take on roles that may actually be a part of their lives (acting as the student government), the central issue is that a problem could be real to someone somewhere. In other words, the problem does not appear to students as a contrived, school-based exercise.

Compare the following two tasks for their authenticity:

a. Create and present an oral presentation on any topic you like. You will speak for between five and seven minutes, and you must use at least two visual aids.
b. After completing your investigation into the issues surrounding the transportation of nuclear waste through our city, present your recommendations to the City Council. The Council allows speakers only seven minutes each, so you will need to organize your presentation carefully. You may find it helpful to reinforce your presentation with visual aids, such as charts and graphs.

In example *a*, students are given clear boundaries for their work, but the task is the stuff of classic school exercises: no sense of audience or purpose or passion. Example *b* has students doing much the same task, but this task is framed as a real-life issue, a situation the students could face one day and a situation the students could witness at City Hall next week. The authenticity motivates students.

Significance. Not all that glitters is gold. The fact that a problem situation seems relevant to children and authentic does not mean it is worth spending the time that PBL (done right) requires. As a problem designer, you should ask yourself and your colleagues if the particular problem you have in mind contains enough significance to devote the time and energy needed to create the PBL experience.

Of course, significance is a range concept (from little to much) rather than a categorical concept (yes or no). And significance, like beauty, is, to some extent, in the eye of the beholder. Still, professionals are always making decisions about what to teach (remember the Afrocentric curriculum problem?); they are always making judgments of the value of learning experiences. Every time we choose to do one thing in a classroom, we are choosing *not* to do an infinite array of other things. Given the fact that a teacher cannot do everything, it is important that a teacher chooses significant things to do.

Consider the choices of Mr. Willis. He wants his fifth-graders to learn to be critical thinkers, and he also knows they need to learn something about U.S. history. He has time this term to implement one PBL experience related to U.S. history, a topic large enough to generate thousands of problems. His colleague, Ms. Valenzuela, convinces him that a PBL unit based on transportation would be worthwhile. She suggests that they jointly create an experience that has students design and build a mock Conestoga wagon—and she has the shell of a wagon to work with. But Mr. Willis has misgivings. Surely such a task would be engaging to his students, but is it something worth the amount of time it requires? On the other hand, he has an idea for a different problem, based on the selection of a rail system or a canal system for a developing community. Though he lacks the materials for this idea, it strikes him as being more significant in that it raises questions about the role of transportation in developing the country, the role of communication and networking, and so on. How does he decide?

One way to think about this is to ask the following question: What would a "critical friend" say about each unit? Which has greater significance in terms of leading students to think about big ideas, powerful ideas of the discipline? Despite the greater difficulty in designing a PBL experience around systems of transportation, Mr. Willis decides this is more significant than an experience in packing a wagon— though each experience promises to be engaging and to make history come alive.

Contextualization.   One of the issues raised in the previous chapter was the danger of focusing too much on the details of the problem itself instead of the larger learning issue the problem represents. The reason why this even becomes a problem is that a good problem is rich in contextual detail. In selecting a problem, the designer should make certain that the problem provides the potential to generate contextual detail, but that it also sends the students beyond the details provided to find a solution.

Consider the problem of what to do about Andy (Chapter 3). This particular problem was supported by documents from teachers, family members, the school psychologist, and official records. Rich details were available, but it's doubtful anyone could find the solution in that mix of documents. For one thing, what does the law actually say about special education? That was nowhere to be found in the documents. What is the difference between a learning disability and limited English proficiency? One has to go beyond the problem documents for such information.

In the same way, when you are designing a problem for your students, consider whether the problem invites the creation of artifacts (documents, realia, artwork, and so on) that will give a context for students. However, a prime goal of the PBL process is getting learners to ask questions and seek information. A good problem will not have all the answers right there, because a good problem will generate questions even the designer hasn't anticipated. Here's a good rule of thumb: A good problem will always have more information than is needed to solve it, but never enough to solve it. When you work through the paradox of that statement, you'll have a good sense of the balance of details in a PBL experience.

Ill-structured.   This descriptive phrase makes it sound as though the problem designer is incautious or haphazard. Clearly, that is not the intention. A problem designer must be very deliberate and cautious, and the goal is to design a problem that has the potential to generate multiple solutions, arising from multiple solution paths.

Perhaps the best way to think about this is to recall some of the science labs you may have experienced as a student. Often such labs are "cookbook" experiences, where the learners follow a prescribed path (the steps are laid out by the instructor), and the teacher crosses her fingers, hoping that the students get the "correct" results (and students often do not!). Atkinson and Delamont (1984) describe this sort of experience as a "mock-up," and they question whether any real learning is going on. Teachers design labs that students dutifully execute, and then teachers are left to explain why the labs didn't work.

In contrast, current thinking about problem solving emphasizes students' selection and justification of a solution path (see recommendations from the National Council of Teachers of Mathematics and the National Science Teachers Association). Good problems for PBL experiences are those that do not suggest only one way to go about solving them. Indeed, good problems for PBL experiences call on students to dig around the details before even defining what the problem is, let alone how to solve it. Thus, "ill-structured" refers not to a lack of care on the part of the designer, but to tremendous care in selecting problems that will permit students to devise solution paths. Gallagher (1997) uses the paradoxical phrase "well-constructed, ill-structured problem" (p. 337) to indicate this complexity.

Embedded Targets.   Finally, a good problem for a PBL unit must connect to the curriculum mandate each teacher faces. Teachers should not be arbitrary about selecting learning experiences; each teacher answers to someone for the curricular choices he or she makes. Whether the mandate comes from a district guide, a school or department's "scope and sequence," state standards, or the proclamations of a professional organization, there is a larger community that helps define what students ought to know and be able to do. We ignore this mandate at our peril.

A good problem is one that connects to the mandate by embedding important learning targets in the problem. Generally, connecting to the curricular mandate is not a matter of teaching a particular discrete fact or skill. If the state says you must teach the capitals of all fifty states, that is probably *not* the stuff of problem-based learning. Teach the capitals, but use a more appropriate means. The important embedded target for a good problem is what we might call a big idea, or what Wiggins and McTighe (1998) call an "enduring understanding." For example, if your mandate says something to the effect that students should understand science as an inquiry process (which is roughly what the first science standard the state of Arizona calls for), you can readily design a PBL experience in which students experience science as inquiry rather than science as the memorization of a bunch of facts someone else discovered. A PBL experience in which students look into the alarming increase in mosquito populations (see Torp and Sage, 1998) allows such inquiry, giving the learning process credibility due to embedded targets.

Each of the above characteristics is important for selecting worthwhile problems to develop. True to the nature of problem solving, no problem is likely to be perfect for every characteristic, so the designers must make judgments about the value of specific possibilities. To assist with this, the following rating scale (Figure 13.2) provides systematic attention to each characteristic. The best use of this scale is to have more than one teacher consider and rate a problem before developing all the support documents and resources. After rating the potential problem, teachers join together in a discussion of the potential benefits to students of creating

FIGURE 13.2   Rating Scale for Potential Problems

Problem Synopsis: _____

_____

Features of Effective Problems	Score						
	Low			**Medium**			**High**
1. Students will be **interested** in the problem (relevance).	1	2	3	4	5	6	7
2. Students will perceive the problem as like **"real life."**	1	2	3	4	5	6	7
3. Outsiders would see the problem as a **significant** issue, worth spending time on.	1	2	3	4	5	6	7
4. The problem can be **contextualized** through documents, but still provide opportunities for students to **inquire beyond** these documents.	1	2	3	4	5	6	7
5. The problem is **messy** enough to allow multiple solutions and solution paths.	1	2	3	4	5	6	7
6. The problem has important **learning targets** **(standards)** embedded in it.	1	2	3	4	5	6	7

Score	Reasonable Response
34–42	Looks very promising. Now work together to create the PBL.
22–33	There is potential here, but enough doubt to cause you to reconsider. Could the problem be adapted to improve its potential?
6–21	There is never enough time to teach. You can do better things with your time than this.

and implementing the problem. There is no magic number or score that determines the worth of a problem, but a rough guide is provided with the scale. Remember that professionals make judgments and justify them according to professional standards and criteria.

Sources of Problems

Where do problems come from? There are several sources available. One can find problems through some of the exemplars published in current texts (Delisle, 1997; Torp & Sage, 1998); there are also online sources, such as the Center for Problem-Based Learning, based in the Illinois Math and Science Academy (www.imsa.edu). Textbooks themselves suggest problems, though it is unlikely any text will actually present material in a PBL format; the creative teacher must see how to transform texts into resources for engaging learning rather than seeing them as repositories of facts that dictate course structure.

Given the importance of relevance to the students' lives, perhaps local issues provide the best source for problems. For example, in the Association for Supervision and Curriculum Development's videotapes on problem-based learning (1997a; 1997b), students pursue problems related to traffic flow and the building of a bridge in one community, while other students address a problem of turning a prison facility into a public building. Every community has issues that bring to life the learning targets of our subject areas—indeed, it is in seeing the usefulness of school subjects for solving life's problems that students find reasons to learn. The astute teacher, sensitive to creating powerful learning experiences, is always on the lookout for potential problems that can engage students while accomplishing the goals of instruction. At times teachers will design problems around local issues that "could have been." For example, one team of middle school teachers, recognizing the conflict in their area concerning anthropological digs, devised a "could have been" problem that had students determine the rightful ownership of what may have been a grave site in a farmer's field. When issues arise in the local community, problem-solvers will apply the very skills you want your students to learn in reaching a resolution.

Teachers can profit from conversations with their peers about potential problems, both as these problems arise from local events and concerns and as the problems emerge from the curriculum in place. Jacobs (1997) describes a curriculum mapping process that can assist teachers in finding common ground in their curriculums to use as the basis for cooperatively developed PBL experiences. The mapping process helps teachers see the bigger picture of their students' learning, identifying gaps and overlapping topics.

Connections among Problems

As you are selecting problems, one of the tacit considerations you will make is how to connect problems to one another and to other aspects of the curriculum (Hmelo, 1998). As indicated in Chapter 1, some courses are organized so that all learning is done through PBL. Other courses are organized along a "post-hole" model

(Stepien & Gallagher, 1993), whereby key PBL experiences anchor other learning experiences. This model is the one employed in the Integrated Secondary Teacher Education Program (I-STEP) at Northern Arizona University (Figure 13.3). Typically, the post-hole model allows teachers to use some problem-based learning without completely revising their curricula.

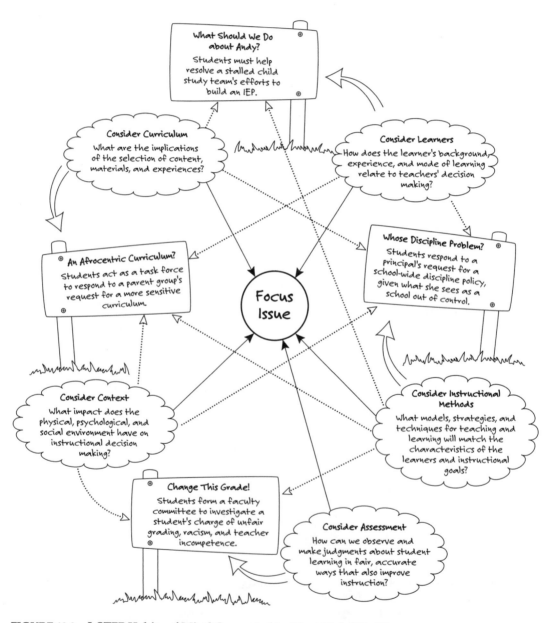

FIGURE 13.3   I-STEP Habits of Mind Connected to "Post-Hole" Problems

The post-hole model used in I-STEP works as follows. The conceptual framework of I-STEP focuses on five "habits of mind" that future teachers use to examine each issue they encounter in their professional education. The five areas of focus ask students to consider the *learners,* the *context* of the environment, the *curriculum, assessment,* and instructional *methods.* Thus, if the focus issue for the week is the organization of schools, I-STEP students examine each of the five habits of mind in relation to the question of organization.

Post-hole problems highlight these areas well. However, the nature of real-life problems is such that there is inevitably overlap among the focal points. The problem of Andy's IEP (Chapter 3, "What Should We Do about Andy?") has special emphasis on considering the learner. Of course, dealing with this problem demands an exploration of instructional methods, curriculum, and assessment to a lessor degree. The preparation of future secondary teachers is enhanced by the post-hole problems that interact with the habits of mind indicated in Figure 13.3.

One approach to making connections among PBL experiences, whether in a single classroom or in an interdisciplinary context, is to develop a concept map of the relationship of PBL experiences to the flow of the course and the "big ideas" of the course. A generic map is provided in Figure 13.4. It is not necessary to have the complete picture to implement a PBL experience. In fact, success with one experience will often lead teachers to create more PBL units, which then demand attention to the connections among units. A series of fragmented PBL units, though engaging, will not benefit students as much as a carefully designed progression of experiences.

PRESENTING THE PROBLEM SITUATION

You have selected a problem that is worthwhile and now you need to develop it into an experience for your students. One of your early considerations ought to be how you will present the problematic situation.

Even before this, you would do well to recall that for most students, the learning experience in PBL is not like typical school learning. That is, for many students, learning has been a matter of finding out what the teacher wants and then doing some memorization. For students who have been successful in this traditional model, PBL will be uncomfortable. Recall some of the activities from Chapter 2 that helped prepare you for your work as a PBL student. These can be readily adapted to K–12 learners. For example, you would do well to have your students role-play confronting a student who does not do his or her share of the work before that situation actually arises.

Assuming you prepare your students to be successful in PBL, you still must introduce each problem to them. This step of the process is well worth some extra thought. In their book, *Understanding by Design,* Wiggins and McTighe (1998) present a helpful acronym for judging the quality of a unit of instruction: WHERE. Briefly, the W stands for where are we going and why, the H stands for a hook to get the students' attention, the E stands for engaging instruction that will equip and enable students to perform, the R stands for reflection, and the final E stands

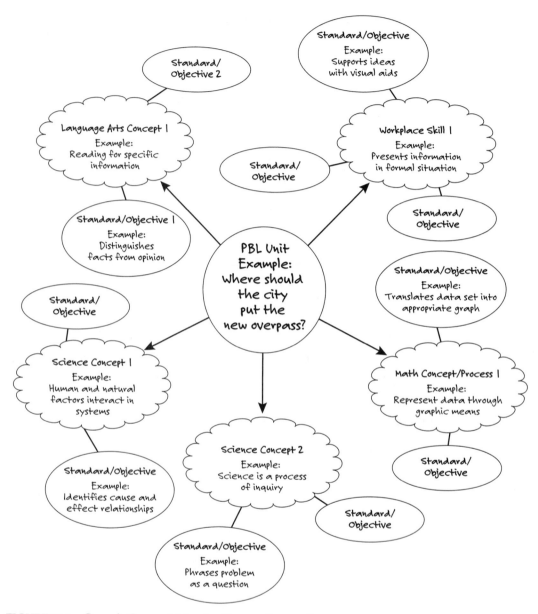

FIGURE 13.4   Generic Concept Map for Course Connections

for exhibit and evaluate. For the purposes of presenting the problem situation, the hook is of greatest importance.

Wiggins and McTighe (1998) speak of several types of hooks. A teacher can present students with a puzzling situation that demands explanation; a teacher can present students with a provocative question or an anomaly; the teacher can provide a story or puzzle, a far-out theory, or a role play. In some respects, the hook is similar to what Alfred North Whitehead (1929) referred to as the "romance" stage of instruction (his three stages were romance, precision, and generalization). We need to create a sense of romance and excitement.

Torp and Sage (1998) use the phrase "meet the problem" to describe the students' first encounter in a PBL unit. The personal connection suggested by "meet the problem" is appropriate—a metaphor that reminds us of meeting a new person. It suggests we will just get at the edges of a whole new relationship, and that there is much more to come.

Perhaps your problem could be best introduced by orally reading a brief, engaging passage, such as a news report (actual or simulated) of a controversial event. Teachers sometimes show brief video clips, such as a scene in which non-violent protestors are confronted by angry and violent police. Do not show the three-hour version of *Gandhi* to hook students into a problem on the role of public protest! Some teachers actually create simulated news reports for videotaped introductions; some teachers use graphics, such as a photograph of a crime scene. Whatever means you choose, remember your purpose: to hook students by engaging their curiosity. Introducing the problem must create some sense of mystery or urgency, inviting students to dig deeper. Figure 13.5 provides a means for planning how you will introduce your problem.

FIGURE 13.5   Planning to Meet the Problem

PROBLEM	INTRODUCTORY ACTIVITY	MATERIALS NEEDED
Example: Whose Bones Are These? (An interdisciplinary examination of competing claims at an archeological dig.)	Read newspaper account of adolescent skate-boarders who discovered ancient skeleton on Flagstaff's east side. After discussion, provide first problem document, the letter from the farmer who discovered the bones while plowing.	Newspaper article (*Arizona Daily Sun*) Problem document: farmer's letter.

"AUTHENTIC" DOCUMENTS AND ARTIFACTS

A crucial element of your PBL unit, both at the introductory stage and for the students' determination of what the problem is and how they will inquire into it, is the set of authentic documents or artifacts that students will access. One of the most important tasks for the designer is to assemble or create these documents.

In order to achieve a comprehensive collection of such artifacts a teacher must plan carefully at the outset of the design process. Creating a list of the needed documents and artifacts at the outset helps organize the efforts of a problem

FIGURE 13.6   Document Planning for "Change This Grade!" Problem

DOCUMENT/ARTIFACT	PURPOSE	SPECIAL CONSIDERATIONS	DEVELOPER
Darrin's appeal letter	Provides Darrin's view of the injustice of his situation.	Must appear to be written by a weak high school student.	dk
Ms. Torrence's response letter	Initial justification of grading and teaching practices.	Tone should be positive and confident.	dk
Ms. Torrence's grading system	Documents teacher's perspective on how grades are assigned.	Part of syllabus document; should portray something of her energy and sense of innovation.	dk
Ms. Torrence's Intelligence Portfolio Rubric	Provides evidence of how grades were assigned in part of the course. Include Darrin's scores here.	Ambiguities should be present in her rubric. Insert math error to encourage careful reading.	dk
Newspaper editorial	Establishes a context of emphasizing academic achievement over athletic prowess.	Draw in some of the slogans about excellence.	dk
Clancy Unified School District relevant Board policies	Establish the policies under which the school operates,	Check for alignment with state law and similarities to existing policies.	dk
Principal's memorandum	Lay out the timeline of the appeal and actions.	Include the idea of a faculty meeting.	dk

designer; when problems are created collaboratively, such a list allows for a distribution of labor.

The documents needed for the "Change This Grade!" problem (Chapter 5) are listed in Figure 13.6 as a model for planning. Notice that each document must develop some component of the problem, further student inquiry, or stimulate critical and creative thinking. Following this example, there is a blank planning chart (Figure 13.7).

While all the documents in the grade-appeal problem were simulated, it is conceivable that the problem developer could have used actual documents, such as a

FIGURE 13.7   Planning Chart for Creating/Selecting Documents and Artifacts

DOCUMENT/ARTIFACT	PURPOSE	SPECIAL CONSIDERATIONS	DEVELOPER

practicing teacher's grading system. Obviously, to use actual documents, one must seek permission and preserve the confidentiality of the document's originator. For this reason, it is often more efficient to model documents after existing ones, but to create artifacts that are uniquely suited to the problem situation. In the grade appeal problem, for example, the district policies are modeled after existing policies.

For many problems, documents are not the only appropriate artifacts. In the archeological problem referred to above, students actually visited a dig, which teachers had "salted" with artifacts. Photographs, audiotapes, broken furniture, data tables, polluted water samples, and police drawings are just a sample of the limitless array of items that may be useful to engage students and to induce inquiry.

Another consideration in your artifact planning is the timing of the students' encounter with each document or artifact. It is sometimes appropriate for students to receive all the documents they will be provided at the outset. At other times, it is appropriate to provide documents on an as-needed basis. For example, you may want to disrupt patterns of thinking in the student solution groups. If you find that the students are not giving enough attention to a particular issue as they seek solutions, instead of telling them to redirect their inquiry, you might provide them with another problem document that brings this issue to the surface explicitly. You can build into your plans that after a certain amount of time investigating a problem such as transportation in a national park, you will "leak" an internal park document that reveals crucial information designed to have students broaden their search. (You might even consider leaking contradictory documents, where students must make decisions about credibility.) After all, it is often the case in "real life" that new information comes to light in the midst of a problem-solving process.

RESOURCES

In planning for a PBL unit, a teacher must be sure to provide students with access to the resources necessary to solve the problem. One of the primary appeals of PBL is that this approach to learning helps students learn to inquire, to research, to seek answers. Especially in the early encounters with PBL, teachers should be certain that there are ample resources available for students to use in their inquiry.

Teachers do well to connect with other professionals in their schools and communities in order to build up a list of resources. The teacher-librarian, for example, is a central resource. Teacher-librarians generally delight in helping their colleagues structure student investigations, and often a teacher-librarian will seek sources even outside the school library and media center to assist in this process. Be sure to present your ideas to this colleague early in the process.

Other staff members will have areas of expertise to help you out, also. For example, you may find a counselor or administrator who has a hobby related to your problem. You do not necessarily need to have this person appear as a guest speaker, but you may encourage students to ask questions of your expert peers.

The Internet and e-mail contacts with other students and professionals are terrific resources for your students. Indeed, in the context of inquiring into a problem, learning Internet skills has a purpose that makes the learning more meaning-ful. The important question to ask yourself is this: Are there resources available to allow my students to inquire into this problem? If not, you should seriously recon-sider developing the unit. Of course, you might use this as an occasion to seek fur-ther resources so that you can implement the unit at a later date.

FRAMING THE SOLUTION AND ASSESSMENT

As indicated earlier, you should provide students with the parameters for their solutions when you have them meet the problem. However, thinking through the issue of assessment in problem-based learning is a crucial component of creating effective and enduring experiences for your students. In fact, Wiggins and McTighe (1998) make a case that one of the most important shifts a teacher needs to make is to move from *thinking like an activity designer* to *thinking like an assessor.* An activity designer focuses on what students will do; an assessor focuses on what evidence will demonstrate that students have understood the targeted learning.

From the beginning of the design process, then, a teacher must pay careful attention to the final performance or task that will allow students to demonstrate their understanding. This final performance must be both authentic and valid. That is, the performance must fit within the context established by the problem. It would make no sense, for example, to have students work on solving a trans-portation problem over which the city council has jurisdiction and to write a paper to their teacher. The appropriate and authentic context for their solution is a pre-sentation to a city council. At the same time, the solution must provide opportuni-ties for valid assessment. In the above example, if students are solving a transportation problem that is designed (with embedded targets) to help them learn about city government, data collection and analysis, and presentation skills, the final assessment ought to make judgments about students' achievements in those areas, and not simply whether the students talked to three residents and charted a traffic flow. Both authenticity and validity are important.

Assessing student learning, a topic that goes well beyond the scope of this book, involves sensitivity to both intended and unintended outcomes. Thus, it is essential that the problem developer consider what objectives or outcomes a stu-dent will achieve through the PBL experience. The notion of embedded targets is crucial here. The problem designer selects and creates problems that are connected to important student learning outcomes. At the same time, given the flexibility of this approach and the importance of student control, assessment in PBL needs to allow for learning outside of the intended outcomes.

A good starting point for thinking about assessment is to return to the con-nection between a PBL unit and the curricular mandate. If, for example, your ratio-nale for using PBL involves helping students understand "science as inquiry," that is clearly one of the big ideas that you should assess in the course of the unit. The design task is to make certain that any final performance includes opportunities for students to demonstrate how they used science as inquiry and that any rubric used to judge student performance includes this important outcome.

Consider your experience with the Afrocentric curriculum problem (Chapter 6). This problem asked your group to become a team of educators, charged with looking into a parent group's request to change the school curriculum. The charge for this task force came from the school board to whom the parent group appealed. The solution, then, must be delivered in the form of a presentation to this same school board. Compare the intended outcomes and the rubric for assessing the team presentations (Figure 13.8). What is left out? How could this rubric be improved?

Clearly the assessment suggested by the rubric in Figure 13.8 does not fully address the outcomes listed there. This implies that the problem designer should either revisit the assessment rubric or expand the assessment to include other perspectives—and this is the preferable solution. Assessment in PBL must be carefully designed so that students have a variety of means to demonstrate their achievement of outcomes. Sometimes a final assessment is sufficient, but more often, the problem designer should consider assessment from various perspectives and through various means. For example, one useful means to assess student progress in a PBL is to have students respond to a prompt in the solution-generating stage. Your instructor may have used an example of this in the teaming problem (Chapter 8). This problem asks learners to operate as part of a consulting firm. Midway through the problem, instructors may provide learners with the following prompt, which is a simulated in-progress evaluation by a supervisor:

> The work of this particular CCI team can be characterized as aimless at best. The team has no means of maintaining member or team accountability. The operating procedures are haphazard and unproductive. I find no evidence of progress toward making a defensible recommendation to the Watertown School Board. Indeed, the very reputation of the company (CCI) is threatened by the quality of "work" produced by this team. I suspect that any single consultant could have progressed to the same extent as this team. Perhaps these questionable results are as much an indictment of the CCI move to a team structure as of the members of this particular team. Recommendation: Disband this team and re-assign the contract before it is too late.

Learners are given an opportunity to respond to the criticism of their team, which invites them to engage in self-assessment of their progress. Such ongoing assessments allow the teacher to make more defensible judgments about student learning as it relates to a variety of outcomes. Thus, PBL designers should think of assessment as ongoing and multiple rather than merely as a final judgment. A planning chart for assessment purposes is provided in Figure 13.9.

Whatever assessment a problem designer creates should include opportunities for learners to reflect on their experiences. Bridges and Hallinger (1992; 1995) use problem "talk back" sheets to structure student response to a problem. These talk back forms serve both as a means for the students to process their experiences metacognitively and as a means for the instructor to assess the problem and improve it for future use. Similar to talk back forms, this book has provided questions for reflection that are designed to encourage students to deepen their understanding of

FIGURE 13.8   Learner Outcomes and Sample Assessment Rubric for the Afrocentric Problem

Learning Objectives for the Problem

- Understand impact of diversity of learners

- Understand theories of curriculum development

- Adapt curriculum according to social, philosophical, political, ethical, and historical contexts

- Select appropriate teaching methods for particular contexts

- Appreciate collaboration with peers

- Demonstrate respect for diversity in schools

Sample Rubric

- **4 OUTSTANDING:** All members of the group participated actively in the presentation. The problem was clearly and appropriately defined. Solution presented is supported by three or more "expert" resources, with the research clearly tied to the proposals offered. The solution is realistic and reasonable. Community concerns are addressed, though not necessarily as each interest group would like. "Professionalism" is evident in the group's presentation (through language, supporting documents, presence).

- **3 STRONG:** The presentation may have unequally distributed participation. The problem addressed is clear, if only by implication. Experts are cited in the solution, but may not be explained in a manner appropriate to the audience. The solution is reasonable, though it may not take practical realities (e.g., cost, teacher time) into account. Community concerns are addressed, though not necessarily as each interest group would like. "Professionalism" is inconsistent, with presenters adopting more of a "university classroom" than "practitioner" style.

- **2 ACCEPTABLE:** Participation is not equal, but all group members make some contribution. The problem addressed seems relevant, but it is not clearly identified for the audience. Use of expert resources is vague or superficial. The solution presented has some reasonable elements, but has one or more glaring inconsistencies or unrealistic components. Community concerns may not be adequately addressed (i.e., it may ignore key interest groups). The presentation lacks real-world professionalism, taking on the nature of a course presentation.

- **1 WEAK:** Participation is evidently not equal; some members may dominate while others are uninvolved. The problem is not defined, and it is difficult to connect the solution to a specific problem. The solution presented is unrealistic, inappropriate, or detrimental. Connections to established authorities may be missing or so superficial that the citations do not support the solution. Community concerns may not be addressed. "Professionalism" is lacking in the presentation style, support, and/or interactions of the group.

FIGURE 13.9   **Planning Chart for Assessment Activities**

ASSESSMENT MEANS	RELATION TO OUTCOMES	PLACE IN SEQUENCE AND FORMAT
Example: Oral presentation to school board.	Allows students to synthesize understanding of key curriculum concepts and to simulate important format for school decision making.	At the end of the problem; create rubric.

the important issues raised in each problem and to consider their own development as professionals. As you design your problem assessments, consider how you will provide students with opportunities to reflect on the problem and problem-solving process.

GUIDING THE PROCESS: TUTOR OR TEACHER?

The challenge teachers face once the design of a PBL unit is completed is to redefine their role. Often accustomed to acting as the dispenser of knowledge, a teacher must rethink this role in order to be effective in the problem-based learning experience. Teachers must see themselves as facilitators of learning, tutors of student groups, rather than as providers of answers (Hmelo & Ferrari, 1997). As Shelagh Gallagher (1997) points out, a move to PBL means a change in curriculum (organizing around problems) *and* instruction (relying more on questioning and discussion). Several moves can help the new teacher in assuming this role.

Process Guide.   With the performance end clearly in mind, a teacher has the advantage of perspective. Whereas students have often been socialized into a mentality that sees school work as plodding from one unconnected thing to another, teachers can see the big picture. With this comprehensive view, the facilitator in PBL sees clearly where the process is headed, and can assist groups of students by reminding them of where they are in the process. Ask your students if they have completed the three-part thinking structure: What do we know? What do we need to know? How are we going to find out? Help the problem-solving teams understand where they are in their process and how they can progress to the next level.

Metacognitive Questioning.   The temptation of teachers is to give answers—and if we can resist giving answers, our next favorite ploy is to ask questions that lead directly to answers. Thus, teachers are used to asking cognitive questions, such as "What are the three branches of government?" Problem-based learning, however, aims at having students themselves learn to ask the right kinds of questions. Teachers need to learn to ask *metacognitive* questions (Gallagher, 1997; Hmelo & Ferrari, 1997) that will permit students to take charge of learning. Instead of asking for the names of the branches of government, a good facilitator will ask, "What questions do we need to ask next? Where can we find answers to these questions?" It takes a great deal of discipline for teachers to stay consistent in keeping the focus on metacognitive questioning, but students profit as they learn to question.

Student Relations.   Managing student interactions is always a challenge to teachers, but this is heightened in problem-based learning. Now, instead of a model of individualistic learning (each student's success is independent from every other student's success), students are placed in a cooperative structure where success depends on each member of the group functioning together. As facilitator, the teacher must lead reflection on effective ways of relating to other group members, successful means of heading off and solving conflict. Teachers should maintain a check on the content of the problem, but just as important, teachers must stay proactive in maintaining the relationships among group members. When student groups are working together, the teacher must maintain an awareness of the progress and difficulties of the various groups. Remind the groups of what they learned through role-playing, and keep them focused on their ultimate outcome: the successful solution of the problem.

Learning Issues.   Throughout the PBL process, but especially at the end, the teacher can enhance student learning by reminding pupils that the issues go beyond the particular problem at hand. The teacher, who has the vantage point that permits a view of the whole curriculum, can help students see the issues that are represented in a given problem in order that the student learning does not become so context-bound that no meaningful connections emerge. The power of PBL is in its relevant context, but there comes a time when you must move beyond that context. After the students have worked out a solution to this particular problem with transportation (or animal populations or urban blight or the lockers in the school), it is important to focus on the general principles that one could learn through the process. Guiding student reflection is one way that facilitators work toward transfer of knowledge (Hmelo & Ferrari, 1997).

TOO MUCH FOR BEGINNING TEACHERS?

A beginning teacher might reasonably argue now that it is too early to learn these complex roles. After all, one might say, I have just figured out how to do an effective lecture and an interesting demonstration, why confuse me with another way of teaching? This is a legitimate question. Perhaps the most important response to this concern is a perspective on learning rather than teaching. As a *learner* of teaching practices, should one be presented with a hierarchy of models, each dependent on mastery of the one before it? That is, should a student of teaching master the lecture before proceeding to the demonstration before proceeding to concept attainment and so on? Is this how one learns best?

The best evidence we have now is that learning complex behaviors and concepts does not proceed this way. For example, instead of having young children master the sentence level of writing before going on to the paragraph, and mastering the paragraph before attempting the story, and so on, best practice lets students play with the whole form right from the start. Young writers create stories even before they are certain of what constitutes a sentence, and as they progress through their education, these young writers eventually encounter the components to writing a story.

In a similar way, beginning teachers need an interplay of mastery and experimentation. There is no harm in learning how to organize and deliver an effective lecture; indeed, this would seem like an essential feature of a good teacher. At the same time, the lecture is effective for only certain kinds of learning and in certain contexts, just as direct instruction works best for some situations, cooperative learning for others, simulations for still others, and so on. For a beginning teacher to have the proper perspective on what it means to be a teacher, he or she should have a broad repertoire of teaching techniques. Learning to be a facilitator in the PBL model is on a par with learning to lecture; it is not what follows. Consider the paradox expressed in this statement: "less teaching can yield better learning" (Wiggins & McTighe, 1998). If our ultimate goal is student learning, we need to know more about guiding students toward that goal.

PUT IT ALL TOGETHER

You have examined problem-based learning through a variety of lenses by now. In Part I of this book, you received a fairly traditional exposition of the process and how it is being used. In Part II, you experienced the perspective of a learner who encounters PBL as a means to learn important knowledge and skills for a specific purpose—becoming a competent, well-rounded member of an occupational community. In Part III, you reflected on the process and saw how it can be broken into component parts so that you could design PBL experiences for your own teaching.

It is now time to put it together by creating a PBL unit that you could use with your future students. If possible, you may find this experience particularly valuable if you work with a colleague whose expertise complements your own. Whether you do so alone or collaboratively, consider how your unit will address the following questions:

- How does the problem connect to the curriculum and embed important learning targets?
- How do students meet the problem initially?
- What problem documents will you select or create for the students?
- What resources will you make available?
- How will you structure time so that you can facilitate student inquiry and effective group relations?
- What parameters will you place on the solution and how will you assess student work?
- How will you organize reflection on the experience so that students increase their metacognitive skills and you learn about ways of improving your unit?

The most useful format for creating such units at this point is to write up your PBL unit with enough detail that a well-informed peer could use the unit in his or her own classroom. Remember throughout the process that a good PBL unit will function like a framework. That is, you will give a basic shape to your students' experience, but if the PBL unit is a good one, the students will take it in directions you hadn't even anticipated. The bare framework you provide them will become an opportunity for them to build a unique structure of learning.

And once you've completed such a unit, sharing it with colleagues for feedback is the next logical step. By immersing yourself in a variety of PBL units that you and your peers have created, you will have expanded your vision of what can be done through this model.

When you use a PBL unit in your class, you can anticipate that it will be exciting and interesting for the students, but also awkward and a little risky—and resisted by some. Remember that learners take time to feel comfortable in a new format, just as teachers do. Be patient with the adjustment involved, and persist even through this discomfort. The opportunities you can provide for authentic, meaningful learning for your students are virtually unlimited. Given time for you and them to practice, a healthy environment where you can process your experience with peers and mentors, and a willingness to break some molds in the predictable routines of secondary schools, you can create a powerful and memorable learning community. You will inspire learners, and you will be a model learner yourself.

REFERENCES

Association for Supervision and Curriculum Development. (1997a). *Problem-based learning: Designing problems for learning* [Videorecording]. Alexandria, VA: Association for Supervision and Curriculum Development.

Association for Supervision and Curriculum Development. (1997b). *Problem-based learning: Using problems to learn* [Videorecording]. Alexandria, VA: Association for Supervision and Curriculum Development.

Atkinson, P., & Delamont, S. (1984). Mock-ups and cock-ups: The stage-management of guided discovery instruction. In A. Hargreaves & P. Woods (Eds.), *Classrooms & staffrooms: The sociology of teachers & teaching* (pp. 36–47). Milton Keynes, UK: Open University.

Barrows, H. S. (1996). Problem-based learning in medicine and beyond: A brief overview. In L. Wilkerson & W. H. Gijselaers (Eds.), *Bringing problem-based learning to higher education: Theory and practice* (Vol. 68, pp. 3–12). San Francisco: Jossey-Bass.

Bridges, E. M., & Hallinger, P. (1992). *Problem based learning for administrators.* Eugene, OR: ERIC Clearinghouse on Educational Management.

Bridges, E. M., & Hallinger, P. (1995). *Implementing problem based learning in leadership development.* Eugene, OR: ERIC Clearinghouse on Educational Management.

Delisle, R. (1997). *How to use problem-based learning in the classroom.* Alexandria, VA: Association for Supervision and Curriculum Development.

Gallagher, S. A. (1997). Problem-based learning: Where did it come from, what does it do, and where is it going? *Journal for the Education of the Gifted, 20*(4), 332–362.

Glasgow, N. A. (1997). *New curriculum for new times: A guide to student-centered, problem-based learning.* Thousand Oaks, CA: Corwin.

Hmelo, C. E. (1998). Problem-based learning: Effects on the early acquisition of cognitive skill in medicine. *The Journal of the Learning Sciences, 7*(2), 173–208.

Hmelo, C. E., & Ferrari, M. (1997). The problem-based learning tutorial: Cultivating higher order thinking skills. *Journal for the Education of the Gifted, 20*(4), 401–422.

Jacobs, H. H. (1997). *Mapping the big picture: Integrating curriculum & assessment K–12.* Alexandria, VA: Association for Supervision and Curriculum Development.

Stepien, W., & Gallagher, S. (1993). Problem-based learning: As authentic as it gets. *Educational Leadership, 50*(7), 25–28.

Torp, L., & Sage, S. (1998). *Problems as possibilities: Problem-based learning for K–12 education.* Alexandria, VA: Association for Supervision and Curriculum Development.

Whitehead, A. N. (1929). *The aims of education and other essays.* New York: Free Press.

Wiggins, G., & McTighe, J. (1998). *Understanding by design.* Alexandria, VA: Association for Supervision and Curriculum Development.

INDEX

238

240